Representing Women

Myths of femininity in the popular media

Myra Macdonald

Edward Arnold
A member of the Hodder Headline Group
LONDON NEW YORK SYDNEY AUCKLAND

First published in Great Britain in 1995 by
Edward Arnold, a division of Hodder Headline PLC,
338 Euston Road, London NW1 3BH
175 Fifth Avenue, New York, NY 10010

Distributed exclusively in the USA by
St Martin's Press Inc.
175 Fifth Avenue, New York, NY 10010

British Library Cataloguing in Publication Data
A catalogue record for this book is available from the British Library

Library of Congress Cataloging-in-Publication Data
Applied for

ISBN 0 340 63221 6 (hb)
ISBN 0 340 58016 X (pb)

1 2 3 4 5   95 96 97 98 99

Typeset in 10.5/12.5 Palatino by
Colset Pte Ltd, Singapore
Printed and bound in Great Britain by
J W Arrowsmith Ltd, Bristol

Contents

Acknowledgements

The main unnamed contributors to this book are the Communication and Media students who followed my Women in Media (later, Gender and Representation) course at Glasgow Caledonian University, in its various historical guises. They fuelled my interests and enthusiasms, repeatedly pushed the agenda of the course in new directions, and showed a healthy scepticism about emerging orthodoxies. Their desire for a book that would span different media was the starting-point for this project. Although this only partly meets that need, it owes a debt to their liveliness and commitment.

I am grateful to Glasgow Caledonian University for granting me a two-month period of study leave in 1992 which enabled me to get this book started, and to the staff at the libraries of GCU, Glasgow University, Glasgow's Mitchell Library and the British Library Newspaper Library at Colindale for their unfailing helpfulness. I would like to thank Lesley Riddle for providing constant encouragement and support throughout the long gestation period.

The author and publishers acknowledge the permissions given by the following to reproduce film stills, advertisements and other illustrations: Sigma Film Productions for the still from *A Question of Silence*; Twentieth Century Fox Film Corporation for the stills from *Black Widow*, and *Aliens*; United Artists Pictures and Metro Goldwyn Mayer Inc. for the still from *Baby Boom*; Posy Simmonds and the Peters Fraser & Dunlop Group Ltd for the *Public View* cartoon; Abbott Mead Vickers BBDO for the Tampax advertisement; Lever Brothers for permission to reproduce the Lifebuoy and Knight's Castile advertisements; DFSD Bozell for the Triumph advertisement; Prestige & Collections for the Armani Giò advertisement; TBWA Holmes Knight Ritchie for the Wonderbra advertisement; and Simons Palmer for the Nike advertisement. The film stills are all provided courtesy of BFI Stills, Posters and

ACKNOWLEDGEMENTS

Designs. Glasgow City Libraries' Mitchell Library provided the copy of the Lifebuoy advertisement; the National Library of Scotland the copy of the Knight's Castile advertisement. Every effort has been made to contact copyright holders. The author and publishers would be pleased to hear from any copyright holders they have not been able to contact and to print due acknowledgement in any subsequent edition.

Introduction

In 1993 the most publicly discussed and photographed woman in Britain created a sensation by announcing that she was retiring from public life. She was not a politician, represented no-one, and had made few, if any, memorable public statements. Like a multifaceted hologram, she shifted identity as the light fell on her. Fairy-tale princess, fashion leader, media manipulator, devoted mother, fun-loving girl, jilted lover, compassionate carer, sad bulimic, Princess Diana appeared at times to possess as many personae as designer gowns. Her treatment by the media reminds us how alive and well, if volatile, long-standing myths of what it means to be 'feminine' continue to be. This book explores how such myths, chameleon-like, have the capacity to both change hue and yet to survive. It would be easy, but misleading, to load all the responsibility for this phenomenon onto male shoulders. The more challenging question is why women, many of whom would disown these very myths of femininity if they were presented as explicit points of view, happily collude with them, and indeed find pleasure in them, when they are reproduced in the popular media.

Throughout the book, 'myth' is used in the sense defined by the French cultural critic, Roland Barthes. In his thinking, the term refers to ways of conceptualizing a subject that are widely accepted within a specific culture and historical period, despite having little necessary connection to reality. Myth 'transforms history into Nature' (1972, p. 129), turning complex processes into simple and apparently unmotivated phenomena. The Barthian model claims that the diverse and multifaceted qualities of reality are flattened into routine ways of thinking and talking. In a more graphic analogy, Barthes likens the mythologist to a colonizer, proceeding discreetly and with charm and stealth to rob the natives of their rich heritage (ibid., pp. 131–2). By posing as 'natural' and 'common-sensical', myths obscure their ideological role in helping to shore up systems of belief that sustain the power of the powerful. The diversity of real women, potentially challenging to male authority, is transformed into manageable myths of 'femininity' or 'the feminine'. This book analyses the production and reproduction of these myths by the western popular media in the course of this century. For reasons of accessibility, most of the textual examples cited are British or American.

In taking a broad canvas, I am attempting to trace similarities across the popular media's treatment of women. As someone who cut her professional teeth in a climate of deep antagonisms between 'media studies' and 'film studies', where arguments about the discrete qualities of film and television in particular were often hotly debated, I am well aware of the dangers of this approach. At the same time, bending excessive scholastic rigour may sometimes be the only way of preventing the final rigor of the corpse. While accepting that differences do need to be acknowledged, the growing tendency of the media to refer to each other (whether advertisements to films, television to radio, or music videos to all and sundry) makes it increasingly artificial to draw medium boundaries too tightly. Despite the breadth of the approach, there are inevitable omissions in a book of this length. Its concentration on film, magazines, advertising and, to a lesser extent, television, leaves radio, popular music and the popular press with only passing mentions. The popular media considered are those that appeal principally to an adult audience: it would take another book to do justice to the important area of constructions of gender in child-directed material. The thematic organization of the subject-matter aims to provide some compensation for these defects, by allowing those interested in other areas to relate the arguments in particular chapters to their own knowledge and enthusiasms.

The main title of this book, *Representing Women*, invites two readings. The concept of 'representation' refers both to politics and culture, creating a potential ambiguity but usefully suggesting the relationship between these spheres. Connections between political and cultural rights are most acutely felt by groups who feel socially marginalized. It is no accident that for Afro-Caribbean youths, or Scots, or gay men, cultural self-expression (preferably through mainstream media) becomes a significant method of campaigning for greater political power. Feminists, too, have often put as much energy into lobbying against pornography, or creating their own versions of reality through stage or screen, as into conventional political action. While there is a danger that cultural achievement becomes a surrogate for political change, what is being sought is, significantly, a voice that will not only be heard but listened to. In this sense, the concept of representation, however outmoded in cultural criticism, is still of crucial political importance. Like a recurrent refrain, this book will consider how far women are able through the media to articulate their own perspectives and points of view. To what extent, in other words, do women represent themselves?

In its method of critical analysis, on the other hand, this book rejects the notion that the media merely represent or re-present reality to us. Such an approach requires too many philosophical contortions. We would have to believe, first, that 'reality' is directly knowable and accessible, unfiltered by our own perceptions and beliefs, and capable of being presented through the media in virtually unadulterated form. Although the material characteristics of physical reality may be uncovered by persistent scientific endeavour, social reality is more elusive and more likely to be shaded by the brush of the investigator. Second, we would need to be persuaded that 'reality' is what the media deal in, even when advertisements, magazines or films are clearly, and with varying degrees of persuasiveness, engaging our desires and creating fantasy environments. Third, the reproduction of reality would have to become a desirable objective. When women complain about the lack of realism in the media's representation of themselves, they are criticizing lack of diversity in portraying and defining women's lives and desires, not asking for a hall of mirrors. Realism, especially for non-dominant groups, may amount to no more than a depressing reproduction of how things currently are. By focusing on myths, I will be pursuing a model of the media as helping to construct the topics and concepts that they touch. The media on this reading have a strong ideological role, inviting our consent to ways of talking about reality that are often regarded as normal and acceptable beyond the confines of the media, too.

This focus means that this book makes no pretence to deal with women in their diversity. A non-homogeneous group, women are separated at least by class, age, educational background, sexuality, ethnicity and nationality. Writing as someone who is white, middle-class, heading towards middle age, heterosexual, Scottish, and an academic, I am aware that in most, although not all, of these respects I fall into the dominant group of writers on women and the media. A wider range of other voices needs to be heard, especially in discussions of how women variously respond to myths of femininity in the media. Jacqueline Bobo's article, commenting on the positive responses of black women to Steven Spielberg's *The Color Purple*, remains unique enough to be almost universally cited as evidence of the benefits of attending to a wider range of perspectives. That this was first published in 1988 provides its own comment. It is also true, of course, that women, for reasons I will outline more fully in Chapters 2 and 3, share common experiences. In writing this book, I found myself swinging between writing about women from a position of identification ('as women, we . . .') and talking about women as a separate grouping: a 'they' rather than an 'us'. However uneasy and inconsistent this seems, I decided that leaving this unevenness captures at least the dual pressure that we feel as women both to speak as part of a larger group, with shared structures of feeling, and yet to acknowledge and respect other women's variety and difference.

The book's critical emphasis is on textual analysis but within a cultural and historical framework. Because gender, as a category, has been important in the differential impact of capitalism on men and women, and especially in our differing positioning as male or female consumers, this context has significant implications for the ways in which the media choose to address us. Modes of talking about, or constructing images of, both men and women also predate the arrival of the media, and set an agenda which the media have variously adopted or adapted. To give a full account of these processes, it would be necessary to investigate the production context that shapes media texts, and, more specifically, to outline employment profiles, in terms of gender, within the media industries. Again, this is a bigger topic than a book of this size can handle. The relation between the gender of the producer and gender representations is a complex one, as a moment's glance at the women's section of a popular paper (written by women) or a Kathryn Bigelow film will confirm. A number of institutional and financial pressures inform the relation between producer and text, regardless of gender, making it naïve to give priority to this factor alone. It is only on those limited occasions when women have virtually total control over their own textual production that women-friendly perspectives might be expected to dominate.

Any discussion of the meaning of media texts requires consideration of the audience, spectator or reader. Although this book offers no new empirical evidence about how women respond to media texts, it uses cultural theory, and in particular the movement from modernity to postmodernity, to argue that interpretation processes have undergone at least as radical a shift in the course of this century as forms of representation. Consistency in methods of constructing women does not imply consistency in response. Long used to acting as mothers, working women, friends, housewives or daughters, women now have access to a wider range of representations of themselves than ever before. Men's images, too, are being spasmodically dislodged from their machismo foundations, destabilizing the touchstone against which femininity has been traditionally measured. Media audiences, reared on a diet of fast-moving films, 30-second narratives in advertisements, spectacular graphic and animation techniques on television and, more recently, interactive video and computer games, have a new facility in both recognizing the tricks that are being deployed, and incorporating them into a kaleidoscopic vocabulary. This visual diet of riches familiarizes viewers with illogical juxtapositions, lack of continuity, mismatches and apparently random selection of images, to the extent that contradictions may cease to be perceived as such.

One of the most interesting studies of women's reactions to media texts undertaken over the last ten years was Elizabeth Frazer's research into ideological readings of the teenage magazine *Jackie* by seven groups of adolescent girls. Open discussion with two quite different groups produced strong criticism of the lack of reality in *Jackie*'s problem pages. Asking them to write their own, more realistic, versions produced an unexpected result. Far from concocting radical alternatives, the girls, without exception, reproduced the style of the magazine, in framing both their problems and their replies, despite their awareness of its inadequacies, and their own more supportive and thoughtful analyses of each other's problems in their collective discussion sessions. Frazer concludes that when confronted with a mismatch between the media version and the reality, the girls chose the media version as the most publicly legitimated and widely accepted one. Knowledge derived from experience gives way to ideas lent authority and credibility by the media. Most significantly, she comments that 'it does not seem appropriate to characterize the difference between these two contrasting sorts of discussion of "problems" as *contradiction*. It is more apposite to say that the girls have available more than one way of discussing the topic' (1987, p. 422).

In Marxist terms, the visibility of contradictory ideas produces a dialectical awareness of conflicting ideologies that acts as a time-bomb, exploding eventually into revolution and change. In the postmodern age, surrounded by contradictory and conflicting images and ideas, we may have become more blasé and comfortable with illogicality and incompatibility. Non-dominant groups, especially, often become experts in learning to juggle with different ways of looking and feeling. Women, confronted with images of themselves as regular victims of crime, but also as superwomen with executive briefcases and designer suits, as gun-toting harpies or immaculate mothers, may find the mix confusing, but not necessarily ironic. In an era that multiplies forms of representation, but leaves balances of power fundamentally unaltered, we need to explore responses more carefully before leaping to the conclusion that contradictions in the representations of women (or any other marginalized group) will necessarily be a catalyst for social change.

The book is divided into two sections. The first reviews what we mean by femininity and examines influences that have been important in sustaining myths of femininity against the grain of social change. Chapter 1 outlines a variety of disciplines which have insights to offer on myths of femininity. This may help those readers who are students both to understand their own discipline's specific contribution and to dip into other, less familiar, perspectives. For other readers, this should provide a useful orienteering guide to the vastly expanding literature in the area of gender and culture. Since an important thread in my argument is that women have been given insufficient chance to formulate their own thoughts and ideas about themselves, and to express these through popular media forms, Chapter 2 considers the concepts of the 'public' and 'private' spheres, and how male and female speaking rights and communicative abilities have been defined in relation to these. The third chapter argues that the linking of women with consumerism has been particularly powerful in shaping the development of myths of femininity throughout the twentieth century.

The second part of the book consists of an analysis of four myths of femininity which recur, or have undergone change, in popular culture this century. These four chapters are not meant to provide a comprehensive or definitive account of significant myths. Readers may think of others of their own, and quibble with my choices. The first two, femininity as enigmatic and threatening, and femininity as nurturing and caring, I selected because of their strong lines of continuity, with roots extending back in cultural history to a pre-media age. The final two chapters consider the myths generated around women's sexuality and bodies. I have ended with these, because it is here that the biggest gap opens up between women's changing experiences and awareness, and the media constructions of themselves that they are regularly exposed to. Because as women we can relate what we see and hear to what we practise most sharply in these areas, they provide an interesting focus for thinking through our own responses as audiences and readers.

Terminology is a difficulty in a book like this. Since my aim is to be as understandable as possible, I have tried to avoid using terms that most readers may regard as 'jargon'. At the same time, in order to explain some of the distinctions that I think to be important along the way, I have had at times to resort to specialist terms. Readers will, in any case, encounter these being widely used in some of the other texts to which I refer. To minimize the problem, I have both included an explanation of the term the first time it is used within the book, and provided a glossary at the end to which any reader who misses this first reference can turn.

PART I

Discourse, consumerism, femininity

1

Disciplined approaches: redefining femininity

It is perfectly possible to agree 'in one's head' that certain images of
women might be reactionary or damaging or oppressive, while remaining
committed to them in emotion and desire.
(Jean Grimshaw, 1988, in Jackson, 1993, p. 44)

In a world where women's magazines gave pleasure only to thin women,
romantic fiction offered enjoyment only to non-feminists, and films
such as *Fatal Attraction* appealed only to asexual women, this chapter
would not need to be written. It explores two puzzles. Why do out-of-
date myths of femininity still continue to exert a magnetic pull over us,
and why is it easier to criticize those media that target us than to explain
their fascination? As a closet fan of *Cagney and Lacey* in the mid-1980s,
struggling to reconcile feminist beliefs with pleasure in a series that contrasted Cagney's troubled single state with the richness of Lacey's family
life, and reserved its heroines' most convincing lines for the cocooned
space of the ladies' room, the discovery that other feminists were also
silent admirers seemed curiously liberating. Female students, too, often
find it easier to say what is wrong with women's magazines than to
explain why they enjoy buying and reading them.

It may seem odd to begin a book on myths of femininity with questions about our responses as readers or viewers. Investigating the role
of the producers might seem a more rational starting-point. There are
two reasons for my emphasis. First, most of us, even in an age of
interactive technologies, will encounter the media primarily as consumers and critics, not as producers. Second, we need to recognize the
part we all play in keeping mythologies and ideologies alive. This gets
obliterated in conspiracy-theory accounts that see the media as bastions
of male privilege, spurred on by the mission of keeping feminism at bay.
This tendency dominates in some recent American writing, such as
Naomi Wolf's *The Beauty Myth* (1991) and Susan Faludi's *Backlash*

(1992). Although producers indisputably have primary power in deciding what images we see, and (equally significantly) what images we do not see, arguments that cast us (or, more usually, some other lesser category of viewer or reader) as passive dupes in this process have rightly been increasingly challenged. At the same time, John Fiske's (1989) utopian vision of a democracy of active readers and viewers busily producing their own meanings and undermining those on offer, is equally unconvincing. In relation to myths of femininity, in particular, with their long cultural history, traditions of seeing and responding cannot be so magically overturned.

In this chapter, I will consider the contribution a variety of academic disciplines make towards understanding where myths of femininity come from, and how we deal with them. I will begin with sociology, move through psychology to psychoanalysis and end with the history of art and cultural theory. These are not the only sources of relevant ideas (others would include social anthropology, literary theory and philosophy), but they are sufficiently varied to outline the key debates. Linguistics, since the 1980s, has also come alive to the possibility that men and women speak and think in different languages. The implications of this, both for the production of media representations and for the ways in which we respond to these, are considerable, and will be separately dealt with in the next chapter. I have not included either film or media studies as contributing disciplines, because I view both at their best as multi-disciplinary areas, however fiercely institutional constraints have forced academics to argue otherwise. These are also the areas most likely to be already familiar to readers of this book.

Despite their differences, the approaches I will outline share one feature: almost all the writing of interest on gender has been produced by women, and almost all of it is written from a feminist perspective. Although gay men have produced pioneering work on sexuality, male academic interest in gender (despite some honourable exceptions) has been less developed. Even in the academy, there has been only modest weakening of the prevalent view that the problem of gender is posed essentially by women, not men.

Stereotypes and role models

Mainstream sociology, tackling the issue of gender, focuses on the unequal position of men and women within the social structure. Key areas investigated include the family, work and pay, and sexuality. The devaluation of women's role, whether as mothers, wives, or workers has been a central concern. For the sociologist, femininity is acquired and reproduced through socialization and the development of self-concept. Real-life role models, the exposure in childhood to forms of activity and play that naturalize gender divisions, and the influence of the media and other cultural forms, encourage men and women in adult life both to adopt behaviour that reinforces gender-specific roles, and to internalize the appropriateness of this as part of their own sense of identity.

Gender as a category is often linked by sociologists to other forms of social classification such as class or ethnicity. Results, for example, of a self-attitude test incorporated into interviews with 40 married mothers in Ann Oakley's pioneering study of housework (1974) found that middle-class women tended to base their self-concept on their individual personality characteristics, whereas working-class women were more likely to define themselves in terms of their domestic role. Other studies have challenged white assumptions about the socialization process. Standard accounts of the construction of femininity are accused of ignoring the impact of the specific family structures and work experiences of ethnic minority groups (see, for example, Mirza, 1990).

For the sociologist investigating gender, the media play an important part in setting stereotypes and promoting a limited number of role models. Unlike social psychologists, who mainly adopt a developmental approach to socialization, sociologists concentrate on adult influences. The concept of the stereotype is used to criticize the reduction of the three-dimensional quality of the real to a one-dimensional and distorted form. Particularly when the group being stereotyped is already in a disadvantaged position, the stereotype intensifies the offence. From bra-burning feminists to house-proud housewives, from sex-crazed seductresses to neurotic career-women, the media regularly serve a menu of female stereotypes that stimulates misogynistic taste buds. Yet, as Tessa Perkins pointed out (1979), stereotypes survive by undergoing change, and by convincing us that they are not entirely false, but contain a 'kernel of truth'. Like ideology, the stereotype works by being plausible, and by masking its own value-system. Those who criticize the limitations of the stereotype often also demand a wider range of positive role models, especially for groups that are denigrated or marginalized. The relative lack, for example, of professional women in soap operas, or of fat, disabled or Asian women in women's magazines, attracts frequent censure.

There are, however, a number of problems in relying on stereotypes as a critical tool. First, this approach suggests that the ideal would be for the media to re-present reality as truthfully and accurately as possible. As I indicated in the Introduction, this begs at least two questions: whose version of reality is to be given priority, and what happens in those instances, such as advertising or film, where the producers' stated intention is not to represent reality but to conjure up an appealing fantasy world? Hunting stereotypes can be an entertaining but ultimately unrewarding pastime. It can also be dangerous, if we fail to take account of the play on stereotypes that is increasingly common in the media. The short-lived Scottish feminist magazine *Harpies and Quines* ('quines' is a Scottish dialect word for women) provoked a storm of protest in the early months of 1994 when it used an advertising slogan 'not just for dungaree-clad dykes' over an image of a sexually alluring woman provocatively sporting a low-cut black dress. Perceived by lesbian readers as insulting, and by heterosexual feminists as advocating *Cosmopolitan* glamour values, this advertisement appeared to many readers to negate the magazine's claim that it was intended to be ironical and to poke fun at existing stereotypes.

While sociologists who have transferred from straight sociology to cultural studies have developed important work on the reading and interpretation of images and words, analysis of stereotyping focuses solely on texts. At its crudest, it even disregards how the stereotype is integrated within the text, and is blinkered to the possibility that the same stereotype can be presented within the narrative context of soap opera or film as either a victim or as the protagonist. This distinction in terms of *narrative* role has more impact on our responses than our understanding of the character's *social* role. Listing the media stage entrances of, for example, the 1980s' stereotype of the 'superwoman', effortlessly combining career, children, sexual pleasure and leisure pursuits, tells us nothing about how we are invited to respond to her. To answer this crucial question we need to attend both to her role within the text's structure, and to the varying reactions of different audiences.

Tracing dominant stereotypes historically is more helpful in revealing changing ideologies. Why the 'vamp' should have been popular in the early decades of the century, the 'dumb blond' in the middle, and the 'superwoman' in the last quarter, are issues worth exploring in the quest to understand how myths of femininity have changed. Equally revealing is the continuing imbalance in both the extent and quality of male and female stereotyping in media constructions. Stereotypes of men (e.g. 'macho man') may elicit negative emotions but they do little to dent male authority. Even the 'new man' stereotype, far from weakening male power, has been cynically viewed by some critics as an attempt to shore up masculinity's defences against the erosion of feminism (see, for example, Chapman, 1988).

The sociological approach has been dubbed by its critics the 'images of women' method of analysis (see Byars, 1991, pp. 67–77 for a fuller discussion of this). Inspired by semiotics (the study of meaning-production through verbal and visual signs), and by European structuralism (to be discussed in the cultural theory section at the end of this chapter), these critics argued that it was misleading to look for a correspondence between media characters and real-life women. Instead, the business of criticism was to explore the textual construction of 'woman', either through analysis of codes such as the cinematic shot (which might, for example, establish woman as an object of voyeuristic contemplation), or through inspection of her varying narrative roles. The centre of interest shifted from *what* the media showed to *how* they produced meaning through an interaction between text and reader or viewer. Sociologists who began to engage with these debates in the 1970s helped to found one strand of the British tradition of cultural studies. In terms of analysing the informational media, and sub-cultures, the pioneering work was undertaken by the Birmingham Centre for Contemporary Cultural Studies. In the analysis of fiction, this approach developed primarily within film studies.

Critics from the European-influenced British film journal *Screen* in the 1970s and early 1980s distanced themselves from the approach adopted by American writers such as Marjorie Rosen and Molly Haskell in their sociological surveys of women in the cinema. Both Rosen's *Popcorn Venus* (1973) and Haskell's *From Reverence to Rape* (first published in 1974) examined the chronological development of dominant roles for women in Hollywood films and related this to social developments. Annette Kuhn (1982), herself an erstwhile sociologist, argued against seeking such a simple relationship between film and social change. Instead, she advocated digging beneath the text's surface to explore its hidden structures and to uncover through this process the film's ideological operation. Although disagreeing with Rosen and Haskell's method, she argued for a form of film analysis that would use 'attention to the internal operations of film texts' to 'inform analyses of their institutional, social and historical contexts' (1982, p. 83). The radical difference between their approaches was that Kuhn wanted to start with the text; Rosen and Haskell with the context.

All in the mind

Psychology considers gender, our sense of being male or female, to be one of the primary categories through which we evolve socially appropriate behaviour patterns, develop our expectations about our lives, and interpret our experiences. Psychological approaches agree that the acquisition of gender identity is a developmental process that is virtually complete by the time we reach adulthood. As a result, psychological research into the media has concentrated on the impact of media representations on children and young people. Where the sociologist is interested in the relationship between representation and reality, the psychologist is particularly concerned with psychological effect.

Three main psychological theories exist about how we acquire masculine or feminine identities. The first, which is often referred to as 'biological determinism', argues that femininity and masculinity follow inevitably from our physical differences as males and females. Biological factors act as programmes which circumscribe our ability to move outside a pre-set range of behaviour and attributes. The second, known as social learning theory, claims that we acquire the relevant masculine or feminine skills by imitating others, and adapting our own conduct and attitudes, while the third, cognitive-developmental theory, maintains that masculinity and femininity develop through a process of interaction between our experience of the world and our emerging, but pre-structured, capacity for conceptual thinking.

Biological determinists' view of sexual difference has been labelled 'essentialist'. Essentialism is a philosophical position that believes in intrinsic, material differences between entities. It makes sense in the physical sciences, where elements can be distinguished clearly from each other, but applied to humans its suggestion that innate qualities have a more determining influence than social or cultural factors sparks repeated controversy. Recently, theories of the genetic origins of homosexuality have rekindled debate between biological determinists and those who emphasize the social and cultural construction of sexuality. In relation to gender, the biological determinist argues that the imprints of masculinity and femininity are contained within genes and hormones. Male aggression and female nurturing capacity are seen as innate tendencies, although most biological determinists (e.g. Maccoby and Jacklin, 1974) do accept that biological predisposition may be affected to varying degrees by social factors.

Many feminist psychologists (e.g. Rohrbaugh, 1981; Lott, 1990) reject the prescriptiveness of biological determinism and argue that it has been used, despite its scientific credentials, in a value-loaded way to excuse antisocial male behaviour and devalue women's capacities (as when rapists are seen as 'naturally' requiring sexual release, or women are thought to have 'natural' manual dexterity that makes them good at sewing but not at surgery). Lynda Birke (1986) takes a different stance. While distancing herself from biological determinism, she views whole-sale feminist antagonism to biological accounts of gender development as misguided. She argues instead that psychologists should extend the time-scale of their investigations into gender formation to include the influence of adult biological experiences such as menstruation, child-birth and the menopause on women's sense of identity and femininity. This approach interestingly challenges psychology's tendency to focus on early development, and replaces a deterministic view of biological influence with a more socially interactive model.

More conventionally, both cognitive-developmental and social learn-ing theories concentrate on childhood and adolescence as the periods responsible for forming our adult sense of masculinity and femininity. Cognitive-developmental approaches stress the role of the individual's own processing of information; social learning theorists, on the other hand, emphasize the part played by the individual's social environment in providing role models and stimuli. Cognitive-developmentalists stress that masculinity and femininity are *concepts*, while social learning theorists focus on the learning and adoption of *behaviour* which is thought to be appropriate for men and women.

For the social learning theorist, femininity and masculinity are first recognized, and then imitated in the child's own behaviour. Factors such as schooling, play, family life, and the media are seen as significant influences. Where the theory is weak is in explaining why the child should be motivated to imitate some forms of behaviour and attitude rather than others. In this sense, social learning theory shares the limita-tions of the behaviourist or 'effects' model of media influence. It assumes that exposure to a stimulus results in a predictable influence, and, by concentrating on a single stimulus at a time, it neglects the interactive and potentially contradictory effects of a number of factors operating simultaneously. Cognitive-developmental approaches, as their some-what cumbersome title suggests, take a more complex view of learning (cognition, in psychology, refers to the mental processes involved in perception and the formation of knowledge).

The cognitive-developmentalist most frequently cited in relation to gender is Harvard psychologist, Lawrence Kohlberg, although he has increasingly drawn criticism from feminist psychologists (e.g. Gilligan, 1982) for explaining male development more convincingly than female. Following in the tradition of the Swiss philosopher and psychologist, Jean Piaget, he believes that children progress through stages of conceptual development which are fixed in terms of sequence but more flexible in terms of the age at which they occur in the individual child. Unlike the social learning theorist, Kohlberg contends that the child's own conceptual capacities are deeply involved in processing the knowledge gained from the environment, making an 'imitation' model seem naïve. His research suggests, for example, that young children lack a sense of 'gender constancy', and believe instead that a girl can become a boy by playing boys' games, wearing boys' clothes and having her hair cut in the style of a boy. By the age of six or seven, this has changed and gender constancy is acquired. Children now recognize that boys remain boys and girls remain girls regardless of outward adornment.

Once gender constancy has been reached, Kohlberg claims that boys and girls then identify closely with, and want to imitate, their own gender. His examples of this, revealingly, are drawn from interviews with boys. While it is easy, given the social status of masculinity, to explain why little boys want to develop masculine characteristics, his own findings leave us with a puzzle in relation to girls. All six-year-olds of whichever gender, Kohlberg himself claims (Kohlberg and Ullian, 1974, pp. 212–13), place a high value on aggression, power and smartness, which they identify as masculine characteristics. Why a girl of this age should therefore want to become more feminine remains mysterious. Kohlberg, indeed, indirectly answers his own conundrum by suggesting that, between the ages of about five and eight, girls become temporarily less sex-typed than boys. Beyond this period, girls begin to recognize the social pressures that require them to conform to feminine behaviour, and, by adulthood, Kohlberg's research finds quite sophisticated awareness of how these pressures operate. Kohlberg attributes these shifts to stages in conceptual development. This may describe the mechanisms involved, but it does not explain how children and adolescents learn the relative values of masculinity and femininity. For this, an awareness of socio-cultural influences needs to be added to Kohlberg's account.

Kohlberg's finding that young adults have a clear sense of the gap between the concepts that they carry around in their heads, and the social realities, is of more interest. By about the age of 18, Kohlberg's research subjects appreciated that distinct attributes are only conventionally ascribed to men or women. The possibility of gentleness being a quality in men or aggression in women is now well understood, although this is still perceived as breaching the norms (Kohlberg and Ullian, 1974, p. 222). What this suggests, and it is an important finding for media studies, is that people are perfectly capable of simultaneously balancing two competing sets of ideas about the world:

- how they perceive it to be from their own observations;
- how they think it is generally expected to be and thought to be.

The first type of knowledge is based on experience, the second on an awareness of dominant ideologies. What Kohlberg's research discovers, and it is a finding supported by other media-related research such as Elizabeth Frazer's (see Introduction), is that even when experience challenges the ideological view, experience will not necessarily prevail. The 18-year-old's earlier notions of masculinity and femininity survive encounters with contrary evidence.

The three main psychological approaches to gender development have varying strengths. Least convincing is biological determinism, weakened both by its reliance on dubious comparisons between humans and animals and its energetic body-swerve around cross-cultural evidence that suggests the importance of social and cultural influences. Social learning theorists take these influences on board, but in an unduly instrumental way. The most persuasive account of the interaction between our experience and the development of our thinking and perception is provided by cognitive-developmental theory, but it, too, gives scant attention to the effects of the social and cultural framework within which development occurs. Psychology's focus on individual difference often leads it to undervalue factors such as ethnicity, place within the family, and even sometimes social class and education when accounting for development (for a critique of this see Phoenix, 1987). Gender itself was long neglected, and many feminist psychologists still struggle to raise its profile within the discipline (see Siann, 1994).

One of the best known attempts to redress psychology's gender imbalance was Carol Gilligan's *In a Different Voice* (1982). A student of Kohlberg, she objected to his neglect of women, particularly in his account of moral development. By basing his ideas on men, Gilligan argues, Kohlberg endorsed a morality dominated by rules and principles, and devalued women's moral focus on relationships and the needs of others. Had he instead assumed women to be the norm, Gilligan claims, his conclusions about moral maturity would have been reversed. Her work, although contentious, has been influential beyond the area of morality, supporting theories that women are more other-directed in their social behaviour than men, and that women's ways of thinking are different from men's. As we will see in the next chapter, these views have been controversially echoed in recent decades in the writings of some French feminist theorists.

If psychologists have been reluctant to explore gender issues, they have long been happy to see sex difference as a fixed variable, dividing humans into two irreconcilable camps of male and female. It was the discovery of androgyny that first ruffled these waters. As a specifically psychological term, 'androgyny' first appeared in an article by Sandra Bem in the *Journal of Consulting and Clinical Psychology* (1974). Bem discussed the results of an experiment that tested the degree to which subjects described themselves in terms of masculine and feminine attributes. The scale which she used has become known as the BSRI (Bem Sex Role Inventory), and included 20 adjectives commonly associated with masculinity and 20 commonly associated with femininity. Women who rated highly on the 'masculine' scale or men who rated highly on the 'feminine' scale were regarded as androgynous. As Kevin Durkin has pointed out, this uncovering of androgynous individuals was rapidly incorporated into the ideological arena where it tended to be heralded as a new standard of healthy and liberated personal adjustment (1985, p. 106).

Feminists and other critics who perceive femininity and masculinity to be social constructions were less convinced. They argued that, far from reducing the importance of gender difference as she desired, Bem's lists of opposing attributes ironically reinforced the view that the essential characteristics of masculinity and femininity were fixed and pre-ordained. Critics also complained that Bem ignored the continuing power imbalance between men and women by tacitly implying equal status to an androgynous woman and an androgynous man. Bernice Lott's criticism that androgyny ultimately undermined 'the possibility of degendering behavior' (1981, p. 178) held growing sway in the 1980s, and caused Sandra Bem herself to rethink her ideas.

In the study of gender in the media, the contribution from psychologists has been surprisingly modest. Even in the burgeoning area of adult audience studies, where issues of gender and its impact on our reactions to texts have become prominent in cultural studies (see cultural theory section on page 33), psychological perspectives are underdeveloped. Sonia Livingstone's work, drawing socio-cognitive approaches and Erving Goffman's participation frameworks into audience analysis, is an exception (Livingstone, 1990; Livingstone and Lunt, 1992). Psychology's tendency to treat gender primarily as a developmental issue produces more plentiful studies analysing the effects of the media on children and young people. Early investigations into this, adopting the behaviourist emphasis of social learning theory, tried to establish direct links between gender stereotyping in comics, television programming or advertising and gender-typed behaviour on the part of their young readers and audiences. Most of these studies were inconclusive because they ignored the social circumstances of the children, and underestimated the degree to which young people, like adults, process the information and ideas they are exposed to.

More recent work has acknowledged the role of cognition. Kevin Durkin (1985) argued for extending the cognitive-developmental approach to take account of children's ability to relate what they see on the screen to their other social experiences and knowledge. Referring to this as 'social cognition', he suggests that we should see children as script-writers, making sense of their viewing in complex and interactive ways. More simplistic models of effect, whether of stereotyping or counter-stereotyping (depicting men in traditionally female roles, or women in typically male roles), have, in his view, underestimated the importance of what happens beyond the television set. His approach has also been favoured by psychologists such as Palmer (1986) and Messenger Davies (1989) who challenge pessimistic interpretations of the corrupting influence of television on young minds by demonstrating that television viewing is just one part of a complex social universe with which children learn to deal actively and creatively.

One of the few attempts to apply psychological theory to the interpretation of texts by adults ignores the issue of gender completely. David Bordwell (1985) suggests that cognition and perception theory can be usefully applied to the analysis of films. Pleasure in film viewing, he argues, comes from testing out schemata, or hypotheses about the direction that the story is going to take. Unlike the critical approaches built around psychoanalytical theory, pleasure for David Bordwell remains gender-neutral.

Unconscious desires

If psychology has contributed less than we might expect to our under-standing of either the formation of myths of femininity and masculinity or their appeal for us, the opposite is the case with its sibling rival, psychoanalysis. By probing unconscious desires and motivations, psychoanalysis offers a theory of pleasure that addresses the complex and sometimes contradictory nature of our responses to media texts. In also suggesting that femininity is not a fixed identity acquired with maturity, but a constantly renegotiated set of alliances and identifica-tions, it helps to make conceptual sense of our varying reactions to representations of women in media forms. On the other hand, psycho-analysis (and especially those varieties that take their cue from Freud) serves as a curious analytical prop for women because it tends to perceive the male as the norm, and, by concentrating on unconscious rather than conscious processes, leaves little scope for change. Despite this, feminist cultural criticism, and feminist film criticism in particular, has since the 1970s embraced psychoanalysis, although the relationship has become more strained in recent years.

Up until the 1970s, feminism gave psychoanalysis the wide berth thought appropriate to an essentially patriarchal theory ('patriarchy' refers literally to rule by fathers or male heads of household, but has increasingly been used more loosely to refer to rule by men in general). It was the publication of Juliet Mitchell's *Psychoanalysis and Feminism* in 1974 that signalled a change of perspective. Confronting head-on the charge that Freudian psychoanalysis regarded the male as normal, and the female by implication as abnormal, Juliet Mitchell argued that 'psychoanalysis is not a recommendation *for* a patriarchal society, but an analysis *of* one' (1975, p. xv). Psychoanalysis, in her view, offered the only convincing theory of gender difference, and made up for the deficiencies in this respect of Marxism, still fashionable as a means of exploring social class. In part, Mitchell was reacting against the pre-dominantly sociological explanations of women's oppression in the writings of American feminists of the period. Betty Friedan, Shulamith Firestone, and Kate Millett were all attacked for trying to explain women's relation to femininity through rational and conscious pro-cesses: 'With Millett . . . empiricism run riot denies more than the unconscious; it denies any attribute of the mind other than rationality' (1975, p. 354).

Amongst feminists, Mitchell's views were contentious: seen by some as a dangerously seductive dalliance with the enemy, by others as a productive and illuminating relationship. Within British cultural criticism, the latter view prevailed. This alliance gained support and stimulus from the European influence of structuralism and, later, poststructuralism (see the cultural theory section on page 33 for a fuller discussion). What united all these theories, and shifted debates about gender irrevocably, was their challenge to the supremacy of the rational subject, equated by many feminists, however contentiously, with masculine forms of thought and control. Both poststructuralism and psychoanalysis (at least in its post-Freudian versions) helped to replace the concept of the unified 'subject' with that of fragmented and unstable 'subjectivities'. Although this may sound like a semantic quibble, it marked a profound shift in thinking about the production of knowledge and meaning, with important consequences for gender.

From the eighteenth century, the primacy of reason established by the movement known as the Enlightenment established the thinking individual as the agent of progress. It was believed that, through education, the individual, or subject, would be in control of knowledge and the capable originator of ideas. Maturity was marked by a stable sense of identity and security of place in the world. In the second half of the twentieth century, these certainties, characterized as typically masculine by some feminist critics, have been more widely and systematically undermined. Psychoanalysis and structuralism both suggest that the individual is not in charge of his or her experience, but influenced and in part formed by it. Poststructuralism takes this further. From thinking subjects, consistently directing and in control, we become like the stage or screen actor, changing identity with the scripts we are given, even if we retain the freedom to interpret the words. Since this more precarious and less unified version of what it means to be a subject is fundamentally different from the Enlightenment one, it is often distinguished by the term 'subjectivity'.

Within cultural and film studies, the prime psychoanalytic influences have been Sigmund Freud (1856–1939) and Jacques Lacan (1901–81). Their ideas have been used to account for the differences in male and female viewing positions in relation to film or other visual media, and Lacanian ideas in particular have helped to explain the role of culture in perpetuating subjectivities for women which are split, fragmented and unstable. For Freud, the unconscious mind and infant sexuality were the critical agents in the development of boys' and girls' gender identity. He first explored the processes through which the boy learned to transfer his affections from his mother to women in general, and, later, the processes through which girls learned to transfer their affections from mothers to men. Put in these terms, the relative disadvantage of the girl is transparent. Boys have to make a relatively simple adjustment in their desires: girls have to jump more problematic hurdles.

The key transitional stages which Freud identified he named the Oedipus and castration complexes. For the boy, the early love of the mother (in the Oedipal stage) had to be restrained and resolved, through castration anxiety. Unconsciously fearing that his desire to possess his mother would lead his father to remove his penis, the boy learns to control this desire, holding it in reserve for other women. He develops a strong superego, or moral censor, as awareness of what is socially acceptable tempers the raw passions of the 'id' (Freud's term for unbridled desires). Initially, Freud appeared untroubled that his model could not be applied sensibly to girls. Later, he explained that whereas the castration complex resolved the Oedipus complex for boys, it merely inaugurated this for girls. Realizing that the mother lacked a penis too, the little girl, again unconsciously, learns to despise her mother, and turns to her father, hoping that his ability to give her a baby will compensate for her lack. Feminine identity is won, according to Freud, through an especially perilous process, with numerous pitfalls which increase the chances of neurosis. This can, of course, happen too in the boy's progression towards maturity, but the risk is less.

Femininity generally remained a puzzle to Freud, but this did not prevent him from defining it as a thoroughly undesirable state. Addressing an imaginary audience in a lecture on femininity in 1932 (the lecture was never delivered), Freud commented: 'Throughout history people have knocked their heads against the riddle of the nature of femininity ... Nor will you have escaped worrying over this problem – those of you who are men; to those of you who are women this will not apply – you are yourselves the problem' (1964, p. 113). Narcissism; masochism and passivity; and a weak superego which leads to women having a poor sense of justice, and being more prone to envy and other base instincts, were all seen in the same lecture as characteristics of the feminine.

Contrary to his popular image, Freud does occasionally claim to acknowledge the influence of social factors in directing women towards feminine and men towards masculine behaviour. We must, he comments, 'beware ... of underestimating the influence of social customs, which ... force women into passive situations' (1964, p. 116).

Masochism, likewise, he admits, develops partly in response to social pressure. With tongue-in-cheek modesty, he concludes that 'psychology too is unable to solve the riddle of femininity' (1964, p. 116). Freud may have been more judicious in some of his statements than popular versions of his ideas have indicated, but we need to take disclaimers such as this with a pinch of salt. However indisputable his contention that psychology (and psychoanalysis) cannot by themselves solve the puzzle of femininity, his legacy has been precisely to confirm expectations that they can. By tying gender identity and desire so uniquely to apparently universal sexual processes, Freud effectively blanks out the agency of external social influences or of internal cognitive structuring, however politely and occasionally he nods in their direction.

The chronological span of Freud's writings makes his ideas difficult to summarize. Jacques Lacan poses a different problem of accessibility. Deliberately avoiding the easy intelligibility of Freud's thinking, Lacan challenges his readers with the complex interaction between language and our unconscious processes. This has been masked, he claims, in our routine familiarity with language. For the cultural critic, the abstruse quality of Lacan's writing encourages us to rely excessively on what others have said about his ideas rather than on his own articulation of these. While this poses dangers, it has also had the effect of enhancing Lacan's status as a guru.

Lacan reinterpreted Freud's ideas, replacing Freud's biological emphasis on the penis with an emphasis on the phallus as the symbolic reproducer of patriarchy. The psychic processes which produce gendered subjectivity are still at the forefront of his argument, but he, like the poststructuralists, thinks of subjectivity as fractured and unstable. Freud's pre-Oedipal phase Lacan renamed 'the Imaginary'. Between about six and 18 months, the young child develops an embryonic but deceptive sense of self, in what Lacan refers to as the 'mirror phase'. Either from physically staring in fascination at its actual mirror-image, or getting the warm glow of self-identity from the reactions of other people, the child's initial fragmented vision of self blends into a comforting organic sense of wholeness and completeness. What is haunting about this stage is that it can only be temporary and evanescent, momentarily glimpsed like a mirage. For the rest of our lives, the sense of individual completeness or wholeness must remain tantalizingly Imaginary. For Lacan, the pre-Oedipal stage precedes the entry into language and culture, or, as Lacan expresses it, into 'the Symbolic'. Set for us like a snare, language traps us in the 'Law of the Father', with the phallus (the symbolic penis) the activating spring.

Our acquisition of language, in Lacanian terms, splits us off from others, and fractures the sense of totality which we briefly enjoyed in the mirror stage. A central part of that fracturing comes from recognizing our gender difference, and our relative positioning within the patriarchal structure. Awareness that 'he' is different from 'she' (as well as 'I' from 'you') marks a rite of passage which permanently disables us from ever regaining the state of Imaginary rapture. While for Freud stability of identity is achieved developmentally, for Lacan our continuing encounters and interactions with 'the Symbolic' invite us throughout our lives constantly to renegotiate our relation to it, producing a precarious and shifting set of identifications.

In common with Freud, Lacan was no feminist, but his ideas of 'the Symbolic' and the significance of language and culture in regenerating patriarchy through unconscious processes put a gendered gloss on the increasingly fashionable structuralist and poststructuralist trends in British cultural thought in the 1970s and 1980s. Freud's reinstatement within feminism made Lacan's thinking doubly attractive to feminist cultural critics since he avoided the biological determinism around which feminists had to fence so nimbly. It would be a mistake, however, to pretend that Lacan is any less guilty of determinism than Freud. Replacing the penis with language as the central signifier and reproducer of patriarchy is hardly a blow for liberation. How, as beings obliged to think and communicate through language, can we escape the limitations of our gender, and produce the political and social change that feminism has always seen as its principal objective? The puzzle continues to engage feminists, and to elicit some deft footwork from pro-Lacanians. Jacqueline Rose, for example, argues that the appeal of psychoanalysis to feminists is that it recognizes 'that there is a resistance to identity which lies at the very heart of psychic life' (1990, p. 232). Psychoanalysis, in other words, rejects the conclusion of the self-styled postfeminist that femininity and feminism can be happily blended into a new improved mix, and characterizes women instead as constantly torn between competing identities, restlessly swinging between admiration for a feminine Julia Roberts in *Pretty Woman* one moment, and an adventurous Sigourney Weaver in *Aliens* the next.

Psychoanalysis and film

It was Laura Mulvey who first examined the relevance of Freudian and Lacanian psychoanalysis for the process of viewing films, in an influential article entitled 'Visual Pleasure and Narrative Cinema', published in the British film journal *Screen* in 1975. This was a novel, even revolutionary, idea. Questions of gender in film had mainly centred on representations on the screen, on texts rather than audiences. Sociological analysis of stereotyping formed the dominant approach and, as we saw above, characterized two significant American books on women and film which appeared just before Mulvey's article. Mulvey took the audience, and particularly the audience's pleasure in film, as her starting-point. Instead of examining this empirically, by talking to actual viewers, as later critics were to do (e.g. Pribram, 1988), Mulvey explores the psychodynamic relationship between spectator and text.

She argues that classic American film gives priority to male perspectives, both narratively, by giving male stars the more interesting roles, and visually, by making women the object of a dominant male gaze. This operates on two dimensions: the female characters on the screen tend to be filmed in a way that emphasizes their 'to-be-looked-at-ness', and point of view shots within the frame are predominantly from a male perspective. The spectator swings, in Mulvey's view, between the Freudian process of voyeuristic and erotic gazing from a safe distance (scopophilia) and the close identification with the characters on the screen that reactivates the Lacanian mirror phase. Like the child's intense pleasure in the imaginary self-recognition in the mirror image, identification operates as a seductive and involuntary magnetism drawing the spectator into the space within the frame. Both in viewing from the distance of the darkened auditorium, safe in our invisibility, and in identifying with the dominant male point of view within the frame, it is the male perspective, Mulvey argues, that is privileged.

At the same time, Mulvey observes that the visually stunning woman threatens to activate castration anxiety in the male viewer. Two strategies are used in American film to prevent this destroying his pleasure. One is to turn the woman, again in Freudian terms, into a fetish, thereby distracting attention from her fatal lack of a penis. This might be achieved by draping her in furs or figure-hugging silk or, more dramatically, by placing a phallic weapon in her hand. The second tactic is to ensure that the plot narratively restores the threatening woman to her due place in the patriarchal order by the end of the film either by punishing her or by reintegrating her into a romantic relationship with a man.

A number of problems with Mulvey's ideas were visible right from the start; others have surfaced as mainstream film itself has changed.

Ironically, for an article now widely hailed as the pioneering work in feminist film criticism, Mulvey in 1975 consistently used the male pronoun to refer to the spectator. Attacked for failing to explain adequately how her theories affected women in the audience, Laura Mulvey refined her ideas in an article in 1981. The spectator, she now claimed, was not necessarily male, but *masculine*, adopting a masculine subjectivity or subject position when viewing a film. Reluctant to see this as an imposition, Mulvey argues that film entices women as spectators to enjoy masculine pleasures. It is a lure which women may resist, but only, she implies, through a conscious act of will: 'it is always possible that the female spectator may find herself so out of key with the pleasure on offer, with its "masculinisation", that the spell is broken. On the other hand she may not. She may find herself secretly, unconsciously almost, enjoying the freedom of action and control over the diegetic [fictional] world that identification with a hero provides' (1981, p. 12).

Women's readiness to slip out of a feminine and into a masculine subjectivity was explained, Mulvey believed, by Freud's ideas of the early bisexuality of the individual. Women are socially weaned out of their early familiarity with masculinity, but retain their attraction to it. When the film narrative encourages admiration for the male hero, and the viewing positions on offer reinforce this, women spectators find no initial difficulty in recovering their bisexual origins: 'for women (from childhood onwards) trans-sex identification is a *habit* that very easily becomes *second Nature*'. But, as social pressures urge women to conform to the ideal of femininity, 'this Nature does not sit easily and shifts restlessly in its borrowed transvestite clothes' (1981, p. 13).

Mulvey also recognizes now that there is a question mark over how her theory applies to films where female characters hold centre stage. Evasively, even for 1981, she answers this question with the example of *Duel in the Sun*, a 1940s' melodrama, where the leading female character is perpetually racked by a desire to reactivate the forbidden masculinity of the Freudian childhood. Passion and adventure fight for ascendancy over femininity and romance, but the struggle is one that inevitably ends in tragedy. Mulvey makes no claims for *Duel in the Sun* being typical even of its own genre, and by limiting her argument to this one film she sidesteps the more challenging aspects of films where women are the protagonists and the controllers of the gaze.

By focusing on the psychodynamics of identification, Mulvey also ignores other pleasures that are potentially on offer to women spectators. As Jackie Stacey points out in a thoughtful critique of Mulvey's

ılture where the circulation of idealised and desirable
ıinity constantly surrounds us, the phenomenon of
ween women is hardly surprising' (1988, p. 114). Reduc-
ion to the pleasure of erotic looking misses other oppor-
ight along the way. Recent work has highlighted the
the dress and personal style of female stars as a source
women (Gaines and Herzog, 1990; Gledhill, 1991), and
women derive from female characters' verbal wit remains

ılvey recognizes the existence of the female spectator,
ıriety of social factors which impinge on our viewing
owerfully, on our talking and arguing about films
afterwards. Most surprisingly, given her own emphasis on the play of
erotic and sexual desire, she sidesteps the impact on viewing of the spectator's sexual orientation. To characterize Madonna, Debra Winger and
Sharon Stone as equivalent objects of the male gaze is to elide the very
different pleasures which may be on offer not just to lesbian and
heterosexual women but also to homosexual and heterosexual men.
Writing when she did, Mulvey can be more readily excused for not
exploring the impact on her ideas of the growing tendency in the 1980s,
in advertising, photography and film, to present the male body, too,
as an object of erotic contemplation.

Early tendencies to treat Mulvey's ideas as a new orthodoxy in
film studies have increasingly given way to more sceptical analyses.
Freudian and Lacanian versions of psychoanalysis, however, remain
powerful influences within film studies, even when these are reworked
in new ways (e.g. Creed, 1993). By relying on these psychiatrists'
universalist account of unconscious processes, social, cultural and
historical influences on desire have been eclipsed. The unconscious
mind does not come, like a McDonald's hamburger, in globally standar-
dized shape and texture. Black psychoanalysts have commented that the
Freudian unconscious, with its emphasis on the individual, makes little
sense for black cultures. Even Freud admitted that the unconscious is
not a universal given, but a cupboard where we shove the junk that
our culture discourages us from putting on display. While he concentrates on the role this hidden mess plays in our daily lives, a more
interesting and relevant question is how we decide what can be
displayed, and what should be hidden. We all obey tacit rules about
this in our own homes, variously exhibiting or concealing pots and pans
in the kitchen, tampons in the bathroom, and videotapes on our

bookshelves. These unspoken codes reveal a great deal about our culture, and about our own place within it. For women, strongly affected by material circumstances, these are questions that should not be obliterated by a fascinated peep behind the cupboard door.

Other forms of psychoanalysis have attempted to explore the interaction between social circumstances and the psyche in forming our gendered reactions. Nancy Chodorow (1978), for example, uses an approach known as 'object-relations theory' to investigate the impact of mother–child relations on the psychic structures that pursue us into adulthood. Mothers, she argues, encourage independence and individuality in their sons; bonding and attention to interpersonal relationships in their daughters. This difference is compounded by boys' tendency to seek masculine role models outside the home, while girls focus on those within the domestic sphere. Rejecting both the behaviourist emphasis of psychology's social learning theory, and the individualist emphasis of cognitive-developmental approaches, Chodorow emphasizes the psychic legacy of these early tendencies in preparing daughters, in their turn, for motherhood. At the same time, avoiding the determinism of Freud and Lacan, she argues that the cycle can be broken by involving men more fully in parenting.

Chodorow's ideas have been contentious not least because she has been interpreted by some feminist critics as blaming mothers for society's gender inequalities. Her model of parenting also implies a conventional nuclear family with a working father and a home-based mother. Even in the late 1970s, this was a partial picture of social reality. Yet her evaluation of the relations between mothers and daughters does at least provide a basis for theorizing women's identification with other women in cultural forms that is absent from Freud and Lacan. Despite a gradual acknowledgement of this within cultural criticism (Byars, 1991, for example, acknowledges Chodorow's usefulness in discussing 1950s' female-orientated melodramas), she remains a marginal influence compared with her male predecessors.

Historical ways of seeing

Psychoanalysis, together with psychology, sees our personal and individual history as more significant than our cultural past in forming our consciousness and our unconscious desires. Art historians, on the other hand, stress the collective baggage that our culture invites us to carry with us. This rich inheritance, once tucked away in art galleries and stately homes, now extends its influence into contemporary advertising, photography and pop music videos. For much of this century, art history, in common with most other disciplines, ignored the issue of gender, but since the 1970s a significant body of work has both explored the contribution to art of neglected but influential women, and reviewed the traditions and patterns of women's representation on canvas or in sculpture.

John Berger's *Ways of Seeing*, published in 1972 in conjunction with a BBC television series, pioneered this review, and signalled the different emphases of the art historian and the psychoanalytic critic. Exploring continuities in the visual representation of women from fifteenth-century oil painting through to 1970s' advertising and magazines, Berger argues that women are trained by the traditions of their visual representation in western culture to look at themselves from a masculine perspective. His conclusion is strikingly similar to Laura Mulvey's, but Berger's argument is based on historical precedent rather than unconscious processes. Western art, he claims, poses women, nude or partially clothed, for the benefit of a masculine spectator. Women have internalized those ways of looking at themselves that permeate this tradition:

> In the art-form of the European nude the painters and spectator-owners were usually men and the persons treated as objects, usually women. This unequal relationship is so deeply embedded in our culture that it still structures the consciousness of many women. They do to themselves what men do to them. They survey, like men, their own femininity.
>
> (Berger, 1972, p. 63)

The pattern of looking that Berger outlines anticipates Mulvey's association between activity/looking/masculinity and passivity/being-looked-at/femininity. As a Marxist critic, he differs significantly from her in relating the power structure implicit in these relations not to psychic processes, but to the economic and social structures that allowed this pattern to etch itself on our consciousnesses.

Berger's argument is stronger on polemic than on detail. The same cannot be said of Marina Warner's *Monuments and Maidens* (1987), which is a triumph of rigorous historical scholarship. Warner escorts the reader on a panoramic tour of Greek and Judaeo-Christian myths, through centuries of sculpture and painting, to demonstrate the kaleidoscopic ways in which images of women have repeatedly signified qualities of a symbolic nature. From the Statue of Liberty to Margaret Thatcher, from Joan of Arc to Eve, Warner examines with panache and frequent displays of wit the ease with which women become the bearers of meanings beyond themselves: standing for justice, architecture, liberty, peace, warfare, or the downfall of humanity. The medley is striking. 'Men often appear as themselves, as individuals, but women attest the identity and value of someone or something else . . . Meanings of all kinds flow through the figures of women, and they often do not include who she herself is' (1987, p. 331). Like the shop-window model with her dehumanized body, 'woman' springs to life only when culture decides the apparel through which she is to be seen. Her face, meanwhile, retains wax-like inscrutability.

The mechanisms that enable colourings of femininity to seep into our consciousness are not explained by Warner. She is, though, sufficiently optimistic to believe that women can begin to reverse the process by taking up 'squatters' rights' to the public forms of communication that have traditionally imposed their own meaning on the female form (1987, p. 333). The squatter may never be other than a courageous but vulnerable usurper of space, but, in a related British television series (*Picturing women*, Channel 4, July 1986), Marina Warner cites feminists working in the arts of sculpture, painting, music, fashion and dance as occupiers who will not sit mutely and patiently in the dark.

Other feminist art historians have turned the spotlight on neglected gendered aspects of the canon of 'great art'. Griselda Pollock (1988), adopting a novel feminist perspective on the nineteenth-century artist, Dante Gabriel Rossetti, exposes his tendency to impose a blank expression on the face of his female models. The effect was to represent the woman, in the words of his own sister, Christina, 'not as she is, but as she fills his dream' (from a poem written in 1856, cited in Pollock, 1988, p. 127). The woman's face becomes an empty sign (in semiotics, a sign has a physical form and stands for something other than itself) through which masculine sexual desire can be negotiated. For women artists, unjustly excluded from the canon, narrow definitions of femininity sometimes constrained, but sometimes also stimulated subversion in their work. Rozsika Parker and Griselda Pollock (1981, pp. 38–41) also explore how the American Impressionist painter Mary Cassatt, working in France in the second half of the nineteenth century, unsettled the normal spatial relations of her domestic images to convey the unease and resistance of women placed within this familiar milieu, so revered within bourgeois ideologies of femininity.

Art history highlights conventions in the visual construction of women that predate the mass media. Its fascinating emphasis on continuity does, however, have one significant weakness: it detracts attention from the major historical shifts in technologies, economics, and philosophical outlook that have impinged with particularly powerful force on media representations and cultural attitudes in the course of the twentieth century. To come to terms with these, we have to grapple with contemporary cultural theory.

Cultural theory

The two fault-lines unsettling the terrain of cultural criticism most profoundly during the latter part of this century are the movements from modernism to postmodernism, and the development of structuralism and poststructuralism. While the second of these evolved a philosophical life of its own, postmodernism makes sense only in the context of dramatic economic, technological and social changes, unprecedented in their dynamism, speed and reach. As a number of commentators have pointed out (e.g. Jameson, 1984; Harvey, 1989), the postmodern period (starting roughly in the early 1970s) replaced an economy based on invention and production with one driven by design, marketing and consumption. Simultaneously, time and space differentials collapsed before the whirlwind advance of global technologies, and the old certainties through which people previously made collective sense of their experience and dreamt of future utopias (religious beliefs, for example, or movements such as socialism) gave way to confused fragmentation.

As with *post*structuralism, *post*modernism was a reaction *to*, rather than *against*, its predecessor. Modernism was itself contentious. This broad cultural movement, stretching from the late nineteenth until the mid-twentieth centuries and accompanying the emergence of the modern world, replaced the harmony and coherence of realism with discordant use of time, space and image to forge new ways of seeing (Cubist painting, the music of Schoenberg and the experimental narrative techniques of novelists such as James Joyce are examples of this). Its aim was to stimulate change by preventing the blindness of familiarity. While some critics applauded modernism (and especially the avant-garde) for encouraging an assault on conventional and outmoded values, others condemned it for widening the gap between popular and highbrow culture and for perpetuating élitism. Supporters of modernism criticize its successor for abandoning modernism's political project and for revelling instead in relativism and the mood of the moment. For anti-modernists, on the other hand, postmodernism's intermingling of popular and 'high' culture and its natural kinship with consumerism, spell liberation and new freedoms, especially for marginalized groups.

In relation to cultural communication, postmodernist theorists argue that the technological revolution, the centrality of electronic information sources, and the role of spectacle in contemporary life conspire to detach the semiotic sign from its referent (the reality to which it refers). Signs become depthless and more likely to refer to each other than to any external reality (this is often referred to as 'intertextuality'). The sign of the 'new woman' on this view loses any pretence of bearing a relation to real 1980s' women, and triggers instead a free-floating chain of association with other media and cultural signs of 'woman'. This might allow us to place it relatively (e.g. as 'more chic' or 'less maternal') but not to evaluate its own meaning. Even this relative assessment can only be temporary, as the kaleidoscope of images keeps changing. 'Morphing', the computer animation technique used by advertisers and other cultural producers to relay split-second sequences of, for instance, different body shapes and heads, typifies this process. Visually stunning rather than meaningful, morphing exemplifies what Baudrillard defined as the 'simulacrum'; the postmodern sign functioning as a copy without an original, an illusion without a foundation (Poster, 1988, pp. 166–84). Before we can ask what any of these individual images mean, we are bounced out of the question into admiration for the spectacle.

Within feminist thinking, postmodernism is viewed either as an unprecedented opportunity for women to forge their own identities and explore their own subjectivities, or as a cultural movement that stifles the possibility for meaningful action just as feminism is beginning to make a political and social impact (Nicholson, 1990). Modernism for many feminists is associated with the Enlightenment's establishment of methods of reasoning that were essentially male. If abandoning modernism means escaping from the straitjacket of this form of rationality, many feminists readily welcome it. As lifestyle replaces social class as a marker of status, and style becomes valued over substance, women, more fluent than men in the language of style, are, on a positive reading, optimally placed to benefit from postmodernism. Equally, other critics claim that a celebration of new freedoms of style and appearance belittles the disparities in power that still separate men and women. Women's ebullient visibility in the shopping mall obscures their invisibility in the boardroom; young women's street-wise sophistication is mistaken for an assault on patriarchal structures. What attitude we take in this debate hinges on whether we see experimentation with image and style, encouraged by postmodernism, as meaningless playful fun or, alternatively, as meaningful parody, challenging and resisting male-dominated conventions. Contemporary stars, such as Madonna and Prince, already play within the terms of this controversy, teasing their audiences with shifting gender and sexual identities that offer expectations of meaningfulness, but fail to fulfil them. Later chapters will return to these issues, especially in discussion of fashion and the body.

The other area of cultural theory with particular relevance to this book is the development of structuralism and poststructuralism. Structuralism emerged as a dominant critical philosophy in Europe in the 1960s, influencing British cultural criticism in the 1970s primarily through the Birmingham Centre for Contemporary Cultural Studies and the theoretical film journal, *Screen*. Led by a diverse band of critics and thinkers, including the philosopher Louis Althusser, the cultural critic Roland Barthes and the social-anthropologist Claude Lévi-Strauss, structuralism was an umbrella movement. It rejected humanism's belief that individuals have primary control over their futures, believing instead that social and cultural life is governed by deep-seated structural polarities. Although these are invisible to the surface glance of the observer, their ideological power can be excavated through philosophical enquiry. Femininity, on this approach, can best be understood as the structural opposite of masculinity, with both mythologies deeply embedded in the structures of patriarchy.

These ideas appealed to British cultural academics, disenchanted both with the instrumentalist tradition of American empirical research into media effects, and with the determinist tradition of an ageing Marxism that envisaged culture merely as a 'superstructure', fastened limpet-like to an economic base. Neither approach did justice to the ideological power and apparent autonomy of the media in an electronic age. Although Barthes' thinking influenced methods of textual analysis, Althusser was the structuralist whose ideas on ideology found most favour with British theorists. Despite remaining committed to Marxism, Althusser (1971) weakened its traditional model of economic determinism. Instead, he attributed considerable power to institutions such as education, the family and the media (he termed these 'ideological state apparatuses'), which actively reproduce ideology in their own ways. Applying the Lacanian model of the workings of language and 'the Symbolic' to ideology, Althusser described it as 'interpellating' or 'hailing' the individual. For Althusser, this 'hailing' was comparable to the police shouting 'Hey, you there!' (1971, p. 163): for *Screen* it was transformed, implicitly, into the irresistibly seductive appeal of the lover. Drawing, as we have already seen, on psychoanalytic as well as structuralist theory, *Screen* began to define the lure of the cinema as inscribing spectators into the relations of the text, with little possibility of escape.

That this approach appeared to be replacing the economic determinism of Marxism with the ideological determinism of the text, caused concern among some members of the Birmingham Centre for Contemporary Cultural Studies. Coming to cultural theory from a background mainly in sociology, they stressed the importance of retaining a clear distinction between the textual subject (the position we are invited to take up at the moment of viewing or reading a text) and the social subject (our identities formed and influenced by our other social experiences). Members of the Centre quoted with approval the criticism of aspects of '*Screen* theory' published within that journal in 1978 by Paul Willemen: 'There remains an unbridgeable gap between "real" readers/authors and "inscribed" ones, constructed and marked in and by the text. Real readers are subjects in history, living in social formations, rather than mere subjects of a single text' (cited in Morley, 1980, p. 169).

In relation to gender, Willemen's criticism reminds us that we do not cease to be men or women of a particular age, ethnicity, social class or sexual orientation as texts invite us to adopt masculine, feminine, androgynous or transsexual subjectivities. Substituting the notion of texts *inviting* us to adopt a temporary persona, or a temporary subjectivity, for the notion of them forcing us into a relationship, avoids many of the conceptual problems produced by terms such as 'interpellation'. David Rodowick comments that, even within the psychoanalytic paradigm *Screen* so often employed, it makes sense to talk of an ongoing 'transaction' between spectator and text (1991, p. 136). Other critics reacting against *Screen*'s deterministic phraseology argued for a comparable model of 'negotiation'. Christine Gledhill, renewing the case for this approach, reminds us that it is implicit in the writing of members of the Birmingham Centre as early as the late 1970s (1988, p. 67). Particularly for women, Gledhill suggests, the notion of negotiating meaning avoids the 'colonized, alienated, or masochistic positions of identification' (1988, p. 66) so often implicit in *Screen* criticism in the 1970s.

Those members of the Birmingham Centre who were most vigorously critical of *Screen*'s approach began to explore methods of investigating the reactions of real audiences (Moores, 1993, pp. 12–22). David Morley, in particular, developed the methodology of the ethnographer (observation and open-ended interviews) to survey television viewing responses. Because this approach, originating in social anthropology, requires the investigator to conduct the research in the context in which viewing habitually takes place, television and video are the media most frequently chosen, and families the most accessible guinea pigs. Although David Morley's work on television (1986, 1992), and Ann Gray's on video (1992) have produced fascinating evidence of gender disparity in control of the technology and in viewing preferences, they are less revealing about male and female readings of gender representations. Interviewees find it easier to talk about their viewing choices than about their own responses to texts.

If structuralist theory made most impact on discussions of gender and representation when it was filtered through the psychoanalytic perspectives of *Screen*, it became progressively difficult to draw a line between this development and poststructuralism. While structuralism's main aim was to carry out methodical excavation of the internal organizing principles of cultures or texts, poststructuralism, like psychoanalysis, shifted its enquiry onto the quicksands of subjectivity. Poststructuralism is scathing about the pretences of logical and rational enquiry into meaning and interpretation. If we are all affected by ideology, there is, poststructuralists claim, no position from which we can stand outside it to offer an objective criticism of the texts we encounter. It is only through examining our competing identities, addressed by a myriad of conflicting discourses, that we can begin to grapple with the complex manoeuvrings of power. For the poststructuralist, resistance to that power, in so far as it is possible, lies in *deconstructing* its operation through a method of critical response to texts often referred to as 'reading against the grain', in which the reader resists the obvious textual subjectivities on offer and searches instead for inconsistencies, gaps and illogicalities, to produce a subversive reading.

Poststructuralism is enlightening about femininity when it sees it as the product of competing discourses, but it poses at least three problems if we wish to keep our sights on the possibility of change. First, its concentration on the non-obvious, the silences rather than the speech of the text, turns criticism into a mystique that is inevitably élitist. For women, as for other disadvantaged groups, criticism has the more urgent purpose of stimulating widespread debate out of which change might emerge. Turning it into a mysterious craft is at least a premature luxury. Second, poststructuralism makes us unduly introspective and anxious about the positions from which we offer criticism. Up to a point, this has been helpful, by, for example, alerting us to the value-rating of terms such as 'progressive' and 'regressive' which are meaningless unless we clarify the perspectives from which we employ them. When this sensitivity turns into tongue-tying anxiety, it contradicts its own purpose. As the feminist critic Alison Light tellingly puts it in a slightly different context: 'If the day ever comes that any woman feels she cannot put pen to paper without being conversant with Lacan's mirror phase . . . then we may as well stop the bus and get off' (1989, pp. 27–8). Worrying whether we have any right to offer criticism as 'women', when 'women' may be an essentialist, patriarchal category that denies difference within it, becomes stultifying rather than helpful. While women vary greatly in their temperaments, social needs, outlooks and aspirations, they do nevertheless share a collective identity in terms of their relative lack of power vis-à-vis men in western society. Like the 'brotherhood' of the trade union movement in the nineteenth century, the bonding arises out of, rather than predates, the group's adversarial position. Without a category of 'women' (structurally disadvantaged relative to 'men'), it is hard to see from what position one could argue for the inadequacies of current constructions of femininity.

The third problem with poststructuralist criticism is that it presents the reading process too exclusively as the site of resistance to myths of femininity. Although Michel Foucault (whose work is examined further in the next chapter) argues cogently for the intermeshing of institutional and discursive networks of power, the effect of his thinking has been to focus attention on discourse rather than institutions. In cultural analysis, reading takes priority over the mechanisms that conspire to produce texts. If the text's ideological work is carried out in its gaps rather than its texture, there is little rationale for arguing for changes at institutional and production levels. The effect of poststructuralism has too often been to limit political intervention to deconstructing the terms in which women are talked about or portrayed. Although this may temporarily shift the balance of power for those who are engaged in the deconstruction, it does nothing for other women: 'reading against the grain', after all, leaves the grain exactly where it was.

In conclusion

Out of the approaches I have considered, there is none that uniquely provides a magic answer to the questions posed at the start of the chapter. Our increasing habits of thinking in discrete disciplinary frameworks can make attempts to combine them appear academically sacrilegious. Yet in practice we need to relate our rational processes of understanding and cognition to the working of the unconscious desires that often produce the pleasure of the text. At the precise moment of viewing a film in a darkened auditorium, or idolizing a favoured band in a packed stadium, or even immersing ourselves in a favourite soap opera or magazine, we may, temporarily, become a fully-fledged textual subject (the media, after all, have vested interests in making us lose ourselves imaginatively and emotionally). But in discussions of that experience and that pleasure, we also struggle to make sense of it. Poststructuralism and postmodernism, by refusing a controlling subject, come dangerously close to deriding logic and rationality. If we want to argue for changing, rather than deconstructing, some of the myths of femininity that have lingered for centuries, we need to admit to holding a rational position from which to argue this.

At the same time, as postmodern feminists point out, we need to be prepared to argue through, and re-inspect openly, the cultural and social positions from which we make our evaluations. Women, especially, need to challenge the linearity and certainties of those ways of thinking that have been dubbed 'Enlightenment', and advocate more sceptical, self-aware and responsive forms of discussion. Arguing, as some contemporary feminists do, that we should challenge rationality itself only endangers the baby along with the bath water. We need also to retain a historical approach to issues of identity and representation, while recognizing that our existence in a postmodern culture makes this a complex rather than straightforward undertaking. Although, as this chapter reminds us, we are not wholly in control of our responses to media texts, seeking a psychoanalytic explanation of this in purely psychoanalytic terms ignores the effect on desire of social and cultural history. The unconscious mind makes best sense when seen as moored to culture, and not as a universal, free-floating entity. The reverence for psychoanalytic criticism that infected areas of cultural studies especially in the 1970s and early 1980s encouraged the hijacking of terms and processes that are more available for scrutiny and change when translated back into socio-cultural and historical terms. The

Lacanian construction of women as the 'other', in accordance with the Law of the Father, for example, provides no insights into women's position that had not already been offered by Simone de Beauvoir in the 1940s: 'Now, what peculiarly signalizes the situation of woman is that she – a free and autonomous being like all human creatures – nevertheless finds herself living in a world where men compel her to assume the status of the Other' (1972, p. 29). The difference is that for de Beauvoir, this observation provides a springboard for investigating how women might *make their escape from* the sphere hitherto assigned them' (ibid., my italics).

The comments offered by one of the black women Jacqueline Bobo talked to about Steven Spielberg's *The Color Purple* provide a fitting conclusion to this chapter:

> When I went to the movie, I thought, here I am. I grew up looking at Elvis Presley kissing on all these white girls. . . . And it wasn't that I had anything projected before me on the screen to really give me something that I could grow up to be like. Or even wanted to be. . . . So when I got to the movie, the first thing I said was 'God, this is good acting'. And I liked that. I felt a lot of pride in my Black brothers and sisters.
>
> (Pribram, 1988, p. 102)

This woman's delight in the film arises out of her position as a black woman, long denied positive role models on the screen. If she is 'interpellated' by the text, it is by virtue of her cultural and historical position, not in spite of it. What this quotation above all reminds us is that psychoanalysis has no exclusive rights on desire and pleasure. Our social aspirations, moulded out of our historical circumstances, can be drives as powerful as any Freudian impulse.

2

Voices off: women, discourse and the media

> Women gossip Women giggle
> Women niggle-niggle-niggle
> Men Talk.
> (Liz Lochhead, 'Men Talk' from *True Confessions*, 1986)

> Moving from silence into speech is for the oppressed, the colonized, the exploited, and those who stand and struggle side by side a gesture of defiance that heals, that makes new life and new growth possible.
> (bell hooks, *Talking Back: thinking feminist — thinking black*, 1989)

In our role as viewers and readers, we all have a hand in sustaining myths of femininity. Responsibility for originating these myths is a different matter. Women have historically been excluded from defining how they should talk or be talked about in cultural forms. In this chapter, I will explore this exclusion, comment on the extent to which it is now changing in the media, and consider the advocacy within one strand of feminist theory for an alternative 'feminine discourse'. Language is often ignored or relatively obscured in discussions of the media. As we saw in the last chapter, Lacanian ideas, although predicated on language, were quickly applied to cinema's visual forms of address. Living as we do in a predominantly visual culture, the significance of words can often be overlooked. For many women, at the same time, being able to speak out, *and* be listened to, remains an important political objective.

The Dutch film *De Stilte Rond Christina M.* (1982), retitled *A Question of Silence* in its English language version, dramatically enacts the pressures that society imposes on women to speak only in particular ways, or to remain silent. Focusing on three women accused of the unpremeditated murder of a male boutique owner, it cleverly demonstrates how they adapt their specific form of oppression by male society into an appropriate strategy of resistance. The judicial system, assuming that women committing a spontaneous murder can only be mad, appoints a female psychiatrist to prove their insanity. The film's narrative development follows the psychiatrist's gradual rejection of this thesis as she increasingly identifies with the accused. Threatening her own career and marriage in the process, she, too, discovers the choice of speaking to order or being ostracized. Through her eyes, the audience is drawn into an understanding of the various forms of oppression ticking away like time-bombs in these women's lives, and finally exploding in the act of murder.

Language, instrumental in keeping these women in their place for so long, becomes a central issue in their strategy of defiance. Christine, the downtrodden housewife, never listened to by her husband, refuses to speak to the psychiatrist, but articulates her domestic oppression through stick-figure drawings; Annie, the garrulous café-worker whose loudness is a defence against the daily sexism of her workplace, bluffs her way through the psychiatrist's rhetoric; and Andrea, the intelligent secretary whose incisive perceptions are interpreted by her male boss as a failure to know her place, uses language to tease the psychiatrist and run rings around her professional method of working. Christine's silence is merely the most extreme version of these women's refusal to comply with a male-dominated system trying to construct a rational and humane defence for their crime.

The climax comes in the courtroom scene at the end of the film when the male prosecutor, increasingly frustrated by the psychiatrist's failure to substantiate the insanity thesis, suggests that the case would be no different if three men were being accused of the murder of a woman. The female witnesses (all of whom have colluded in silence by refusing to identify themselves) and the accused begin to laugh quietly. The ripples of merriment gather momentum, with the psychiatrist also joining in, until all the women in the courtroom are rocked by convulsive laughter which spreads infectiously outwards to embrace the women in the audience. The sense of complicity between screen characters and female audience achieves a power at this moment which many male critics (and male viewers) found threatening (Root, 1986). Laughter, rejecting words and substituting a more basic form of mockery, turns into the most effective form of retaliation against a masculine rhetoric which fails totally to understand what any of these women has been trying to say, either through her behaviour or her words. A similar, if less powerful, moment occurs in Steven Spielberg's The Color Purple when Celie's defiance of the man who has been treating her as his slave inspires a contagious burst of laughter from all the women sitting round

Fig. 1 The accuseds' laughter confounds the male prosecutors in Marlene Gorris's *A Question of Silence*, 1982. By kind permission of Sigma Film Productions

the dinner table, each of whom has in her own way suffered male oppression. In a subversion of Mulvey's dominant male gaze, the male characters, here as in *A Question of Silence*, can only look on in impotent bemusement.

Both films, in differing ways, construct societies in which women are denied a public voice (and even in some cases an effective private one), and both films suggest the strategies of resistance and retaliation which women devise to articulate their own feelings and reactions. If *A Question of Silence* is the more powerful film, it is because it challenges our expectations more than *The Color Purple*. In a culture that suppresses black voices generally, the silencing of black women is not surprising: the Dutch film, on the other hand, presents men's failure to listen to women's voices as an intrinsic condition even of white, privileged society. The psychiatrist's journey of discovering the links between power, place, and rights to speak becomes the audience's too.

Language and discourse

What is also clear from these films is that speech, or its silencing, is linked symbiotically to institutional structures of power and authority.

When we think about language and gender, especially in relation to media practice, we are referring less to the grammar and structure of the language; more to the relative entitlement of men and women to speak up and be heard, and to define the world we live in. For this reason, it is helpful to distinguish between 'language' and 'discourse'. Language refers most appropriately to the self-contained linguistic system of vocabulary and grammar. Discourse, on the other hand, connects the pattern of words that we use to systematic ways of thinking about the world, and sees language as embedded in ideology. Language is not, on this model, a neutral or transparent tool. It already carries the imprint of our culture and its values, although we are often unaware of this. Overtly sexist terminology is easy to spot, but the more subtle discrimination hidden within familiar phraseology can most effectively be exposed by applying a commutation test. This works by taking one element in a communication, altering it, and then observing the impact of this change on the overall meaning.

One example would be to change Gillette's advertising slogan 'the best *a man* can get' into 'the best *a woman* can get'. While 'the best a man can get' implies quality and excellence, 'the best a woman can get' suggests a second-best, and even tawdry, product. Substituting a single word produces a complete change of emphasis, not because the word-change is dramatic in itself, but because the frames of reference and understanding through which we make sense of the words contrast sharply. Like a single faulty fuse wire which trips the whole system, a single word or phrase can trigger a startling chain reaction. Discourse, like ideology, has most powerful effect when we are unconscious of its workings. To explain why we have different reactions to the two slogans, we need to go outside language and consider women's historical and cultural accumulation of inferiority. Discourse is particularly relevant to an analysis of gender because it links language to issues of power and the operation of social processes.

Some feminists have wanted to go further than this and argue that language itself is intrinsically male, since men have historically set the rules enshrined in dictionaries and grammar books, obliging women, in Tillie Olsen's memorable phrase, to 'tell it slant' (Spender, 1980, p. 83). Dale Spender, in her evocatively titled *Man Made Language*, has also drawn attention to the wealth of derogatory terms to refer to women, their bodies and, in particular, their genitalia. The 'richness' of this vocabulary has no match in relation to men. So deprived are women of pejorative terminology for men, that they now resort to terms more conventionally used as forms of abuse against women (Graddol and Swann, 1989, p. 111). Whatever initial blame may attach to male lexicographers for encouraging some of these trends in the language, their reproduction and longevity do, however, depend on social factors. As other commentators have noted, apparently neutral terms gathered negative connotations once they became clearly associated with women. Jane Mills' *Womanwords* (1991) traces the fascinating but often depressing history of such transitions. 'Hussy' is a typical example. Originally denoting a housewife, it remained a neutral term until the transference of power from household to state at the time of the industrial revolution turned it into a pejorative term, matching the lowering of housewife status to that of second-class, or non-, citizen. The term itself has remained constant, but its meaning has changed within a changing discursive framework.

The casting of women's voices as inferior to men's is wittily captured in a short rap-style poem called *Men Talk* by the Scottish poet Liz Lochhead. She recites no fewer than 15 derogatory verbs which relate to female forms of speech, including 'prattle', 'witter', 'gossip', 'nag', 'niggle', 'babble' and 'chatter'. Against this unflattering list she poses ironically the single linguistic activity of men: 'talk'. This differentiation by gender filters through into judgements about media genres, with soap opera and women's magazines regarded as 'trivial' and gossipy; news and even sports commentaries as occasions for 'serious' talk. Attitudes to male and female voice pitch have also been a peculiarly powerful tool in determining where and when men and women might be granted speaking rights within the media. Camouflaged as aesthetic rather than social judgements, these attitudes have been difficult to challenge.

Because of their generally higher pitch, women's voices have been claimed to sound shrill, reedy and thin, and connote unreasonableness, silliness or edginess. It is not accidental that the gender with the higher pitch should also be the one associated with hysteria. Lower pitched voices are estimated to be more authoritative, mellower and easier on the ear. Such generalizations overlook the range of voice pitch in both sexes and fail to explain how men with relatively high pitch escape negative evaluation. They have, nevertheless, been extremely influential historically in persuading broadcasting controllers that women would make inadequate newsreaders, and totally unsuitable sports commentators. The discourse that couches this debate in terms of euphony and ease of listening prevents us from attending adequately to its social and ideological dimension. Even powerful women acknowledge the handicap of a 'feminine' voice. When Mrs Thatcher became Prime Minister, she 'feminized' her appearance to enhance her appeal, but she already, as leader of the opposition, had 'masculinized' her voice by undergoing training to lower its pitch. Many of the women who have become prominent on television also possess voices of deeper pitch than the female average.

Mrs Thatcher was astute enough to recognize that women's voices are, by contrast, culturally valued for their sexiness. In her time as Prime Minister in Britain, she was adept at changing her voice to suit the situation: strident at Question Time in the House of Commons; confiding, husky and intimate in the one-to-one televised interview. The pattern of voice-overs on television advertisements highlights with particular vividness the different values placed on male and female voices. Male voices predominate, lending their authority to a variety of products, including many that men will rarely use. Female voices are reserved for the 'soft' areas of baby products, sanpro, washing powders, cat food or, in their most seductive timbres, for luxury goods such as chocolates or perfumes which are targeted primarily at male purchasers. Operating often below the level of the listener's consciousness, advertising voice-overs provide a miniature snap-shot of the status of male and female voices in the media.

Although pitch, simply understood, is purely a technical linguistic issue, how it is evaluated, and how women, as well as men, respond to this evaluation, reveals a great deal about power relations. In this sense, it becomes an issue of discourse. Theories of discourse owe much to the writing of the poststructuralist historian and philosopher, Michel Foucault (1926–84). Foucault argues that it is through discourse that the play of power in western societies is conducted. Our systematic construction of ways of looking at the world through language becomes as politically significant as the actions of élites. In this sense, Foucault democratizes our responsibility for ideology, bringing it out of the clasp of ruling groups, and into the domain of the everyday. In complete antithesis to the conspiracy theorists, who see the media as pawns in the hands of the powerful, Foucault argues that in all spheres of influence in society a jockeying for power takes place between different discourses. New alliances are formed not through a contest between polar opposites, as the structuralists might have thought (masculine vs. feminine; feminism vs. sexism), but through a changing process of gravitational attractions. Feminism may collide with consumerism, masculinism with nationalism, to form new if precarious formations. Discursive construction and reconstruction of power, Foucault argues, is part of the inevitable process of living; a struggle that goes on, for example, in defining our sexual identity to ourselves and others, or in drawing boundaries between insanity and criminality. Media discourses are not detached from ways of talking and thinking that exist elsewhere in society, but selectively promote some while neglecting others.

While the term 'language' sounds neutral, 'discourse' suggests that language and social practices are intertwined and intermeshed; not something that we use but something that we perform. 'Individuals', writes Foucault, 'are the vehicles of power, not its points of application' (1980, p. 98). Foucault's argument changes debates about terminology into contests for rights. Campaigns for non-sexist language have frequently been mocked on the grounds that they are trivial, petty and nit-picking. If we regard the debate purely as one about words, then it might be tempting to agree that changing the generic 'man' to 'person' (as in 'chairperson', 'spokesperson') is of minuscule importance in the struggle to make women's voices more audible. Once this is recast as a debate about power, and assumptions about the likely holders of power, the argument takes on a new dimension. The issue of discourse requires us to see language as one of the material manifestations of how we distribute power in both our institutional and personal lives.

By focusing so exclusively on discourse, Foucault tends, however, to underplay the material sources of power. The silencing of women's voices has been encouraged by (amongst other factors) women's fragile security in the workplace; their dependency on even abusive men in the home; and their absorption in childcare at key points in their lives. In the media, as in other organizations, male-dominated employment procedures discriminated against women in ways that are now being recognized, and slowly addressed, at least within some broadcasting institutions. These material factors cannot be reduced to discourse, although they are inextricably related to it. A particularly pertinent example of how material and conceptual pressures intermesh to affect gender mythology lies in the discursive division of the social universe into 'public' and 'private' spheres. From the time of the industrial revolution, this has had powerful practical consequences in suppressing women's pay, muting their cries for childcare provision, and constructing domestic violence as a purely 'private' matter. These consequences stem from a conceptual and ideological framework that views the public sphere as inherently 'masculine'; the private as intrinsically 'feminine'.

While this pattern is yielding to the material pressure of socio-economic change in the late twentieth century, its discursive reconstruction is less straightforward.

Separate spheres

The distinction between public and private spheres was from the start profoundly ideological. As men moved out of the home to work, and the (male) bourgeoisie acquired increasing power in the course of the nineteenth century, the public world became identified with influence and power, the private with moral value and support. In bourgeois discourse, the split developed gendered attributes, with men thought 'naturally' to occupy the public arena, women the domestic and private. This conceptualization would have made little sense to working-class women, whose lives of necessity traversed, and continue to traverse, both spheres. For many women in families, who daily exhibit skills of management and negotiation more normally associated with the public sphere, the equation of the domestic sphere with powerlessness has also seemed perverse. Women's influence and control within the domestic space has been regularly ignored by society, or curiously transformed into moral strength. This move is a devious one, appearing to recognize worth while removing the threat that women might pose to patriarchy. The private sphere is at once valued as a peaceful sanctuary, and yet devalued as that non-public space which we worry about only when its aberrations filter through into the public arena. Judith Williamson evocatively describes this process as one of colonization:

> Women, the guardians of 'personal life', become a kind of dumping ground for all the values society wants off its back but must be perceived to cherish: a function rather like a zoo, or nature reserve, whereby a culture can proudly proclaim its inclusion of precisely what it has *ex*cluded

> (Williamson 1986b, p. 106)

Margaret Stacey and Marion Price have put this more directly: 'wherever public power has been separated from private power, women have been excluded' (1981, p. 27).

Against this backdrop, those responsible for the development of the public media in the twentieth century felt little incentive to include women's voices. Where these did appear, the motive, as the next chapter explains in more detail, was often commercial: to appeal to advertisers through the assumed attraction to women of serial drama (the origin of soap opera), or beauty or fashion advice, or home-making tips. While women made early inroads into broadcasting in children's programming, and into the press in writing for women's pages or women's magazines, these advances replicated rather than challenged the public/private dichotomy. Even when women became visible and audible in the high-profile media, the handicap of their delayed start meant that they were likely to emulate male voices. To progress professionally meant acquiring the skills that had already been established by male practitioners. Readers in Britain of mass-circulation Sunday newspapers, such as the *News of the World*, were often surprised to learn in the late 1980s that they were edited by women. The transition from male to female editors caused no disruption in these papers' salacious treatment of women. 'Agony aunt' Claire Rayner allegedly left the *Sunday Mirror* in 1988 after disagreeing strongly with its editor, Eve Pollard, over the level of sexual titillation required in readers' letters (*The Guardian*, 2 June 1988). The complexity of writing as a woman, ostensibly for other women, but in a male-orientated medium, is nowhere more visible than in the so-called women's sections in the British daily tabloids. Breasts still become 'boobs', and the latest nightwear is still described as 'naughty lingerie'.

Broadcasting organizations took a long time to overcome their hostility to female newsreaders and reporters. Claims about the lack of authority of high-pitched voices served as a ready excuse. Although these battles have now been won, women's voices in electronic, as in print, news journalism still predominate in the 'soft' areas of health, welfare and education. Kate Adie, reporting from the war-torn zones of the Gulf or Bosnia, is always quoted as the British exception to this rule. A woman correspondent in a flak jacket still attracts attention, not least for the clash between her appearance and the audience's expectations of femininity. When women speak on television, how they look frequently overrules interest in what they say. Anna Ford, ITN's first regular woman newsreader (from 1978), speaking at a conference organized by a women in media pressure group in July 1980, accused the popular press of 'body fascism' because of its obsession with her appearance. On the BBC her opposite number, Angela Rippon (newsreader from 1975), similarly found the media more fascinated by her legs than her newsreading ability after she performed a dance routine on the Morecambe and Wise Christmas show in 1976 (Holland, 1987). More recently, Fiona Armstrong, a presenter on GMTV's breakfast programme, was forced out of her job in 1993 after a spate of scathing comments in the popular papers on her inadequate dress sense and her unwillingness to reveal her legs. A report from the Broadcasting Standards Council (1994) discovered that the proportion of men to women appearing on national news programmes (in any capacity) in one week of 1993 was 4:1.

Radio and the magazine press have found it easier to give voice to women. Both were catering for segmented audiences long before television, and both are more intimate in their modes of address than the mass appeal media. The popularity of Radio 4's *Woman's Hour* (broadcast from 1946) was measured by the storm of protest that greeted its removal from early afternoon to mid-morning slot in 1991. The barrage of opposition ensured that it retained its identity as a women-orientated programme, despite a stiff challenge from BBC management. The supposedly innovatory Channel 4, committed to alternative and minority programming from its start in 1982, has, by contrast, shuffled women's programming in and out of the schedules with lightning-speed alacrity. Even in radio and the magazine press, however, 'women's material' has often been defined in consumer terms, related to lifestyle and traditional feminine interests. The difficulties of allowing women's voices off the leash in prime-time broadcasting or within the pages of the serious press remain. Even in the broadsheet papers in Britain, the controversial ghettos of the women's pages have increasingly been disguised as 'style' or 'living' sections.

The historical impact of the traditional separation of public and private spheres has been weakening in recent years, but in a way that has offered little help to women. As broadcasting and the tabloid press have come under stronger commercial pressure to compete for audiences and readers, residual hesitancy about investigating the private lives of public individuals has disappeared. In Britain, the combined lack of a freedom of information act and of a privacy law also makes the bedroom an easier and more inviting target for the investigative journalist than the boardroom. Exposures in the tabloid press about the private relationships of members of the royal family and of politicians, together with the revelations offered by chat shows and confessional life accounts on television, have muddied the distinction between public and private spheres. Women have often, though, been the victims of this process, with mistresses particularly reviled by a tabloid press content to reproduce the dishonest cliché that male adulterers are 'virile', while female ones are 'sluts' or 'whores'.

Even areas of broadcasting that might have loosened up access to women's voices in a redrafting of private/public boundaries have been slow to do so. Both the television chat show and the DJ-led programmes on radio, in their straddling of private and public discourse, might have seemed fertile ground for female presenters. Instead, women remain very much on the margins. Because chat normally occurs in private spaces while shows are public spectacles, the chat show has to be at once a performance and an intimate dialogue. In celebrity shows, as Andrew Tolson points out, the development of banter between interviewer and interviewee has been one technique for resolving the potential conflict between (public) exhibitionism and (private) self-revelation (1991, pp. 181–5). Women, thought to be more skilled in flaunting their bodies than their verbal wit, are still perceived to be ill-suited to the role of repartee leader. In the chat show structured around confessional exposure, on the other hand, Oprah Winfrey has been the trend-setter. Through well-publicized willingness to reveal aspects of her own private feelings and her own past, Oprah capitalizes on women's perceived talents as agony aunts and confession-mongers. Despite this, many of her imitators, from Phil Donahue in the United States to Robert Kilroy-Silk in Britain, are men.

Disc jockeys, too, remain predominantly male, despite the cultivation of a synthetic intimacy between speaker and listener that emulates private rather than public discourse (Karpf, 1987). Because this intimacy depends on sexual chemistry and sexual innuendo, women are thought to be inappropriate initiators. Flirting on the air waves is permissible for women only in response to a male lead. Research into how male DJs and their programme controllers explained this gender imbalance discovered that women's voices, and the imagined level of tolerance of these among the audience, featured prominently. 'Shrill' or 'dusky' female voices were both thought unsuitable, especially for daytime DJs. This mirrors, as the author points out, the negative characterization of women as 'nags' or *femmes fatales*' (Gill, 1993).

However far the boundaries between private and public spheres are shifting more generally, they remain tenacious in setting gender expectations. When advertising of sanpro (sanitary towels and tampons) moved out of the private world of women's magazines into the public sphere of television in the 1980s, the ensuing controversy was heated and acrimonious. Early trials of television advertising in 1972 and 1980 were short-lived because of the volume of complaints. A third experiment on Channel 4 in 1987 met less public resistance and allowed the word 'period' to enter television advertising rhetoric for the first time, but advertisers were still obliged to follow guidelines which, amongst other restrictions, prohibited the showing of the unwrapped product. Even in the 1990s, advertisements for sanpro are not allowed on British channels (except for Channel 4) at 'family viewing times'. A relaxation of the rules in 1990 now permits the product to be shown, but Saatchi and Saatchi's advertisements for Vespré Silhouette Plus, featuring agony aunt Claire Rayner flaunting a towel with wings before a studio audience, still proved too much for many, with women leading the complaints lobby (*The Guardian*, 17 March 1992). The problems of sanpro advertising on television have led to some brands preferring the sponsorship option (Lil-lets in 1994 opted for sponsoring a series of films featuring 'leading ladies' in American film).

This suggests that women are still encouraged through socialization and cultural experience to internalize the discursive rules of the public and private spheres. While offensive rhetoric about women's bodies is acceptable in public exchange, periods are unmentionables, rating only at most a passing mention even in the 'intimate' discourse of soap opera. The themes of secrecy and freedom from embarrassment run through the history of sanpro advertising (Treneman, 1988). Creative energies are expended on designing discreet wrappings and packaging that ensure that the real purpose of the product is effectively camouflaged. Lil-lets ran a series of advertisements in the 1980s featuring a ball and chain, and stressing the liberating quality of its product, captioned as 'the small key to freedom'. The emphasis on the need for secrecy reinforces the age-old belief that periods are unnatural, shameful and dirty, even if a dressing of quasi-feminist terminology is now applied. The Tampax advertisement (*see* Fig. 2) offers discretion, freedom, and the ability to lead a full life, by reminding us at the same time that avoidance of this product will cause shame, discomfort and constraint.

As the British comedian Ben Elton humorously pointed out (*Saturday Live*, Channel 4, 7 February 1987), if men had periods the situation would be transformed. Then, menstruation would become 'a big laugh . . . a subject for after-dinner conversation'. Alternatively, in the words of a sanpro advertisement of the 1980s (Dr White's) 'the cry would go up for the three-week month'. The caption 'Have you ever wondered how men would carry on if they had periods?' was answered in the accompanying image of a self-pityingly posed young man clad in women's underwear and offering a variety of excuses for his feebleness. Excluding menstruation from acceptable discourses has wider social

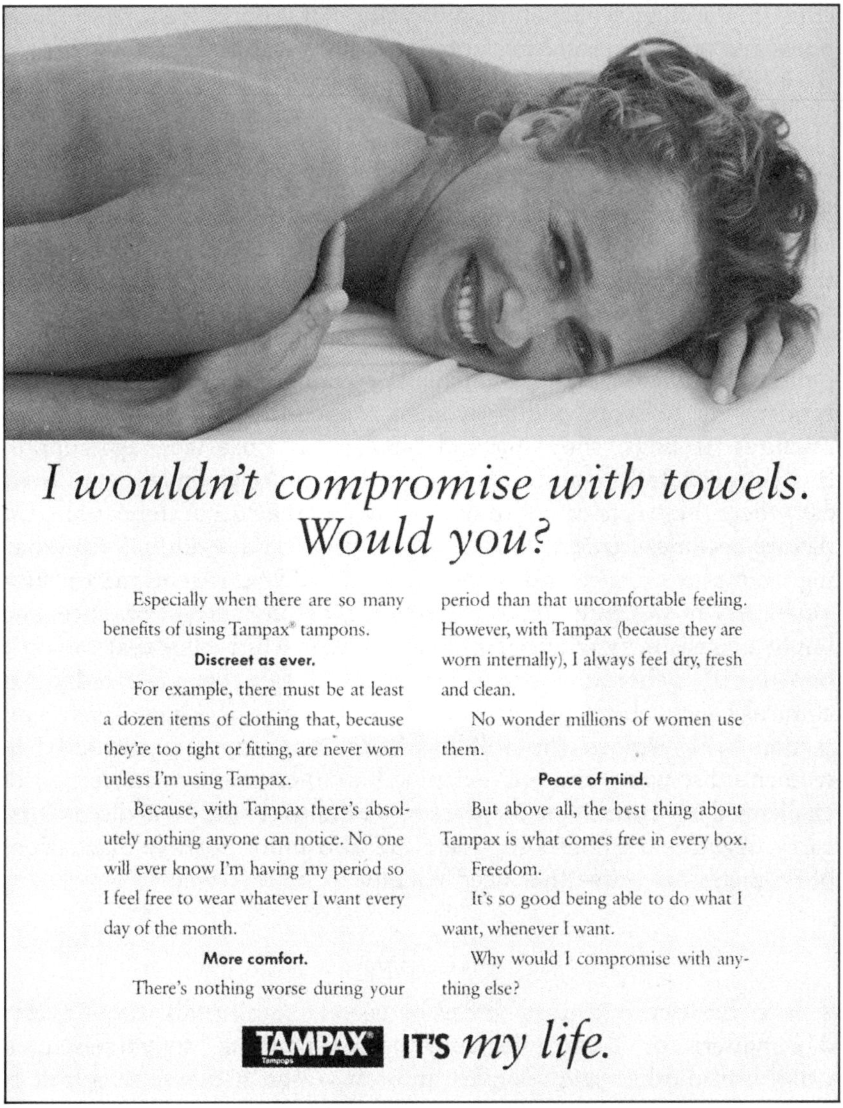

I wouldn't compromise with towels. Would you?

Especially when there are so many benefits of using Tampax® tampons.

Discreet as ever.

For example, there must be at least a dozen items of clothing that, because they're too tight or fitting, are never worn unless I'm using Tampax.

Because, with Tampax there's absolutely nothing anyone can notice. No one will ever know I'm having my period so I feel free to wear whatever I want every day of the month.

More comfort.

There's nothing worse during your period than that uncomfortable feeling. However, with Tampax (because they are worn internally), I always feel dry, fresh and clean.

No wonder millions of women use them.

Peace of mind.

But above all, the best thing about Tampax is what comes free in every box.

Freedom.

It's so good being able to do what I want, whenever I want.

Why would I compromise with anything else?

TAMPAX IT'S *my life.*

Fig. 2 1993 Tampax advertisement

effects, in muting debate about the taxation of sanpro, the safety of tampons, and pollution resulting from inadequate disposal. Periods, even in the 1990s, remain 'women's talk', and consequently women's problem.

Folklinguistics, gender and the media

So far I have been suggesting the need to include a wider range of 'women's voices' or 'women's discourse' in the media, as if the terms themselves were unproblematic. A moment's thought will suggest otherwise. Ready reckoners of the characteristics of male and female discourse do, of course, exist: men supposedly talk about sport, women, politics and work, and use language competitively, aggressively and egotistically to score points; women supposedly talk about personal relations, feelings, shopping and families, and use language supportively, anecdotally, and to explore issues in an open-ended way. If we ask where these lists come from, or to whom they accurately apply, the picture becomes fuzzier. None of us is likely to have difficulty producing examples of men and women who would be exceptions to these 'rules'. Myths of gender discourse survive, despite current practice, and imply a consistency within the category of male or female that can only be artificial. Deborah Cameron and Jennifer Coates have referred to our cultural beliefs about patterns of language use as 'folklinguistics'. This section will explore the folklinguistics that apply particularly to women's discourse, and will examine how these are reproduced in, or challenged by, current media practice. Although those I will discuss first carry negative connotations, there are also more positive evaluations of women's discourse that need equally to be reviewed.

Gossip

'Gossip' has two meanings. It can be used to signify talk about everyday matters, or it can refer to voyeuristic prying, sometimes maliciously, into other people's lives. In both senses, it is seen as a trait of female rather than male discourse. The very term can be a means of belittling communication about everyday domestic matters for which women, whether working outside the home or not, still have primary and undervalued responsibility. Women's claimed tendency to gossip each time they talk together has often been used as a means to put them down. Although gossip for women can be a means of asserting their own community, like all women's strengths, as Deborah Jones puts it, it is prone to being 'discounted and attacked' (1990, p. 245).

In the media, the association between gossip and the 'women's genre' of soap opera is often used to endorse its designation as 'women's talk'. This argument is not only circular; it also neglects the narrative functions of gossip in soaps. Gossip fills in part-time viewers on developments of the plot, enabling the audience to outstrip the characters in their awareness of the events and machinations taking place. The character identified as the main exponent of gossip often provides comic relief. Although in British soaps this role is most frequently filled by a female character, older men with time on their hands also qualify. What this suggests is that gossip (whether malicious or not) is more a product of a closed environment than of a particularly gendered sphere. The synthetic community of the neighbourhood British soap, sealed off to a large extent from the larger world and prone to navel-gazing, is an ideal breeding-ground for gossip, whatever the gender of its originators.

Similarly, gossip in the 'women's film' becomes a dominant mode of interaction only in those films set in a tightly-defined community, such as *Steel Magnolias* (1989). Gossip generally lacks a narrative purpose in films, since their plots depend more on action than on dialogue. In *Steel Magnolias*, the beauty parlour run by Turvy (Dolly Parton) serves as a theatre for the enactment of a myriad emotional dramas. Gossiping, as the role of the crotchety but kind-hearted Ouiser (Shirley MacLaine) makes clear, is a means of sustaining community against the variety of onslaughts that threaten to destabilize it. *Steel Magnolias*, like soap opera at times, places a positive value on women's gossip by setting it against the male characters' incompetence in expressing their feelings. Women's films that have avoided a community setting tend to avoid gossip. *Thelma and Louise* (1991), for example, largely set out on the open highway, replaces inconsequential chit-chat with an alternating mixture of resounding soundtrack and laconic and understated exchanges between the principal characters.

Bitching and nagging

Accusing women of gossiping is one way of demeaning their communication: attacking them for bitching or nagging is another. Jane Mills points out that the word 'bitch' had, as early as the fifteenth century, 'become standard English as a term used opprobriously of a woman, strictly one considered to be lewd or sensual' (1991, p. 27). The

term could then be applied also to men, although with less severe connotations: by the eighteenth century, it had narrowed into a form of
abuse directed at women alone. Standing in direct opposition to the
feminist ideal of supportive sisterhood, bitchiness implies that women,
given half a chance, will progress from gossip to a more bitterly vindic-
tive attack on each other. In nagging, hostility is most often targeted
at relatives. For men, there are no equivalent terms. This should alert
us to the possibility that 'nagging' and 'bitching' are frustrated reactions
to women's lack of power. Instead, their absence from descriptions of
male language elevates men to a plane of greater verbal control and
self-restraint. Men may be snide, but not, it seems, bitchy. Snideness
implies rational reasoning and control; bitchiness raw and uncontrolled
emotion.

'Bitchiness' and 'nagging', like 'gossip', are social rather than linguistic
constructs. Their recognition depends as much on the listener's labelling
of the language and non-verbal activity taking place as on identifiable
features of the speaker's practice. In media terms, both, revealingly, are
associated with situation comedy. Women's speech becomes a source
of laughter by virtue of appearing excessive, either in terms of its insults
or its relentlessness. The BBC's *Birds of a Feather* (created by Laurence
Marks and Maurice Gran, and first broadcast in 1989), regularly
portrays bitchiness between the three main characters: two sisters, who
are sharing a house while their husbands languish in prison, and their
pretentious, man-hunting neighbour, Dorien. The more sophisticated
sister, Tracey, complains repeatedly about Sharon's lifestyle and
attitude. In a typical episode, Tracey's attempts to improve Sharon's
table manners and housekeeping skills are met with the charge: 'you're
turning into a right nag, you are, Trace', while Sharon's humour at
Tracey's expense leads Tracey to dub her sister a 'sarkie cow' (BBC1,
11 October 1990). The US sitcom *The Golden Girls* also shows the four
house-sharing women characters regularly hurling insults at each other.
In the more recent British comedy *Absolutely Fabulous* (1992–), written
by Jennifer Saunders and starring both herself and Joanna Lumley as
luminaries of the fashion world, vituperation flows as freely as the
champagne. The 'nag' in this sitcom is, paradoxically, the adolescent
daughter, Saffron, who, in a reversal of the usual mother/daughter relationship, rails at the mother (Saunders) for her laziness, debauched
habits and poor choice of friends. Sober Saffron earns her mother's
wrath only for being too industrious, frumpily dressed, and disappointingly virginal.

Evidence suggests that one of the reasons for the astounding success of *Absolutely Fabulous* lies in the licence it gives its central characters to be outrageous linguistically. Patsy (Lumley) emerged spontaneously as one of the positive representations of women in the Broadcasting Standards Council enquiry into women's attitudes to television. As one respondent put it, 'she says things you'd like to say, but you don't' (1994, p. 16). Contained within the ritualistic narrative frame of each episode, the verbal slanging matches in all of these sitcoms comfortingly pose little threat to the solidity of the relationships they depict. Generically, situation comedy ensures that the character interactions remain predictable, however the situation changes around them. In *The Golden Girls*, the women's age, allowing flashbacks and shared reminiscences, provides additional bonding; in *Birds of a Feather*, the working-class credentials of the central characters and their shared situation act as ballast against the vituperation they hurl at each other. Insults flying across the designer kitchen in *Absolutely Fabulous* often fall on ears deafened either by hangovers, crises at work or in personal lives, or, in Saffron's case, by bored resignation. The potentially explosive enmity between Edina's friend Patsy and Saffron fails to blow the series apart because both are linked inextricably to the mother.

Verbal skirmishes in situation comedies are not, of course, unique to women-only samples of the genre. The BBC's *Steptoe and Son*, or ITV's *Home to Roost*, both of which centred on father–son relationships, were capable of slanging-matches (especially in the case of *Steptoe*) that surpassed the women's sitcoms in ferocity and vulgarity. Neither was, however, perceived to be about 'nagging' or 'bitching'. *Steptoe* is remembered precisely for its crossing of the boundaries between the speakable and the unspeakable. Its excesses were not perceived as breaches of the boundaries of acceptable *male* discourse, but of acceptable *social* discourse, as the bigoted central character vented his spleen on the vulnerable and disadvantaged. Male discourse, in parallel with masculinity, is regarded as so natural that its excesses are seen as those of society in general, not men alone.

Joke-telling

Women, such as Carla Lane and Jennifer Saunders in Britain, have had some notable success as writers of situation comedy. Telling jokes, on the other hand, has long been characterized as a primarily male skill, with women more likely to be the butts of one-liners than their originators. Although women are acknowledged to be capable of bitingly acerbic wit and hilarious mimicry in the private sphere, occupying the public space as a female comic can still be seen as an act of transgression. Partly, this stems from the predominantly male tradition of working-men's clubs that used to (and to some extent still do) form the training ground for would-be comedians, partly from the folklinguistic view that women are more polite and deferential than men. The picture is, though, slowly changing. The family-orientated atmosphere of television, with its tamer studio audience, provides an easier environment for the female comedian, even though television still depends on the comedy circuit for her discovery.

Despite the growing presence of female comedians on television, equality with male comedians is still remote. As Jennifer Saunders points out, women have to write their own material if they are to find roles that they want to play (cited in interview in *Radio Times*, 7–13 November 1992). In addition, television demands visual rather than purely verbal performance from those women who intrude into its public spaces. In comedy, this means that women are pushed further in the direction of character and situational comedy. Lacking opportunities for ready-made visual humour (a male performer in drag taps into a history of comic effect denied to female performers dressed in male attire), women comedians tend to concentrate their talents of mimicry on other women, thereby appearing at times to send up female rather than male discourse.

Stand-up comedians often exploit the female tradition of self-deprecation as a means of winning over the audience. Jo Brand plays on her size ('I know what you're thinking' – pause while she pats her hips – 'here's one of those supermodels from London', cited in *The Guardian*, 10 November 1993); Joan Rivers draws a laugh by commenting on her appearance ('they show my picture to men on death row to keep their minds off women', cited in Goodman, 1992, pp. 289–90). Women's alleged neuroses feature similarly in several of the sketches of the British comedy duo, French and Saunders. One that strikes a chord with many middle-class women focuses on the antics of an overwrought Jennifer Saunders as she prepares an important dinner party for her husband's boss and his wife. Her exaggerated and restless gestures and verbal asides, culminating in her sending her guests home halfway through a disastrous meal, draw attention to the absurdities of the normally accepted ritual as she brings the private traumas of the kitchen clattering into the sacred space of the cosmetically ordered dinner table.

Because of its status as 'other', femininity still causes problems for women comedians in a way that masculinity, viewed as the norm, fails to do for men. Women have to decide on the extent to which their womanliness impinges on their act. Some, such as Whoopi Goldberg, claim that this is not at issue: 'I don't talk about myself as a woman, I don't talk about myself as being black because for other people that's a problem. . . . I can do anything and that's how I proceed' (quote from 1991 Canadian documentary film, *Wisecracks*, directed by Gail Singer). Others worry more about being labelled as 'feminists' or 'manbashers'. The respected status of masculine discourse in our culture means it is easier to alienate the male section of the audience than the female. Such a fate befell the British comedian Jenny Lecoat when she presented *Watch the Woman*, a short-lived Channel 4 series broadcast in 1985, which raised male hackles by, amongst other outrages, running a cactus award for the 'prickle of the week'. Immensely enjoyed by most of its female addicts (and some male ones), it was so savagely panned by the critics that Channel 4, had it been more courageous, might have deemed it a success. Jenny Lecoat subsequently tried to redefine her role without abandoning her feminism. Anxious to explore the tensions many women feel between 'right-on' feminist attitudes and, as she put it, 'crying because you've put on five pounds', she describes such comedy source material as even 'more dangerous because I can see myself falling into all sorts of "sell out" traps, but it's something that I've got to do' (quoted in Banks and Swift, 1987, p. 30).

So far, the folklinguistics considered in relation to gender are ones that value men's language over women's. Men, the mythology tells us, against the evidence of our daily interactions, don't gossip, nag or bitch, and are natural joke-tellers. The picture is not all one-sided, however. Women's discourse is also put on a pedestal for the qualities of politeness and the ability to express feelings. There appears to be an uneasy alliance in this respect between folklinguistic mythology and the views of feminists who advocate the promotion of 'women's discourse' as a means of redressing the imbalances of patriarchy. These views will be discussed further in the final section of this chapter. To some extent, this alliance is more apparent than real, with folklinguistics, unlike feminism, offering women only a barbed compliment.

Politeness

The claim that women are more polite and formal in their use of language than men implies praise but also suggests that women are instinctively deferential and submissive. The linguistic evidence is at best controversial. A prime example of the difficulty is the debate over women's use of 'tag questions' (e.g. 'isn't it?', 'wouldn't you?', 'don't you think so?', tagged on at the end of statements) which some commentators have taken as a sign of women's hesitancy and willingness to yield to others (Lakoff, 1975, pp. 14–19). More recent research contests the theory that women employ tag questions more often than men, and suggests that the category of 'tag question' is in itself linguistically unhelpful since the tagged-on question may be performing a variety of functions. If, for example, I say to a student, 'You will hand your course-work in on time, won't you?', I am using the tag question for emphasis, not to suggest deference. My relative power in this situation has to be taken into account in interpreting the meaning. Seeing women's use of the tag question as a sign of their inferiority reveals more about the prejudices of the listener than about the intrinsic quality of the linguistic feature.

Further support for the deferential nature of women's discourse centres on their reputed unwillingness to interrupt in mixed-sex groupings, or at least their failure to persist when they do venture to break into the conversation. Research into interruption rates in patient/doctor relationships by Candace West concluded that gender was a primary influence on these, taking precedence over social or professional position. Unremarkably, she discovered that male doctors frequently interrupted their female patients, but she also found that female doctors were regularly interrupted by their male patients, despite the patients' relative lack of power in this situation (Graddol and Swann, 1989, pp. 77–80). Although these results have been disputed by others using a slightly different definition of the term, Margaret Thatcher, even as Prime Minister, experienced a higher rate of (attempted) interruption than her male predecessors.

Assumptions that women 'naturally' tend to use higher-status forms of language than men is challenged by evidence that when women's working lives parallel men's, their language patterns coincide. Studies undertaken by Lesley Milroy in Belfast in the 1970s demonstrated that when women were integrated into the close employment networks more traditionally enjoyed by men, they began to use similar vernacular forms. She found particular consistency between the characteristics of working-class men's speech in areas of the city where male employment was still strong, and those of working-class women in areas where male unemployment and high rates of female employment dominated (Coates, 1986, pp. 81–5). Although Lesley Milroy confined her analysis to phonetic features of speech, it seems probable that her findings apply equally to the wider discursive features of use of vocabulary, style of delivery, or ability to tell jokes.

In the media, deference and submissiveness are marked by the absence rather than by the presence of women's voices. Deferential women in media representations are, by definition, quickly forgotten, with the most pernicious and memorable type historically being the black 'mammy'. She appeared in many 1920s and 1930s films as the semi-comic but ultimately faithful servant whose frequently superior moral perceptions were quashed by a servility born as much out of racial as gender discrimination. From Mae West and Bette Davis in the early cinema to Ena Sharples in the 1960s' *Coronation Street*; from the lyrics of a Madonna video to the outspoken features on sexual issues in young women's magazines, women's voices have been most memorable, but also most unique, when they have refused to yield the floor.

Ability to express feelings and offer emotional support

The view that women are naturally co-operative and mutually suppor-tive sits oddly with the stereotype of the woman as bitch. Yet woman in her role as cultural symbol typically gyrates between extremes: virgin or whore; saint or sinner; supportive ally or destructive fiend. Myth defies logic in allowing polar opposites to co-exist without discomfort (a similar pattern emerges in mythologies of childhood, with children being viewed at one and the same time as pure and innocent angels and as devil-inspired monsters). The myths of women's discourse parallel closely the diverse myths of femininity as simultaneously other-centred, gentle and kind, but also prone to jealousy and pettiness.

The complimentary view that women are more likely than men to co-operate and support each other in verbal interaction also hides a flip-side. It endorses women's nurturing role and re-emphasizes the importance of relationships in their lives. Deborah Tannen, in a study graphically entitled *You Just Don't Understand* claims that 'for most women, the language of conversation is primarily a language of rapport: a way of establishing connections and negotiating relationships' while 'for most men, talk is primarily a means to preserve independence and negotiate and maintain status in a hierarchical social order' (1991, p. 77). This is a sweeping generalization, which Tannen documents mainly from anecdotal evidence. The distinction between 'rapport-talk' (appropriate to the private sphere) and 'report-talk' (intrinsic to the public domain) reinforces myths of femininity and masculinity that need to be questioned. Male managers, sales*men*, team-playing sports*men*, do, after all, need also to 'establish connections and negotiate relationships', and many women work hard within their traditional location of the family, and in the workplace, to 'preserve independence and negotiate and maintain status'.

Like women's supposedly natural facility for cooking, dishwashing or childcare, women's strengths in maintaining relationships can be used to place an additional burden on them. The work of smoothing over family disagreements, or of organizing festivities like Christmas or Thanksgiving, fall heavily on women, as the communicators with the 'natural' talent for bringing people together and ensuring harmony. Instead of seeing women's co-operativeness as a natural trait to be applauded, some feminists prefer Pamela Fishman's graphic claim that women perform the 'interactional shitwork' of communication (Cameron, 1992, p. 72). Putting a more positive gloss on this process, we could also say that women acquire excellent 'negotiating skills' in the course of managing family and relationships. This discourse rejects the idea that women are innately morally superior (a formulation that, as I have already pointed out, often keeps woman in her private place), and emphasizes instead the acquired qualities that are valued in the workplace. Women returning to education or work after having a family often suffer the crisis of confidence that comes from having their expertise devalued both materially and discursively. As the demographic pattern changes, employers and educators are slowly beginning to acknowledge that women's domestic interaction may be valuable training for work and that the terms in which we conventionally talk about it need a radical overhaul.

What is clear is that each of these interpretations of women's supportive speech depends on different ideological versions of femininity. It is difficult, if not impossible, to pinpoint the linguistic markers of 'co-operation', especially when any particular feature is open to variable interpretation. Research shows, for example, that women's capacity to listen is often heard by men as agreement with what is being said. When women intersperse their listening with 'uh-uh', 'um' or other signals, from their perspective, that they are merely attending to what is being said, men will frequently interpret these as indications of support. The mismatch is one that tells us more about male and female *discourse*, and relative assumptions about power, than about language in a more technical sense.

Equally, women's openness in expressing their feelings, at least in the company of other women, is a discursive rather than a purely linguistic phenomenon. It depends on practices of intimacy and support formed in childhood. In an often-cited paper reviewing the effects of single-sex play on the interactional styles of men and women, Daniel Maltz and Ruth Borker found that boys prefer competitive and hierarchical strategies, girls the supportive and intimate interaction with their best friends (Cameron, 1992, p. 73). Forms of bullying often differ similarly along gender lines, with boys choosing to intimidate other boys physically, and girls to isolate and socially humiliate their one-time friends. In adulthood men's relative lack of practice in openly expressing their feelings and women's relative lack of practice in asserting their own desires accentuate communication problems between the sexes. Socialization and mythology combine to blinker each gender's vision.

This problem has increasingly been recognized in popular discourse, with the growth in writings such as Tannen's (1991), and forms of popular counselling in women's magazines, radio and television programmes such as *The Oprah Winfrey Show*. It is, indeed, common now for communication problems, rather than sexual difficulties, to be identified as the key source of relationship breakdown between men and women. The burden of putting this right has not yet been equalized (see, for example, the discussion of problem pages in women's magazines in Chapter 6). Recognition of men's relative ineffectiveness in expressing their emotions has let them off the hook, and helped, as some critics have argued, to shore up their power by making them appear more invulnerable and less temperamental than women (see, for example, Cameron, 1992, p. 77). The imbalance in responsibility is one that women increasingly have begun to question.

When Shere Hite, the American cultural historian, published the third volume in her enquiry into female and male sexuality in 1987, its most astonishing findings were that women were much more dissatisfied with their emotional relationships with their partners than with their sexual lives. A staggering 98 per cent of women in the study said 'they would like more verbal closeness with the men they love; they want the men in their lives to talk more about their own personal thoughts, feelings, plans, and questions, and to ask them about theirs' (1987, p. 5). Of those women in the sample who had undergone a divorce, 91 per cent claimed that the primary reason was not inadequate sex but emotional isolation within the relationship (p. 459). While some men have attempted to adapt their behaviour in response to these discoveries and the earlier demands of feminism, the more widely publicized reaction has been the 1980s' vogue for male emotional therapy work-outs advocated by Robert Bly (1991). Bly significantly rejects the other-directedness of the men's groups established in the 1970s and 1980s in support of feminist ideals. 1990s' men, he suggests, need to get in touch with their feelings, but in order to reassert their male tribalism, not to prepare them for sharing the emotional work in relationships. Turned into soft, yoghurt-eating wimps by strident feminists, men, Bly argues, need to regain their raw masculinity.

Second-wave feminism endorsed the notion of women's supportiveness by stressing the values of 'sisterhood'. Valuing this as a source of positive solidarity, and ignoring its negative connotations of sibling rivalry, feminists achieved considerable local impact in encouraging less hierarchical and competitive methods of interacting in meetings and at work. Women's groups, established to raise consciousness of women's subordinated position, especially endeavoured to make communication between the participants more open, egalitarian and democratic. Men who were sympathetic to the feminist movement, and as yet untainted by Bly rhetoric, also began to review their own practices. Just as 'penis envy' might arguably be replaced by 'womb' or 'breast envy', so, it was suggested, men might profitably adapt their linguistic practices by learning from women's culture. In popular media terms, however, feminist sisterhood mutated into sentimentalism, as the difficult task of building solidarity and campaigning for change in organizational and personal practice was reduced to a matter of emotional bonding.

Symbolically, when 'sisterly' discourse appeared in the popular media of the 1970s and 1980s, the location where it occurred was typically marked out as a private space. When Cagney and Lacey wanted to express their feelings to each other, they removed themselves to the locker room, or used their car as a substitute private capsule. In the public space of the police-station, feelings were more subtly and indirectly conveyed. A similar distinction applies towards the end of Scorsese's 1974 film, *Alice Doesn't Live Here Any More*. Alice (Ellen

Burstyn) confesses her unhappiness to her close female friend and colleague in the confidential space of the toilet. Tears give way to laughter
as they jointly decide that insouciance and independence are the sensible
response to the fickleness of men. This scene, shot in tight framing, is
almost immediately undermined by the wide-angled scenes which
follow in the café, as Alice succumbs once again to the charms of David
(Kris Kristofferson). In the public space, the resolution and strength of
female solidarity gives way to conventional romantic responses.

Media portrayal of caring relationships between women will be further considered in Chapter 5, but, in terms of discourse, it is significant
that one recent popular film depicting women's friendship, *Thelma and
Louise* (1991), prevents its characters from wallowing in emotional out-
pourings. The avoidance of stereotypical 'women's talk' undoubtedly
increases its unisex appeal. Although Thelma gives us some insight into
the misery of her life with her husband, the more streetwise Louise
remains reticent. Louise's reaction to the attempted rape of Thelma, the
event that transforms the two friends' carefree weekend into an event-
packed flight from the law, is, we learn, explained at least in part by
her having been raped herself years before. But this crisis in her life
remains off limits, even with her closest friend. When Thelma works
out what has happened, and tries to talk to her about it, Louise rejects
the overture:

L: Hey, now look. I'm warning you. Just drop it. I'm not goin' to talk
   about that. D'you understand?
T: Yeah.
L: I'm not talkin' about it.
T: Okay.
L: D'you understand?
T: Yeah. Okay, Louise. It's okay, it's okay.

This laconic interchange temporarily suspends the triumphant mood of
the film. Gloomily lit, and with the distance between the two women
highlighted by the frame of the car window cutting diagonally across
the space that normally unites them, this scene temporarily freezes the
film's action. The subject of rape is never reopened. To what extent this
departure from the free-floating emotionalism more characteristic of
'women's films' results from the film having a female scriptwriter, Callie
Khouri, is hard to judge, but it finely captures the respect for the
borderline between sharing and privacy that often typifies female
friendships.

What, then, is clear from this brief survey of the supposed characteristics of 'women's discourse' as refracted through the media is that
there is now more variability and more challenge to prevailing assumptions of gendered 'folklinguistics' than might at first be supposed. Less
subject to change are the audience's and critics' *perceptions* of women's
discourse in those instances when it appears with a high profile. Soaps
are still seen as heavily dependent on women's discourse, although the
evidence does not always support this contention. Women who defy the
norms of female discourse, such as female comedians, continue to be
seen as unruly and unfeminine. The 'women's film' is shunned by many
male cinema-goers who believe that it will be dominated by sentimental
chit-chat and tear-jerking scenes. Historically, 'women's films' were
referred to as 'weepies', as if no western or war movie ever left an
audience with tears in their eyes at the end of a screening. While there
is still some justice in the view that American mainstream films featuring relationships between female characters will reproduce a romanticized version of sisterhood in both their narrative development and
their discourse, this, too, is beginning to be challenged.

Women's discourse: a cause for celebration?

The difficulties of separating out the actual qualities of women's voices
from the folklinguistic versions complicates the advocacy of 'women's
discourse' as a means of destabilizing the primacy of 'men's discourse'.
Key initiators of this debate since the 1970s have been two French
feminist thinkers, Hélène Cixous and Luce Irigaray, who, in differing
ways, have suggested that society would benefit from a wider accep-
tance of women's ways of talking and thinking. Both seek to avoid
implying that men and women are intrinsically and irreversibly different from each other (the essentialist position), and, by defining their
vision as utopian, they try to distance themselves from current stereotypes of women's talk.

Cixous argues that feminine writing (*écriture féminine*) has a potential
openness, variety and responsiveness to the rhythms of the body which
endow it with greater humanity. The feminine voice, when it can be
persuaded to articulate itself in writing as well as speech, is capable of
overcoming the defensiveness of the Lacanian Symbolic realm, and
regaining something of the wholeness and spontaneity of the Imaginary
phase. Avoiding an essentialist position, Cixous contends that the
feminine voice does not necessarily belong to a biologically female

writer, and that not all women will write in a feminine manner. On the contrary, she claims that most women, through the conventions of writing which have been developed by men, adopt a masculine voice in the written word. Her own writing has a fluidity, a love of associations and rhythmic patterns which challenge the conventional linear and logical form of academic discourse.

Irigaray's arguments are related, but different. Originally closely associated with the work of Jacques Lacan, she was expelled from his institute when she published her controversial *Speculum de l'Autre Femme* in 1974. Playing on the idea of the 'speculum', a concave mirror employed in vaginal examinations, Irigaray argues that male discourse prevents women from thinking of themselves in other than male terms. Constituted irrevocably as 'the other', outside discourse, women perceive themselves merely in the refracted images of themselves which men project. 'Womanspeak' (*parler-femme*) exists according to Irigaray whenever women meet in single-sex groupings, but it cannot be described or talked about, since this would draw women's discourse back within the mechanisms of patriarchal culture. Irigaray differs from Cixous in arguing that one of the defences which women do possess against being formed totally in the image of men is to mimic masculine discourse in a way that draws attention to its constructedness.

Critics have commented on the logical problem of Irigaray's position. If women's discourse is so at variance with the conventional logic of patriarchy, then from what authority can a female academic herself speak? There is also the danger that the style of writing recommended and practised by these critics confirms prejudices about the illogicality, allusiveness and intuitiveness of female discourse, and thereby reinforces its debased status. As Toril Moi puts it, in a succinct critique of these writers, 'it is after all patriarchy, not feminism, that insists on labelling women as emotional, intuitive and imaginative, while jealously converting reason and rationality into an exclusively male preserve' (1988, p. 123). While re-evaluating women's current patterns of discourse is an urgent task, a view of a future utopia that privileges feminine speaking or writing, as if these would remain unchanged under new social conditions, seems harder for feminists to sustain. The concept of discourse reminds us that forms of talking and speaking are intrinsically related to forms of social organization. If the position of women changes, then so will their discursive practices. This should remove the gender connotations of forms of interaction such as assertiveness or emotional expressiveness, not reverse the status of 'masculine' and 'feminine' positions by privileging 'womanspeak'. Cixous and Irigaray want to retain arguments for social change while applauding elements of women's discourse which have been forged out of a position of disadvantage. If this is not paradoxical, it is at least idealistic.

Because they concentrate on language, these theoreticians have been principally influential within the field of women's writing. Similar arguments have, however, become increasingly orthodox in discussions of melodrama and of television soap operas. The view that soaps are a 'women's genre', reproducing 'feminine discourse' (Brown, 1990), offering a 'sense of being "down among the women"' (Geraghty, 1991), or communicating 'a great deal about . . . women's "collective fantasies"' (Modleski, 1982) has become so often repeated as to appear incontestable. These critical approaches reinstate aspects of communication that have been denigrated because of their association with women, but they also prop up a version of women's discourse that shares many features with the mythologies of folklinguistics. In addition, the patterns of interaction in current soap operas suggest that the distinctions in terms of gender discourse are waning rather than solidifying. If soaps are being deemed 'feminine' *because* they deal with everyday problem-solving and emotional crises, and *because* they are set primarily in the private sphere, then the supposition that these are essentially women's concerns is strengthened rather than questioned.

Soap operas, unlike the rest of television drama, clearly do focus on the everyday, and on personal relationships dramatized principally through talk rather than action. A prime source of our enjoyment in viewing soaps arises from our position of superior knowledge. More fully informed than any of the participants about who is doing what to whom, and why, we evaluate the decisions that individual characters make, and guess ahead as to what the consequences will be. Why this pleasure should be regarded as 'feminine' is less clear. To justify this, we need to argue that women find the processes of identifying with others more satisfying than men, and that women are better at interpreting the interpersonal information that these programmes offer. This may describe current realities, but labelling such activities as 'feminine' also perpetuates the idea that this is 'naturally' women's work.

Contrary to folklinguistics, soap operas do, to some extent, show men as well as women gossiping, supporting each other, and being willing to talk about their feelings, even if these remain primarily female modes of discourse. The gendered nature of discourse appears more sharply in soaps when they contrast women's readiness to discuss a difficult situation with men's apparently instinctive desire to resort to action-based solutions. Examples of this abound in British soaps, but the male and female reactions in *EastEnders* to Kathy Beale's retrospective accounts of the times she was raped, both as a teenager and as a mature woman, illustrate the cycle. Kathy and her female friends discuss her feelings at length, acknowledging the need for long-term support and the impossibility of quick solutions. Kathy's male partners, on both occasions, react by wanting to seek direct revenge through action. It is, then, possible to argue that soap operas offer particular pleasures to women viewers by emphasizing their skills as communicators, while accentuating men's deficiencies, but this again reinforces a status quo that is at odds both with feminism's general objectives and with the type of utopian 'feminine' language that the French theorists want to see promoted.

Soaps have also been classified as a women's genre because of their focus on the private sphere. When they do venture into the world of work, that too has an uncanny knack of appearing as an extension of the domestic realm. Service jobs in shops, pubs, launderettes and cafés predominate; family networks among employees are not uncommon; and even urban soaps (for reasons of financial economy on set expenditure and location filming) are contained within a confined community. Male, as well as female, characters are mainly employed in the service sector, although the men tend to occupy the managerial positions while the women characters clean, serve, cook or launder. The Channel 4 soap opera *Brookside*, which set out to challenge the conventions of the genre when it began in 1982, has ventured into the arena of (male) industrial disputes and tensions and, more daringly, into the arena of sexual harassment at work. Its relative retreat from this position (although these issues are still spasmodically aired) has accompanied the opening of a neighbourhood shopping centre, where, in defiance of realism, most of the inhabitants of the mixed-class Brookside Close now work. Representations of work in soaps tend to fit into the paradigm of domesticity and personal relationships more normally associated with the private sphere, but when we align this with 'femininity' we are reinforcing an alliance that is increasingly being challenged in reality.

When the focus shifts from representations to reception by audiences, analyses suggest that soap opera's particular appeal for women arises out of parallels between soaps and women's lives. Mary Ellen Brown applauds the genre for giving credit to women's rich but invisible oral heritage (1990). Arguing that women's gossip should be viewed positively, Brown stretches her case to suggest that this tradition of speech also contains the ingredients of parody. Drawing a direct parallel with Bakhtin's notion of the subversive power of the carnival in relation to the dominance of the medieval church, she claims that female soap opera fans, in gaining pleasure from their playful appropriation of the characteristics of soap dialogue, succeed in undermining patriarchy. While ethnographic audience studies support the view that playful interaction with soaps does take place, it is much less clear that this subverts dominant discourses. Mary Ellen Brown herself admits that the parody may be visible only to the subordinate group.

Tania Modleski argues that soap opera's fragmented structure echoes the pattern of a woman's daily grind, and allows for the distracted pattern of viewing which is supposedly characteristically 'feminine'. This belief has been strengthened by ethnographic research which shows that, at least in many of the households investigated, men control the viewing of the main television set and the use of the video (e.g. Morley, 1986; Gray, 1992). Women, busy with family or housework, can only devote fleeting attention to the box in the corner.

Such arguments not only imply that all women viewers are mothers and housewives; they also help to perpetuate the negative stereotype of women as scatterbrained and unable to concentrate, by referring to the 'state of distraction' (Modleski, 1982, p. 102) in which this form of viewing occurs. This is a peculiarly negative formulation for a feminist critic, because it obscures (just as dominant discourse does) the facility that women, balancing a variety of roles, often develop in attending receptively to more than one claim on their attention at a time. Research into sports watching and masculinity in the United States also challenges the view that distracted viewing is uniquely or even especially feminine. Male viewers of sport, too, in a manner akin to the viewers of soaps, are invited to move between moments of multiple identification and moments of loss of attention (Rose and Friedman, 1994).

While feminist cultural criticism has raised the status of soap opera, its definition of soap as reproducing women's discourse is more controversial. Although audience research suggests, unsurprisingly, that the female audience for soap operas exceeds the male, the gap is not as wide as might be supposed. A week's survey of television viewing in 1990 discovered that soap operas featured in five out of ten of the top ten programmes watched by women, but also in three out of ten of those watched by men (Beere, 1991, pp. 54–5). In Britain, the soap opera *EastEnders* was deliberately conceived by the BBC in 1985 to appeal to a male as well as a female audience. The purpose of this was unashamedly commercial: to lure a young unisex audience away from the attractions of ITV programming. A wide diversity of male characters was introduced, and given as strong characterization and roles as the female characters. Recent work has also suggested that analogies exist on a variety of levels between soap operas and sports programmes. O'Connor and Boyle (1993) draw attention to the similarities in terms of audience loyalty; the significance of each in women's and men's daily talk; and their shared textual emphasis on personalities and on constructing appeal to the audience's emotions. Characterizing one as a 'feminine' and the other as a 'masculine' pleasure, far from validating male and female experience, merely reproduces constructions of femininity and masculinity that are ultimately conservative.

Feminist critics who have cautiously welcomed soap opera's ability to address the competencies and perspectives of women have sometimes been over-optimistic about the radical potential of the pleasures on offer. To the extent that these pleasures contrast with absent voices elsewhere on television, and with dominant paradigms of action-driven drama, they are expansively liberating. But to go further than this with a textual analysis which suggests that the method of narrative construction is 'feminine', or the dialogue indicative of 'women's discourse', is to distort the evidence of many contemporary soaps, and to be in danger of confirming mythologies of the feminine which can only hook women back into the net within which they have been conventionally ensnared. Attention to those areas of popular programming that particularly address feminine subjectivities also obscures the degree to which women's voices remain absent or marginal in other areas of broadcasting and the media. Current affairs discussions, and even panels on the arts and culture, follow a traditional mould of agenda-driven discussion that is seen by many women as typically male. It is rare on television to have access to a group of women talking about serious issues on their own, and in their own way. While women do this all the time *off* the television screen, with wit, humour, and tangential references back and forth between the 'public' and the 'private', this remains invisible from public view. Small wonder, under these circumstances, that when women discuss rape or lesbian relations in peak-time soap opera, it should seem so remarkable.

In conclusion

The second section of this book will return frequently to the need for women to define themselves and their own attitudes and perspectives through the media. Although women's voices have, numerically, been increasing in the media in the course of this century, they have almost invariably failed to become the dominant discourse. As Kaja Silverman (1988) and Amy Lawrence (1991) have both observed in relation to film, women's voices have classically been constructed instead as a problem, and a source of anxiety.

Arguing for a new value to be put on 'women's discourse' is not, however, problem-free. 'Women's discourse' can neither be constant nor transparent. The term will evoke different connotations for feminists, anti-feminists and those indifferent to feminism. It will also imply divergent realities, and inspire divergent versions of utopia, for white and ethnic minority women, or for middle-class and working-class women. Neither Cixous nor Irigaray makes this diversity sufficiently clear. In addition, by implying that social progress can be effected through change in the status of women's language, they ignore the ties that bind social processes and discourse inextricably together. For 'womanspeak' to gain dominance, women would already need to possess power and authority within the social structure. Belief that the nature of 'womanspeak' would remain the same under these new conditions defies the logic of how discourse works.

What we can agree as women is that our diverse voices are still granted insufficient authority within the media. We need more voices on, and fewer voices off. Although I have been critical of what I regard as a feminist romanticism about soap opera, one of the reasons why it is so valued by women is precisely that, regularly and frequently, it beams across the air waves a variety of women's voices. Scottish Television in 1994 pioneered a new series, hosted by Sheena McDonald, enabling 100 women each week to debate topical issues. If this moves beyond the menu of typical 'women's topics', it will mark modest progress. Moving from silence into speech, is, as bell hooks reminds us, the single most liberating step for any human being.

3

From Mrs Happyman to kissing chaps goodbye: advertising reconstructs femininity

Shopping is to a woman what getting drunk is to a man.
(Columnist Dorothy Dix in *Daily Mirror*, 19 December 1935)

A new traditionalism, centered on family life, is in the offing. . . .
Romance and courtship will be back in favor, so sales of cut flowers
are sure to rise . . . a return to home-making will mean a rise in
supermarket sales.
(Jib Fowles, in *New York Times*, 1988, quoted in Faludi, 1992, p. 36)

Women, since at least the late nineteenth century, have been particularly associated with consumerism. The 1980s' film *Pretty Woman*
is only one in a long list of cultural celebrations of the link between
shopping and women's sexual desires. If food is reputedly the route
to the male heart, shopping, preferably on an unlimited budget, is the
imagined pathway to a woman's. The French language makes the point
succinctly: *'consommation'* refers equally to consuming and sexual con-
summation. As evidence grew in the early decades of the twentieth century that the developing arts of retailing and advertising were attracting
a predominantly female clientele, marketers and advertisers became
significant definers of twentieth-century women's desires and aspirations. The media's interest in attracting women as readers or viewers was
often motivated first by their perceived commercial value as consumers.

This chapter will explore the part that consumer discourses have
played in endorsing and reproducing particular models of femininity in
the course of this century. As early as the interwar period, long before
poststructuralism had been heard of, advertising was constructing
multiple possible identities for women in an effort to enhance their spending power. Women who saw themselves as self-sacrificing mothers *and*
as occasionally self-indulgent pleasure-seekers were going to be better
consumers than those who related to one persona only. Where consumerism saw increased purchasing potential, feminism saw the creation

of a multifaceted and artificial feminine mystique. Anxious to explore instead the common experiences that united women, and, more gradually, the real political differences that separated them, such as class, sexuality and ethnicity, second-wave feminism in the 1960s and 1970s had little in common with consumerism. Postfeminism, in the 1980s and 1990s, has been hailed as an accommodation, however uneasy, between these two old enemies. The last part of this chapter will consider how persuasive this theory is.

Women, the media and consumption in the interwar period

With the growth in department stores, such as Macy's in New York (established as early as 1860) and Selfridge's in London (established in 1909), middle-class women were enticed out of their domestic cloisters and into the public sphere. Outings by bourgeois women had long been legitimate in the interests of finding a marriage partner, as Jane Austen's exquisitely detailed and witty early nineteenth-century accounts of balls and promenades as methods of feminine self-display demonstrate. Venturing out of the home was also allowed in the course of that century for the dispensing of philanthropy to the poor or the sick. Going out to indulge in the pleasure of looking and buying, with woman the surveyor rather than the surveyed, marked a revolutionary innovation (Bowlby, 1985).

Women's supremacy in the field of consumption quickly had its effect on the emerging mass media both in Britain and the USA. 1930s' advertising trade journals in the United States regularly attributed between 80 and 85 per cent of all consumption to women, and as early as the 1920s identified women as a coherent target group. The class-differentiated 'Colonel's Lady and Judy O'Grady' were, advertisers were pithily known to remark, 'sisters under the skin' (Marchand, 1985, pp. 65–6). The growing band of press advertisers eagerly exploited opportunities to coax women out of their feminine caution into a desire to spend. By 1926, the high-selling *Ladies' Home Journal* was already devoting over half its 270 pages to advertisements (Marchand, 1985, p. 7).

In Britain, Alfred Harmsworth (later Lord Northcliffe) was the first to capitalize on the attraction of women to advertisers. In the 1890s, he launched two popular women's weekly magazines, one with a title, *Home Chat*, which neatly encapsulated current thinking about the feminine sphere and feminine discourse. In 1903 he took the more pioneering step of setting up the *Daily Mirror* as a newspaper 'for gentlewomen'. The aim was commercial success rather than support for feminism, even though Northcliffe's entrepreneurial zest persuaded him to appoint a majority of female journalists. The failure of this project reputedly enhanced Northcliffe's disillusionment with women's intelligence and abilities: 'Women can't write and don't want to read', he is alleged to have 'growled' (Williams, 1969, p. 93). The immediate result was the sacking of the female staff, and the transformation of the *Daily Mirror* into a successful general-interest picture paper.

This experience did not deter Northcliffe from including a women's section in his newspapers. He had initiated this in the *Daily Mail* in 1896, and by 1909 was warning its editor, Marlowe, to ensure the continuing femininity of the magazine page, as competition for women readers intensified from the *Daily Express* (LeMahieu, 1988, p. 33). Their function as bait for advertisers encouraged women's pages (particularly in the more popular papers) to experiment with layout and typography ahead of the rest of the paper. Northcliffe's alleged claim that 'women are the holders of the domestic purse-strings . . . They are the real buyers. Men buy what women tell them to' (quoted in LeMahieu, 1988, p. 34) was to find many echoes as the twentieth century progressed, in the film as well as the press industry.

Charles Eckert (1978), Jane Gaines and Charlotte Herzog (Gaines and Herzog, 1990; Herzog and Gaines, 1991), amongst others, have documented the interaction between the selling of movies and the selling of goods in 1930s' America. Women, again, were the principal target. Hollywood films acted as showcases for the latest feminine fashions, which, by the 1930s, were being promoted and sold in tandem with the film's opening. Newspapers and magazines, on both sides of the Atlantic, helped to promote the fashion of the stars by running features on their dresses or costume designers, and by treating female stars as the first source of glamour pictures. In the mid-1930s, the *Daily Mirror*, reviewing the fortunes of women over the previous 30 years, identified film stars as the most powerful influence. 'Here we are', commented the writer Cecile Leslie, 'thanks to the Dietrichs, Harlows, Garbos and Colberts. . . . For it is the film stars who are in great degree responsible for us of 1935. They have shown us how to make the best of whatever type of face and figure we possess.' Stars were, in the words of the article's introduction, responsible for defining the rules of 'that amusing game – the game of being a Woman' (*Daily Mirror*, 17 December 1935).

Films also helped to promote cosmetics and beauty products. Lux soap was the most widely publicized product in the 1930s to use star appeal to sell itself to admiring fans. Daily newspapers in Britain, as well as film magazines, carried a series of advertisements extolling the benefits of the brand to named actresses, including Bette Davis and Myrna Loy. The unrelenting rigours of the cinematic close-up were cited as evidence of the soap's ability to prove its qualities of gentleness and deep-cleansing softness. Film idols set standards of appearance that influenced many women's choices as consumers. Jackie Stacey's (1991) fascinating discovery of the extent to which female fans of the 1940s and 1950s identified with the stars beyond the screen, constructing them as objects of desire and imitating their hairstyles and clothes, would almost certainly have been true of the interwar period also.

Financial incentives prompted radio, too, to dream up ways of targeting women listeners, especially in the United States, where commercial motivation flourished earlier than in the regulated British environment. Soap opera was the most obvious result, combining the selling of the sponsor's products (Procter & Gamble toiletries) with a narrative structure designed to keep women compulsively tuned in. By the 1930s the custom of equating women with domestic consumption and control of the family budget was so well established that it was etched into most forms of media, and was almost single-handedly responsible for the burgeoning of the women's magazine press. It encouraged the establishment in Britain of two increasingly successful weekly magazines (*Woman's Own* in 1932 and *Woman* in 1937), while in the United States *McCalls* changed its format in 1932 to improve the visibility of its advertisements (McCracken, 1993, pp. 65–6). Contemporary statistics about gender and purchasing decisions, taken together with the plethora of diverse products now being manufactured for domestic use, made women the obvious group to become the first holder of the successful 'market niche' award, even if marketing terminology had not yet evolved the term.

That amusing game of being a woman

Advertising discourses of the interwar period evolved a personal style of appeal, or personal mode of address, to their assumed readers. Whereas in everyday life we adapt the ways we talk according to our knowledge of the people we are speaking to, being playful or ironic with some and formal and serious with others, media modes of address have to rely on assumptions about their intended audiences. For this reason, they have been described as addressing an implied, rather than an actual, reader and as playing a significant role in *constructing* subjectivities for the audience or readers (Brunt, 1990).

During the interwar period, three constructions of feminine identity dominated in advertising discourse: the capable household manager; the guilt-ridden mother; and the self-indulgent 'flapper'. These were not self-contained categories of actual women, but manufactured versions of feminine responsibilities or aspirations that had particular resonance for women of the period. While the first two principally spoke to women in the domestic sphere, they also had wider ideological influence in sustaining the importance of the home against the new libertarianism of the 'jazz era'. The pleasure-seeking 'flapper' most obviously addressed a generation of young women exploring the new leisure opportunities of the period, but it also provided a dream of escape for the housebound married woman. The modes of address, as we will see, were sometimes directed at men rather than women, but the constructions of femininity remained constant.

The capable household manager

In the interwar period, a number of developments conspired to redefine women's domestic responsibilities as a science or a skilled craft. Women had to be enticed back to the home, whether from their brief taste of industrial life during World War I, or from their pre-marriage employment in the professions, many of which operated a marriage bar. The growth of suburbia broke up women's traditional social networks, and turned sparkling new homes into potential shrines, just as domestic servants became increasingly hard to find. If this was not enough to motivate a new ideological status for household management, domestic chores were potentially shrinking because of the increasing production of labour-saving devices, and the growing availability of ready-made clothing and prepackaged foods. While working-class women still juggled jobs outside the home with domestic responsibilities, unaided by either servants or electrical gadgets, middle-class women were ready to take a novel pride in managing their homes with minimum outside help.

Training for this new 'career' mushroomed during the period, with the growth of domestic science courses and a steady stream of manuals offering advice and instruction. Some of these made explicit links between the time and motion studies being carried out in the industrial sphere and the desirability of introducing similar principles of efficiency into the domestic realm (Lewis, 1984, p. 116). Women themselves, still largely accepting their prime responsibility for hearth and home, applied pressure for better access to the new technologies and improved training through campaigning organizations such as the Electrical Association for Women, founded by Caroline Haslett in 1924 (Davidson, 1982, pp. 40–3). Women in Britain were conscious that they were not gaining maximum advantage out of the rapid spread of the electrical supply in the 1930s. While in the United States, refrigerators and vacuum cleaners were already well established, in Britain only relatively small percentages of the population owned these by 1939 (although the possibility of hiring equipment increased their distribution to some extent). Cookers (electric and gas) and small appliances such as irons were more widely available.

Analogies between women's domestic skills and the qualities expected in industry and the professions began to appear in newspapers and women's magazines as early as the 1920s. Helena Normanton, described as a law student and a brilliant young feminist, wrote in the *Daily Express* (6 September 1920) of the discipline and discrimination involved in cookery: 'The same gifts that enable a woman to be a methodical and balanced teacher, writer, doctor, or nurse will make her into a good cook if she wishes them to do so. Economy, plan, method, judgment, and proportion are all called into play'. Her view was echoed by a 1925 article in the same newspaper (this time on the women's page) entitled 'What is Household Science?' The writer, Mary Evelyn, comments that 'the kitchen is the cook's laboratory or place where experiments are made' (*Daily Express*, 17 June 1925). Housework had never before been awarded such a high status.

Advertising discourses caught the mood, using flattery to hail women as experts well versed in the finer points of household management. Advertisements for Electrolux vacuum cleaners turned the housewife into a scientific educator, able to interpret diagrams explaining the advantages of the Electrolux filter and dust-collection system:

To the ordinary eye clean and dirty air look much the same. But science has proved, as you can see from these diagrams, what a difference there is – and the Electrolux made the difference! By means of its chemically-treated pad through which all the air in the room is passed, the Electrolux removes the dangerous germs and bacteria and leaves the air germ-free and wholesome.

(*Daily Express*, 27 March 1930)

Science was evoked repeatedly in advertisements for new cleaning agents. 'Do you use Persil the right way?', advertisements asked, as the product's chemical properties were outlined: 'it's the oxygen set free by Persil which does the work' (*Daily Mirror*, 9 June 1925). Advertising also acknowledged that women shared information and ideas as well as gossip. Household tips from female friends, relatives or named experts were regularly included in women's pages and frequently used in advertisements to endorse products. Of obvious commercial value, these also suggested a bank of feminine knowledge and information which was recognized and valued in no other public discourse of the time.

Science in the kitchen became symptomatic of modernity. Advertisements for cleaning agents particularly stressed the connection between the modern and the scientific. Women, freed from 'drudgery' (the advertisers' favourite 'boo' word for domestic chores) could enjoy the modern pastimes of the age. Repeatedly, advertisements for labour-saving machines such as vacuum-cleaners and thermostatically controlled cookers implied that the woman released periodically from the kitchen would make a more exciting companion. Men were cajoled into purchasing (or hiring) vacuum cleaners to save their wives (often described, with a nuanced reminder of sexual delights, as 'brides') from the toil of housework. An advertisement for Goblin cleaners asked pointedly, 'SIR! Is your wife cheerful when you get home tired?' (*Daily Mail*, 14 March 1930). If not, the solution was obvious. Hoover enticed husbands, too, by claiming that leisure was what a woman needed 'to keep herself daintily dressed and up-to-date' (*Daily Record*, 15 December 1930). New World Regulo-controlled gas cookers allowed an elegantly dressed woman to provide her own testimonial: 'I used to spend half my morning in the kitchen (looked and felt like it, too . . .). Now . . . I can just leave the whole dinner to cook itself . . . whilst I trot out and do my shopping or see my friends, or enjoy myself in lots of ways I never had time to do before'. The advantages were palpable: 'John says it's made a New Woman of me!' (*Scottish Daily Express*, 4 March 1935).

Redesigning housework as scientific management did not quite succeed in making it glamorous, but it did make it compatible with the spirit of modernism. The contrasting subjectivities of the 'housewife' and the 'New Woman' could be blended into one. 'Mrs Happyman' embodied the combination. She was the modern advocate for Electrolux, responsible as we saw earlier for demonstrating its scientific advantages, but her priorities were unashamedly conventional: 'Look, everybody', she exclaimed with delight, 'Homes transformed and beautified – the servant problem solved – and every husband a Happy man, like mine. That's what this really wonderful machine will do for you'. (*Daily Express*, 25 March 1930).

As Christina Hardyment ruefully points out, the 'businesslike gloss' that discourses of household management put 'on the mundane matter of housework' helped to distract women from dreams of participating more fully in the public sphere (1988, p. 187). Management skills in women, and familiarity with science and technology were to be encouraged as long as they remained confined within the home. Although the time released by labour-saving foods, ready-made clothes or domestic appliances was frequently depicted as enhancing women's leisure opportunities, it was rarely seen as enabling women to combine the roles of homemaker and worker outside the home. A 1930 advertisement for Vim was an exception. 'Our Mothers', its advocate explained, 'could not have managed both housekeeping and business', but now it was possible to combine both with ease – and with a cleaning lady employed for only 'a couple of hours' (*Daily Mail*, 6 March 1930).

Guilty mothers

While technology reconstituted housework for modernity, women's roles as mothers invited a more traditional approach. Women's capacity for guilt was ruthlessly exploited by advertisers in the interwar period. Even when the problem to be solved by the advertised product was women's exhaustion, women were invited to take the blame. An advertisement for Wincarnis tonic stressed that a relaxed and stress-free atmosphere in the home was the woman's responsibility. Based on worries that female 'fatigue and anaemia' were capable of wrecking marriages, the first-person text repeatedly underlined this thesis. One 'young Mayfair wife' admitted, 'although I didn't realise it, I was to blame. Nine times out of ten the woman is' (*Daily Express*, 6 December 1935).

In both Britain and the USA, advertisers homed in on mothers' insecurities about the quality of their childcare. Ruth Schwartz Cowan cites a content analysis of advertisements in the *Ladies' Home Journal* between the wars which demonstrated that appeal to guilt was a favourite tactic (Cowan, 1983, footnote, p. 187). The tricky economic situation, together with the growing attention to child psychology, provided a fertile breeding ground for maternal anxieties. The quality of nourishment mothers were providing for their children was one of the worries advertisers encouraged, especially in advertisements for the new breakfast cereals and food supplements. What Roland Marchand refers to in the States as the parables of the 'Unraised Hand' in the classroom and the 'Skinny Kid' (1985, pp. 296–9) were echoed in British advertising, as women were urged to identify with the mother whose son was not 'good enough for the team' until she fed him Grape-Nuts (*Daily Mail*, 17 June 1925) or the mother whose baby did not look as strong as others (advertisement for Scotts Brand Emulsion, *Daily Mirror*, 6 December 1935).

Fears about hygiene were a second and potent source of concern. At a time when penicillin had not been heard of, and diseases such as tuberculosis claimed many young lives, this anxiety was readily evoked. Since germs, as advertisers frequently emphasized, were invisible, the housewife could never be totally sure that she had exterminated them. In Britain throughout the 1920s and 1930s, Lifebuoy soap advertisements vividly described dust as the 'invisible enemy' (*see* Fig. 3), and graphically enacted domestic scenes where children were at risk from lurking microbes, while Vim piously declared 'it's not original sin but original dirt we have to fight' (*Daily Mirror*, 19 March 1930). The Victorian moral crusade had moved unceremoniously from the temperance hall to the kitchen floor. When motherly angst wore thin, fear of scorn from neighbours or friends could be equally effective. Harpic advertisements in the 1930s featured a pair of disapproving eyes, with a caption guaranteed to strike terror into the reader: 'Are you SURE your lavatory never offends? Friends won't tell you about your lavatory' (*Scottish Daily Express*, 7 March 1935). Shock tactics in advertising discourse were softened, however, by reassurance. Experts and advisers were frequently quoted within the advertisement, encouraging trust. Doctors and nurses (real or fictitious) were favoured sources of confidential advice. With such support, women could embrace the caring burden with confidence and enthusiasm.

Flappers invade the public sphere

For the new generation of cosmetic and luxury products coming onto the market in the interwar period, a thoroughly modernist version of femininity needed to be constructed. The unmarried 'modern miss', designated in the 1920s as the 'flapper' woman, loved to enjoy and indulge herself, participating in sport, dancing or driving open-topped motor cars. Her spending power was earned by working in the public sphere, most probably as an office employee, or sales assistant. With bobbed hair, and clothes which gave an androgynous look to her svelte figure, her sophistication was symbolized by her elegantly displayed cigarette. As Billie Melman (1988) observes, the term 'flapper' shared the history of other words that acquired pejorative connotations when applied to women. Although outgoing and lively, the flapper was also irresponsible and flighty. She occupied the public domain of the street or the dancehall while her married sister kindled the domestic hearth. Although a creature of modernity, the flapper was often caricatured as replaying the traditional characteristics of femininity in new garb. Her display of feminine manipulation, narcissism and coquettishness was a frequent theme in Haselden's cartoon strips in the *Daily Mirror*, published prominently on the editorial page. Her association with leisure pursuits rather than serious activities helped to devalue her social and, especially, her political status.

This process was particularly visible in the public discourses surrounding the introduction of votes for all women over 21 in late 1920s' Britain. Pejoratively referred to in the press as the 'Flapper Bill' or the 'Rule-by-Women Bill', this long overdue extension of the franchise raised spectres of incompatibility between femininity and citizenship rights. The age-group to be enfranchised (21 to 29, women over 30 having already been given the vote in 1918) provided the excuse for forgetting about women's capacities and selflessness in the domestic sphere and for highlighting instead their fickleness and self-indulgent silliness. The disdain in which the new voter was held was typified by a cartoon in the Scottish *Daily Record* (18 May 1929) during the election campaign. 'Here is the latest election story', it quipped: 'A canvasser calling on a woman elector asked if she was interested in the Liberal Party. "Yes, of course!" she replied. "Where are they having it?"' (18 May 1929).

For the advertisers of the expanding range of cosmetic and beauty products, or of artificial fabrics such as rayon, the flapper was the ideal icon. The selfless concerns of the wife and mother were replaced by a self-directed attention to image. Soap advertising exemplified both approaches, with a clear dividing line between those brands (such as Lifebuoy and Sunlight) destined to offer protection to others by fighting household germs, and those (such as Lux or Knight's Castile) guaranteed to stimulate personal fantasies (*see* Figs. 3 and 4). Cartoon strips, such as the Knight's Castile one in Fig. 4, had become a popular means by

Fig. 3 Address to the anxious mother in a Lifebuoy advertisement (*Scottish Daily Express*, 11 September 1935). By kind permission of Lever Brothers

Fig. 4 Address to the image-conscious young woman in a Knight's Castile advertisement (*Daily Herald*, 12 December 1935). By kind permission of Lever Brothers

the 1930s of indulging desires already fanned by romantic fiction and women's magazines. Germs may have been the obstacle to utopia confronting the mature woman, but the obstacles to romance were more intimidating to the young, competing (because of the wartime toll on available men) for a marriage partner. Bad breath, body hair and body odours were graphically depicted as major hazards to be defeated by the array of chemical remedies being produced in the new light-industry factories. Blemishes bestowed by nature could also be masked by seductive lingerie, silk stockings or careful attention to dress.

The flapper image of the 'new woman' as playful, self-indulgent, sexually aware, and adventurous also suited the advertisers of cigarettes, perfume, chocolates, motor-cars and other luxury goods. Although many of these targeted male purchasers, the association of the product with women helped to enhance its seductive aura. Advertising for Nippy chocolates in newspapers of the 1930s featured female open-topped car drivers and female motor-cyclists. This daring outdoor image contrasted with the version of femininity on offer from Rowntree's advertisements in the run-up to Christmas in 1935. Addressed to men, the text focused on box appeal: 'Choose among the hundreds of delightful designs, knowing that Rowntree's Chocolates are those which a girl loves best, and that long after they have vanished the box will be used for her little personal knick-knacks' (*Daily Record*, 21 December 1935).

Although the flapper image accorded ill with women's increasing claims for political recognition, her outgoing modernity allowed advertisers to align her independence of spirit with women's rights campaigns. As an advertisement in the States for toothpaste suggested in the early 1930s, deciding which brand to favour could become a surrogate political act (Marchand, 1985, pp. 186–7). Following a lead caption 'When lovely women vote', the text concludes that their inevitable choice is Listerine toothpaste. The woman romantically represented in the illustration is, we are told, 'charming, educated, well-to-do' and *'prominent in the social and civic life of her city'* (my italics). That her main concern should be her choice of an appropriate brand of toothpaste is not meant to surprise us. When the American Tobacco Company consulted Edward Bernays (nephew of Sigmund Freud and pioneer of public relations) about the best method of encouraging women to smoke, he suggested equating cigarette smoking with women's rights. With the support of feminist Ruth Hale, he negotiated the inclusion of ten cigarette-smoking young women in the 1929 Easter

Parade in New York 'as a protest against women's inequality' (Ewen, 1976, pp. 160–1). Equality might be co-opted as a device to sell goods, but it gained little practical support from the period's emphasis on female consumerism. As Christine Frederick, a contemporary home economist and advertising adviser, observed in *Selling Mrs Consumer* (1929), 'Woman is ... powerful in buying because of her secondary position to men' (Ewen, 1976, p. 170).

In the interwar years, the different subjectivities constructed for women in consumer discourses coexisted without friction. The technology-freed housewife could become the 'new woman' in her newly discovered leisure hours, while the youthful flapper might mature contentedly into the caring, guilt-ridden mother. Modernity added excitement to the domestic role, without fundamentally disturbing its status. The Gramscian theory of 'hegemony' offers some help in understanding this process. Gramsci argues that dominant ideologies do not impose themselves coercively on our consciousness: instead, they dovetail into ways of thinking that we are comfortable with, that make sense to us and may even seem to acknowledge important truths about our lives. Women's role in the domestic sphere was given a new lease of life in advertising discourses that turned unpaid labourers into technologically sophisticated craft-workers with special competencies and skills. By redrafting discourses of domestic labour, advertising both brought them into line with modernity and flattered women into taking pride in their traditional place within the home.

That hegemony, given a further boost by the advertising and women's magazine discourses of the consumer boom years of the 1950s, was sharply challenged by the second wave of feminism in the 1960s and 1970s. Led by Betty Friedan's *The Feminine Mystique* (first published in 1963), feminism charged consumerism with constructing identities for women that were deeply conservative. Initially adopting Friedan's manipulative model of the media, feminists set up consciousness-raising groups to extend women's awareness of the relationship between their own experiences and the social structures underpinning these. By this means, they also extended politics to include the subjective and the experiential. With the slogan 'the personal is political', a new agenda was set to include personal relationships, sexuality, and even fashion and personal style. Throughout the 1970s, feminist and consumerist ideologies and discourses were ranged implacably against each other, sparring from time to time, but occasionally also learning each other's tricks.

Independent but still feminine

During the 1970s, feminists began to wage guerrilla war on advertising's sexism. Stickers accusing advertisers of degrading women appeared on the London Underground and graffiti slogans were sprayed on street posters, humorously and effectively parodying consumerism's masculine discourse. A Fiat advertisement, sporting an elegant woman lying on the car roof and exclaiming 'it's so practical, darling', attracted the riposte, 'When I'm not lying on cars I'm a brain surgeon' (Posener, 1986).

Feminist appeals for change were less successful when channelled through the official advertising monitoring bodies. The Advertising Standards Authority, responsible in Britain for all advertisements other than broadcast ones, was unimpressed by feminist complaints in the 1970s. Retaliating with its own research, published in 1982 as *Herself Appraised*, the ASA demonstrated that most women were content with current representations. Although accused of bad faith for focusing solely on advertisements printed in women's magazines, which were least likely to cause concern, this report fuelled suspicions that feminists were paranoid whingers, totally lacking, despite their witty graffiti campaigns, in a sense of humour. Feminists were criticized for ignoring 'the existing facts of life, i.e. that the majority of women still see themselves as housewives *and that a high proportion of products are aimed at women in their traditional role rather than in their business role*' (ASA spokesperson quoted in *The Guardian*, 26 June 1978, my italics). The second part of this defence confirms that the prime motivation keeping the domestic emphasis alive was commercial rather than purely ideological.

Advertising in the 1970s was not, however, entirely impervious to the debate about women's changing roles and aspirations. Despite its reluctance to accede to feminist demands, the Advertising Standards Authority did clamp down on the most blatant abuse of women's bodies as sales gimmicks for products such as motor cycles or industrial tools. More subtly, advertising itself began to take stock of the evidence that women wished to be regarded as individuals rather than as roles. The tone was set by the up-beat modes of address in the new generation of 'liberated' young women's magazines (such as *Honey* (1960), *19* (1968) and *Cosmopolitan*, making its British début in 1972). Advertisers who addressed young women as unique in their style and aspirations encouraged wider consumption of cosmetics and fashion. By blending harmoniously with the environment and discourse of the new magazines, advertising also benefited from the intimacy and trust that these publications established with their readers.

Recognition of women's individualism began to feature in 1970s' advertisements, although it became more pronounced in the following decades. In the 1970s, Triumph advertised bras 'for the way you are', but the images were still of feminine women, 'woman-shaped and proud of it' (*Cosmopolitan*, November 1978) or 'the very picture of serenity' (*She*, November 1978). By the mid-1980s, the caption remained the same, but the images identified a wider range of subjectivities, from tender mother, to sun-seeking holiday-maker, to art-loving sophisticate. The *Daily Mail*, in its campaign to woo more women readers, also exploited a varied set of identities to illustrate its caption 'behind every successful woman there's a *Daily Mail*'. In an odd inversion of readership expectations, an advertisement for that paper in *Cosmopolitan* (November, 1978) depicts a mother being applauded by adoring children as she bears a three-tiered birthday cake to a table already groaning with labour-intensive goodies; while in the same month, the more domestically orientated *She* features a young woman, with two male companions, participating enthusiastically in a yachting expedition. Perfumes, too, caught the individualistic fever. Cachet featured snap-shot images of eight different women to accentuate its caption: 'A fragrance as individual as you are' (*She*, November 1978). Max Factor's Blasé also featured a range of individualistic women to bear witness to its slogan: 'It's not what you wear: it's the way you wear it'.

The other hint that feminism was in the air came from the advertising agencies' sudden cultivation of stylistic androgyny. This began with Revlon's fragrance, Charlie, launched first in the United States in February 1973 and soon established as an international brand leader. 'Charlie' was clad in trousers, always striding confidently along, but aware of her own sexual appeal. On film or in still pose, her gaze was directed knowingly towards the camera. She was to be seen, as the caption instructed us, as 'gorgeous, sexy, young'. Revlon was careful to retain Charlie's feminine credentials: 'Independent and not needing a man, but still feminine, not into women's lib' (cited in Myers, 1986, p. 77). Although Charlie wafted a breath of fresh air across Revlon's other creation of the period, the 'sensual, but not too far from innocence' woman of Jontue's cloyingly romantic campaign, her femininity was never in doubt. Other feminine women in masculine attire followed, most notably in Chanel no. 19's Gentleman's Club campaign, where the sophisticated young woman takes the male club by storm, literally letting her hair down as she capsizes into the traditional leather armchair to read her *Financial Times*.

This use of male dress was novel in advertising, but, in common with its appearance in the cinema, it worked to increase the sexual appeal of the woman rather than the reverse. It had little to do with a feminism that was already wary of trick suggestions that women's equality meant becoming more like a man. Feminism may ultimately have been more influential in the 1970s in encouraging advertisers to expand the product areas that were thought appropriate to female consumption. New arrivals included cars; drinks previously thought of as male; and banks, building societies and insurance companies.

With the eye-catching caption 'Sex has never been a problem for us', an advertisement for the British Leyland Mini in the mid-1970s makes heavy weather of the attributes of the car (such as stylishness, or the luxury that 'pampers the gentle sex') that cannot be talked about in an era conscious of 'sex discrimination' (*Observer Magazine*, 13 June 1976). Car advertisements in women's magazines often appealed to women as mothers, trying to pack the family shopping and baby gear into inadequately sized boots. A Citroën Estate advertisement used the image of a toddler with the caption 'she takes up more room than two adults' to catch the reader's eye (*She*, November 1978). Guinness was marketed for women who had already 'pinched' men's pullovers, aftershave and trousers (*She*, February 1974), or for women who could even 'look stunning dressed in a boiler suit' (*Nova*, September 1975). Money management advertisements used more traditional appeals either to women's concern about their families' well-being or to their romantic desires.

At the same time, many advertisements of the 1970s ignored feminism entirely, reproducing the caring images of good wives and mothers, or the sexually titillating images of women that were familiar from other media discourses of the decade such as the 'page three girls' in the Rupert Murdoch *Sun*. Although advertising had not yet caught up with the notion of the 'superwoman' identified in Shirley Conran's book of that title in 1975, it had begun to extend the repertoire of feminine subjectivities likely to encourage consumption. Advertising remained uncertain about the direction that women themselves wished to follow. Confident that feminism was not the favoured route, they toyed with a variety of contrasting identities.

Advertisers generally lagged behind women's magazines in the cultivation of new modes of address, even when the evidence suggested that commercial advantages could be gained from modernizing their approach. Shortly before the publication of the ASA's report in 1982, the Equal Opportunities Commission in Britain published its own research into women's thoughts on contemporary advertising (Hamilton *et al.*, 1982). This research, humorously entitled *Adman and Eve*, compared women's reactions to four 'traditional' and four 'modern' advertisements for the same products. Its aim was to measure their relative persuasiveness in encouraging women to make a purchase. Including among the four test cases the *Daily Mail* 'birthday mother' advertisement, it found, not surprisingly, that women preferred the more up-to-date approach.

Advertisers were not persuaded. One of the campaigns tested as an example of the modern 'category' was the early 1980s' television advertisement for Camay soap, in which a young, elegant and affluent woman steps from her Porsche into her executive flat, and ignores a ringing telephone to lavish attention on herself in the bath. This advertisement, written by an all-woman team, allows the answering machine to deal with her male friend's telephone call in the intermission between the two-part slogan, spoken by a male voice-over: 'rich creamy Camay . . . for women who choose to please themselves'. Despite the finding of the EOC study that this was much preferred to an earlier, non-narrative, campaign, the advertising agency had by 1983 reintroduced a man to this advertisement, in response to their own market research findings that most women wanted its romantic connotations to be more explicitly articulated (cited in BBC2 programme, *Washes Whiter*, 22 April 1990). Pleasing oneself, if one was a woman, was still not acceptable within advertising discourse, especially if this involved rejecting a man.

Postfeminist utopias

By the later 1980s and 1990s, consumer discourses were taking a new approach to feminism. Believing both that feminism's battles had been won, and that its ideology was now harmless by virtue of being out of date, advertisers invented 'postfeminism' as a utopia where women could do whatever they pleased, provided they had sufficient will and enthusiasm. The feminist's overburdened woman juggling the demands of career and childcare with the pleasures on offer in the gym or bedroom was magically transformed into the executive superwoman, always on the move and always in complete control. Jet-setting, caring for children, revelling in an exciting social life were all easily compatible. Yet another in the procession of twentieth-century 'New Women' had been born.

Pleasing oneself, freedom and self-sufficiency all moved up the copywriting hierarchy. 'Making the most of oneself' became as mandatory a consumerist goal as looking after others. Those with goods and services to sell to women caught up with the message of freedom and self-fulfilment advocated by feminism and rejoiced, before the political implications of its demands could ricochet off the walls. Consumer discourses in both advertising and the women's monthly magazine press now eagerly absorbed the terminology of self-assertiveness and achievement, transforming feminism's challenging collective programme into atomized acts of individual consumption. For the new superwoman to combine career and home, cultivate independence while maintaining family relationships, remain sexually alluring but also convincingly businesslike, a panoply of material aids and services was required. From microwave ovens to massage oils, from linen suits to silk lingerie, from aerobics to assertiveness-training classes, her iconography depended on spending money. This new version of consumerism, claiming feminist credentials, undoubtedly strengthened many women's perception that feminism was an essentially middle-class movement. Advertisers' slogans which picked up surface aspects of feminist discourse muddied the waters of feminist campaigning.

Borrowing from an alternative discourse to add zest to your creativity is a regular trick in advertising and other forms of popular culture. Known in cultural studies as a process of 'recuperation' (Brunsdon, 1986, pp. 119–20), 'co-option' or 'incorporation', this manoeuvre pretends to respond to the competing ideology but ignores its ideological challenge. Environmental and ecological concerns have been subject to similar treatment. Happy to incorporate 'green' issues when they aid consumption (whether of unleaded petrol or of eco-friendly toilet cleaners), advertising agencies understandably baulk at the more radical suggestion that we should all reduce our consumption or abandon our cars in order to protect the future of the planet. Ignoring counter-discourses such as those of feminism or ecology has never made good commercial sense, especially in media aimed primarily at young people: fully accepting and integrating their implications is, however, equally unsound financially. The compromise is to adopt the surface terminology, without taking on board the ideology that underpins it. As Charlotte Brunsdon claims, the effects of 'recuperation' are misleading: 'Not only do the oppositional ideas and practices lose their bite, but they can function to make it appear as if change has been effected' (1986, p. 120).

The concept of 'recuperation' is not universally accepted. Foucault rejected it as giving too concrete and definitive a form to the continuing process of struggle between discourses (Foucault, 1980, pp. 56–7). His view is coloured by a misperception of the finality of the recuperative process. Recuperation is not a single action, but an ongoing process, subject to constant review. What Foucault does rightly suggest, however, is that recuperation may be viewed more ambiguously than Brunsdon implies. Co-opting even selective elements of feminist discourses might also be regarded as a gesture in their direction. 'Making the most of yourself' does begin to transform the passivity of narcissistic self-contemplation into the dream of active and dynamic self-fulfilment even as it reins that dream back into the feminine activity of 'going shopping'.

Later chapters will explore these different perspectives more fully. Although my own preference is for Brunsdon's position, I also accept that for many women feminism is now thought of as a historical rather than a current ideology, and their primary contact with its objectives may often be through the discourses of consumerism. If this is a distorted refraction, it may nevertheless be significant in stimulating debate about gender roles and expectations. Against this background, the remainder of this chapter will consider three forms of co-option of feminist ideas and ideology that emerged in consumer discourses in the 1980s and 1990s. These are as follows:

- the appropriation of quasi-feminist concepts;
- the redrafting of 'caring' to make it compatible with self-fulfilment; and
- the acknowledgement of female fantasies.

Freedom to kiss the chaps goodbye

Advertisers in the later 1980s and 1990s happily made use of concepts that had acquired new status thanks to the feminist and other civil liberties movements. 'Freedom', 'independence' and 'pleasure', all problematic terms within political and cultural theory, were reduced to matters of lifestyle and consumption. Women could now 'do their own thing', without worrying about male reactions, even though men often continued to hover anxiously in the background. The fast cutting of television advertisements was especially suited to capturing the panache of the latest 'new woman' in action. Supersoft hairspray proved its ability to protect and hold the hair against the elements as its owner jetted between Heathrow and same-day appointments in Berlin and Rome. Sunsilk styling mousse allowed women to 'take control' and put an end to 'wrestling' with their hair. Self-confident women dominated the action in both these commercials, but the voice-over was still distinctively male. Women were occasionally, however, granted the last word, as in the Volkswagen Golf 1980s' advertisement where a jilted woman discards the jewellery and fur coat given to her by her lover, but keeps the car keys as her passport to independence.

In magazine advertising, connotations of feminist influence were more subdued, but being 'comfortable with who you are' (a caption on Hush Puppies shoe advertisements in 1994) was a common implicit injunction. The accompanying aspirational images made it clear that this was a command to fulfil your potential, not rest on your laurels. Men became commodities who could help or hinder progress, but they were not yet superfluous to requirements. A Boots 17 advertisement aimed at young women in 1992 teased its readers by running two images in sequence: one a facial close-up of a beautiful young model with her lips pursed in a kiss, and the caption 'how to kiss chaps'; the second, an extreme close-up of her nose and mouth, with lipstick being applied nonchalantly to the lips, and the caption now reading, simply, 'goodbye'. Before the reader had time to wonder at a campaign advocating celibacy or lesbianism, the word-play on 'chapped' lips was revealed.

This advertisement offers alternative subjectivities to the reader. The immediate address is to the conventional heterosexual desires of young women, anxious to learn how to please their men. But over the page, we are projected momentarily into a contrary universe of independence, self-reliance and self-sufficiency. Before a blow can be struck for feminism, however, the joke takes over. The playfulness of this and other advertisements of the 1980s and 1990s encourages us to laugh at traditional versions of femininity, but stops well short of openly challenging them. Triumph adopted a similar strategy in the 1990s. Its 1993 campaign featured an ecstatically cheerful model, sporting an independently-minded new hairstyle, new look and new bra. Although the small print tells us that the black lace product is called 'Amourette', the main caption declares men to be part of the trappings of lifestyle that can be readily exchanged when desired (see Fig. 5). This is more jocular and tongue-in-cheek than Triumph's earlier campaigns, but, while it departs from the commonly romantic or sexually servile

New hair, new look, new bra. And if he doesn't like it, new boyfriend.

Fig. 5 1993 Triumph advertisement

discourse of lingerie advertising, the independence of spirit that is captured here still implies that *a* boyfriend is a necessary part of the image.

In the postfeminist era, traditional female preoccupations such as men or body-care were not abandoned, but women were now urged to travel light and indulge themselves, not others. As we will see in Chapter 7, this perspective also dominated in the health and fitness discourses of the period. While women of earlier decades were invited to spend hours in front of the mirror, the new instruction was, in the words of the Vidal Sassoon advertisements, to 'Wash and Go'. The encouragement to be oneself did, however, have limits. In contrast to feminism's dawning recognition of the importance of cultural difference, consumerism offered choices that were supposedly universal. Most of the models in British advertising remained white and young: in the United States, because of the greater commercial power of the non-white ethnic communities, there was somewhat greater diversity. Yet even in that country, the balance in the general women's magazine press was unevenly struck, and tensions often erupted between the white-look aspirations of beauty features and African-Americans' desire to celebrate their own appearance. In Britain, where black models were used, they tended to appear in advertisements for clothes, not beauty products. As in the shopping mall that promises to each and everyone that it will satisfy a variety of tastes, but is the most uniform transnational space that most of us will ever encounter, conformity is exciting only when it masquerades as difference.

Caring for me, too

In the interwar years, caring was still associated with guilt and self-sacrifice. Even though labour-saving advances in the kitchen released spare time for women, their new leisure activities remained firmly off-stage. In the 1950s, in the wake of World War II, official rhetoric encouraged women to desert the public sphere and devote their energies once more to being ideal wives and mothers. Advertisers and women's magazines, supported by more sophisticated market research and an economic boom that stimulated spending on the home, readily colluded with this campaign, even though its ideological hegemony bore little relation to the realities of life for many women, financially driven to part-time, low-paid work.

Feminist thinking questioned women's 'natural' talent for caring, and reconstructed it as a social imposition placed on women for men's convenience. Feminists encouraged women to get out of the home to develop their full potential. While feminism's criticism was targeted at the structural and social roots of the problem, an unintended and paradoxical by-product was to lower yet further the status of the domestic sphere. Initially derided by feminism, the area of fashion has been recently integrated within a feminist perspective (the arguments will be considered in detail in Chapter 7). No similar reconstruction has been carried out on women's domestic role, cast too all-inclusively as the infection that stops the wound of male oppression from healing. In contrast to fashion, domesticity's subversive power appears restricted. Cake moulds mocking the phallus or celebrating the lesbian symbol do not form part of the average ironmonger's stock. If domestic activity is characterized solely as cleaning the toilet, doing the washing up, as endless cooking for unappreciative families or changing nappies on unresponsive babies, pleasure is easily omitted from the reckoning. But more creative aspects of domestic life do exist, and are seen by some women who have chosen to stay at home, or who find domestic chores a relaxing alternative to work outside the home, as rewarding and pleasurable. Baking, decorating and interior design, entertaining or gardening are amongst these.

French novelist and essayist Annie Leclerc was attacked by fellow feminists for arguing in the 1970s that the denial of the pleasures of domestic activity owed much to the power of a male-led language to devalue women's interests (1987, pp. 76–7). A similar point was made by British journalist Mary Stott, commenting on television quiz shows' readiness to include questions on male hobbies (such as sports or woodwork), but not on women-related domestic crafts such as embroidery or baking (*The Guardian*, 9 January 1992). The former, she claimed, were regarded as 'general knowledge'; the latter as too specific and esoteric. Christine Delphy, on the other hand, accuses Leclerc of ignoring the role of housework in sustaining women's oppression (1987, pp. 80–109). While this is an important argument, it is not incompatible with recognizing the possibility of pleasure in domestic activity when that is consciously chosen by women rather than structurally enforced. In recent years, women's creativity in crafts such as tapestry and weaving has been reclaimed by feminists (e.g. Parker, 1984) anxious to ensure these achieve the same recognition and status as traditional male handiwork, but female creativity in domestic management continues to be seen as tainted by the pejorative connotations of the private sphere itself. In this sense, feminism and dominant ideology appear curiously united.

Partly because of this problem, feminism gained limited support from those women who identified positively with the domestic sphere. Mistaking its attack on structural inequalities for an assault on their interests and preoccupations, they felt doubly devalued: both by dominant ideology and by a movement purporting to support them. Advertising, still anxious to sell domestic products primarily to women, was able to exploit these feelings and offer its own compensations. The reinstatement of the home was achieved in part by filling it with rounded human beings, more emotionally complete than the stultified if glamorous models who, in the words of the L'Oréal Plénitude advertisements 'moved with the times'. In the United States in particular, this movement within consumer culture quickly infected other areas of popular culture. Dubbed 'new traditionalism', it has been seen as part of the backlash against women's advances (Faludi, 1992).

In Britain, the Oxo family was recreated in the mid-1980s after market research suggested that the terms most women associated with the family were not 'love', 'peace' or 'harmony' but 'squabbling', 'isolation', 'fatigue' and 'drudgery'. Katie, whose tasty casseroles had been simmering on and off the boil since the 1950s, now held together a family prone to bickering and selfishness, who treated their home as a hotel and their mother as a piece of the furniture. Often harassed and constantly undervalued, Katie, granted a vaguely defined life of her own outside the home, constantly retains the sparkle in her eye, at least to share complicitly with the viewer at home. Her pride in her lively but unregenerate family is at once deeply conservative, but potentially vindicated by audience memories of cardboard cut-out children from earlier commercials. In the manner of soap opera characters, the Oxo family has evolved, but left the ideology of the family intact.

The soap opera techniques of the Oxo narratives have also been adopted in other caring advertisements of the 1980s and 1990s. Allowed secret access to the mother's point of view, women viewers can identify with her frustrations as well as her triumphs. A Hotpoint advertisement for state-of-the-art domestic appliances presents a mother busy in the kitchen while her self-absorbed family leave one by one to pursue their own interests. Only then do we realize that she, too, is planning her escape to play tennis with her girlfriend while the preprogrammed machines get to work. This scarcely amounts to liberation, but it does allow a minute crack to appear in the self-sufficient pleasures of caring.

Mothers were beginning to ask to be noticed, even if the sound-level had barely risen above a whisper. Changes in Flora margarine advertising typify the trend. Its advertising campaign in the early 1980s became famous for persuading the public that polyunsaturated fats were much healthier than butter. It achieved this with graphic images of male torsos, and captions addressed to women, such as 'Is it time to change your husband?', or 'How soon will all your men be Flora men?' By 1986, however, Flora advertisements featured sensible-looking 'thirty-something' women photographed against a backdrop of fresh flowers. The verbal text now took a different tack: 'Of course, I like the light, delicate taste of Flora. My whole family does. But I have a much better reason for eating it. That reason is me.'

The 'reason that was me' was concurrently being shouted from the rooftops in cosmetic and body-product advertising. Within the domestic sphere, traditionalism seemed hardly to have been challenged sufficiently to be dubbed already as 'new'. If there was a noticeable change in 1980s' consumer signifiers of caring, it came through the depiction of caring men, rather than through a redrafting of women's role. Young 'new men' were shown wheeling baby buggies and shopping trolleys, or popping Lean Cuisine menus for two into the microwave. This phenomenon will be considered further in Chapter 5, but it is worth noting for the moment that when men became carers in advertisements, caring was suggested either to be beyond them, or to be so simple that anyone could do it. Even although the appearance of men in the kitchen was to be welcomed, it perversely reinforced the belief that women complained unduly about their lot.

From secret gardens to women on top

When feminism declared that the personal was political, it triggered a new interest in women's desires. If psychoanalysis was the main tool in the cultural theorist's enquiry, a more populist approach was taken by Nancy Friday. Starting with *My Secret Garden* in 1973, she documented the hitherto unspoken evidence of female sexual fantasies, relying to a large extent on women's own accounts. Her first volume, as its title implies, found guilt a major obstacle to free expression, turning the dominant voice into that of the confessional. By her 1991 volume, indicatively titled *Women on Top*, confession and guilt have given way to celebration of women's right to sexual pleasure. Friday takes an uncomplicated and positive view of this, perceiving fantasy as a self-contained gold-mine waiting to be quarried.

Fantasies, and particularly women's fantasies, become more complex if we ask where they come from and who has shaped them. If the formation of our fantasies is linked, as the formation of our conscious thoughts is, to the culture in which we operate, then the ownership and origins of 'women's' fantasies become problematic. As Lisa Tickner points out, it is a mistake to argue that women's sexual feelings and desires were merely repressed by a dominant male culture, when their very articulation was conducted historically in male terms. After centuries of male definition, women have difficulty, for example, in reclaiming the discourse through which they have been encouraged to think about their own sexuality (Tickner, 1987, pp. 237–8). This is also acknowledged, in stridently evangelical terms, in the attempts of Mary Daly (in, for example, *Gyn/Ecology*, 1978) to exorcize the demonology of patriarchy and restore positive energies to the hags, crones, harpies, furies and amazons who have become embodiments of men's fears about women. While Nancy Friday believes in the value of unlocking fantasies repressed within the female psyche (even when these include the notorious accounts of 'rape fantasy'), Mary Daly argues that in order to reclaim metaphors and symbols for women's own self-expression we must first appropriate them.

Women's fantasies have historically been represented in advertising discourses as private, mysterious and incommunicable. Disembodied, and unknowable, these fantasies intensify connotations of the feminine woman as enigmatic and narcissistic, inhabiting a private universe that makes her a convenient repository for male rather than female imaginings (this will be further explored in the next chapter). In recent years, women's fantasies played out in advertising mini-narratives, and indeed in the longer narratives of films such as *Thelma and Louise*, have incorporated more active revenge themes. Nancy Friday remarks on this shift in *Women on Top*, noting that the fantasies that women had in the 1970s of being seduced by strong powerful men (the controversial 'rape' fantasy) had given way increasingly to fantasies of female retaliation, including the scenario of the woman forcing the man to have sex with her. The degree to which these can be seen as a response to feminist discourses is less certain. The ambiguity of the revenge fantasy is indicated in two recent advertisements on British television. One (an advertisement for shoes) depicts a woman metaphorically castrating her boss: the other (for a bra) creates a micro-narrative around female vengeance classically produced by jealousy over a man.

The advertisement for K Shoes casts the avenger in smart office suit severing the balls on her boss's executive toy. This is a woman who hands in her notice with panache, style and a sardonic sense of humour. As she makes her final exit from the office, her triumph is momentarily undercut as a close-up focuses on her heel trapped in a grid in the floor. Unlike the film noir, where such an event would signal the beginning of the end for the woman, this dilemma marks the start of a further victory. Nonchalantly lifting the grid, detaching it from her shoe, and handing the offending item to her boss's secretary, she inspires revolt in her too. In a striking blow for solidarity, the secretary grimaces in the direction of her boss, turns on her K Shoe heels, and marches out in dignified step with her new-found sister. If this narrative has a feminist moral, its humorous touches modify its threat to the masculine viewer. The excessively mimed reactions of the boss and his male partner, squirming when metaphorically under attack, smirking when appearing to triumph, act like the clown's extravagant gestures to deflect male pain and humiliation.

The Gossard Ultrabra fantasy rejects any feminist trappings. Here the heroine, distinguished by her striking cleavage, seeks her revenge on the woman who is trying to steal the affections of her boyfriend at a select party. Humiliation strikes the interloper when she is 'rescued' from an incipient sneeze by the Ultrabra woman reaching into her rival's bosom and extracting yards of tissue that have been used for artificial padding. Throughout, the complicity between the heroine and her boyfriend is maintained through his refusal to have his gaze distracted from her Ultrabra-adorned cleavage. The fantasy is one of jealous bitchiness rather than feminist-inspired self-assertiveness.

In the postfeminist era, romantic fantasies are enacted, as here, with a new playfulness or with a new style and sophistication. Chanel no. 5 television advertisements resorted to hyperreal settings and enigmatic narrative structures in the late 1980s in a bold attempt to span the chasm between romance and postmodernism. Fantasies of doing without men entirely are rarer in consumer discourses, but exceptions are beginning to appear, particularly in car advertisements. Even in the interwar period, the car could symbolize escape for women. In the wake of *Thelma and Louise's* box-office success, Peugeot's agency devised a campaign for its 106 model featuring two British women discarding the trappings of their consumer lifestyles and the security of their past for a carefree life on the open road in the American West.

In conclusion

Postfeminism takes the sting out of feminism. The subjectivities of femininity, presented seriously earlier in the century, are reincarnated towards its end with a twist of humour and a dash of self-conscious parody. The outwardly caring woman willingly shares the lapses in her devotion, with a wink in the direction of the audience. The superwoman is so sophisticated that she looks poised to leave the planet and return as a *Blade Runner* replicant. Fantasies of taking our revenge against men, and getting away with it, are the most daring dreams on offer, but allying this with the selling of feminine heels undercuts the euphoria.

What this chapter suggests is that within advertising discourses, the range of what it means to be feminine has been surprisingly stagnant throughout the century, despite the profound cultural and social changes, and despite the commercial advantages to be gained from brand-differentiating the consumer as much as the product. What most clearly distinguishes the advertising discourses of the postmodern era from their modernist predecessors is the jokiness of their approach and their willingness to cast women as heroines of their mini-narratives. It is difficult to describe either of these as a postmodernist development.

Woman's long history of acting as a depthless sign, responsive to masculine whim, makes her peculiarly resistant to sharp transformation from modernist meaningfulness to postmodern emptiness. The fantasies in which she appears may have become more exciting, less mundane, as special effects and visual tricks replace the heavy-handed techniques of early print advertising, but her kaleidoscopic ability to whet whatever appetite the viewer fancies stretches like a continuum from the 1920s to the present.

What is new, however, is the advertiser's recognition that the perception of the viewer, and especially of the female viewer, has undergone a radical transition in this time. No longer easily coaxed to believe that her life mission is to scrub grates or even to spend dreamy afternoons driving along country lanes, women, it is assumed, will now respond more favourably to constructions that collude, however superficially, with their upbeat, outgoing perception of their lives. Hence the wink and the joke, the refusal to take motherhood too seriously, that sets the gap between the 1950s' Persil advertisements (risible to a contemporary audience in their zealous and class-bound moralizing) and the 1990s' Oxo family.

Advertisers, too, always in tune with aspirational thinking, know that women increasingly want to be 'on top'. It is hard to imagine a contemporary advertiser choosing to replay in any straight form the Knight's Castile romantic narrative, with the woman in a purely passive role, awaiting male attention. Romance still features, but it has either been rendered exotic, or spiced with danger. Occasionally, as we have seen, women can step into the shoes of the heroine, and get the better of men; a safe strategy in selling products aimed uniquely at women, but deploying it in car advertising is more daring, and, as a means of changing the image of a traditionally masculine drink, bolder still. A recent advertisement for Tennent's Lager depicts four young women on a lunchtime outing sending up the amorous attentions of an Italian waiter. Although the stereotyping of the male allows the sensibilities of traditional Tennent's drinkers to be protected from the ridicule of the young women's laughter, this marks a new approach in lager advertising. Allowing women sporadic triumphs may have begun to blur the gender boundaries, but reversing femininity's value as a malleable sign is not readily accomplished.

Unsettling masculinity's stability as a sign might speed up the pace of change. To date, masculinity has been extended by men appearing foolish (usually in role reversal contexts), occasionally caring (especially of babies), or displaying virile bodies emphasizing their strength and carefully developed physique. If the last reverses the pattern of the 'male gaze', it does not reverse the status of masculinity. Mr Happywoman, delighting in his partner's pleasure, is still some way off.

This chapter has focused on *textual* manifestations of consumer discourses. Consumption *as an activity* presents a different picture, with sharper movement between modernist and postmodernist periods. Feminist cultural criticism has been quick to examine the degree to which consuming, as something that we do, provides a space in the postmodern era 'for transgressing traditional boundaries of sexual difference and for flouting anachronistic notions of femininity' (Stuart, 1990, p. 33). By focusing on texts, rather than practices, this chapter leaves these questions on hold. I will return to them particularly in Chapter 7, in considering the relation between women's practices and discourses of the body and fashion in contemporary culture.

PART II

Feminine myths: replay or fast forward?

4

Enigma variations

Who is Sylvia? what is she?
(Shakespeare, *The Two Gentlemen of Verona*, sixteenth century)

Who is Giò?
(Armani perfume advertisement, 1993)

Nothing is impossible, not for she devils.
Peel away the wife, the mother, find the woman, and there the she devil is.
(Fay Weldon, *The Life and Loves of a She Devil*, 1983)

One of the sharpest defences against understanding groups or ideas that challenge our prejudices and assumptions is to construct these as unknowable and mysterious. Both femininity, and more recently feminism, have suffered this fate. Freud's question, 'What do women want?' does not wait for women's answer. Instead, it enables women to become the repository for male fantasies: either idealized as goddesses, or dreaded as man-devouring monsters. Since the domestic sphere is constructed as women's 'natural' habitat, to appear enigmatic, woman has to be extrapolated from her familial context, or at the very least inhabit that space restlessly and uneasily. Her voice must either be muffled, or misleading.

This chapter will argue that the location within which woman is set, and the authority or lack of it with which she speaks, are key ingredients in the construction of the enigma of femininity. The areas of the media it will focus on are disparate, yet connected in their denial of the woman's voice. Fashion photography and perfume advertising often decontextualize their models, depriving them both of a specific setting and of individual personality features. The 'supermodel' and 'superstar', on the other hand, share the mystery of the flamboyant spectacle, teasing us with meaning before changing shape before our eyes. In film, 1940s' film noir gave memorable narrative shape to the enigma of femininity. The *femme fatale* has been refashioned in the remakes of the 1980s and 1990s, and joined by a new urbanized moral monster, mysterious in her motives and irrational in her behaviour. Driven by a desire for a 'normal' family, the 'mad woman' descends from the attic into the heart of American domesticity. As women have in real life become more articulate about their wants and desires, the cultural survival of the enigmatic woman poses particular questions. Is she still a blocking device, protecting audiences from acknowledging the variety of women's own agenda; or in an age of postmodernism, is she merely the ultimate simulacrum, meaning nothing, but fun to consume?

Still puzzles

Central signifiers of women's mystery in a range of still images across media and cultural forms are the dreamlike context, the coy pose, the averted gaze and the wax-like absence of facial expression. Each denies individuality, refuses access to the woman's own view of herself, and enables the looker to admire the woman as an aesthetic or erotic object. Woman is removed from history, and becomes instead a symbol, a sign for something beyond herself. As Marina Warner has demonstrated (see Chapter 1), this emptying of selfhood allows eternal values such as liberty, justice, peace or wisdom, to be spoken through the sculpted female form (1987, *passim*).

By averting her gaze from the spectator, the woman in the still image invites speculation and possessiveness. We (and more particularly, men) can stare unchallenged. As John Berger points out, the oil painting offers many templates of the poses still evident in fashion features, pornography and print advertisements (1972, pp. 35–64). The decontextualized woman, engaged in no activity other than narcissistic self-contemplation, evokes our interest in narrative speculation. Unlike the male subject, often posed with the trappings of activity (such as dog, horse or gun), the female subject of the oil painting offers few clues about her situation. Only her dress allows us to place her within the class system as lady or servant.

For woman to signify symbolically, her personality must be obscured. Facial expression, as one of the key encoders of personality, needs to be obliterated and replaced with a wax-like mask. The photographer Cecil Beaton reputedly became tired in the 1930s of taking pictures of fashion models 'who survived just as long as their faces showed no sign of character' (cited in Craik, 1994, p. 78). It is often assumed that older women are excluded from advertising, fashion or pornographic representation principally because their bodies are no longer aesthetically pleasing. Even if aesthetic judgements could be so easily separated from social influences, this view ignores the specific difficulty of masking the older woman's personality. Older faces, both male and female, have gripped photographers' and viewers' attention precisely because experience is etched on their faces. In the evolution of men's visual representation of women the repeated removal of history from the woman's face ensures that woman ceases to be real and becomes instead an approximation of the religious icon, offered for mysterious contemplation, even when sexual appeal substitutes for sacred adoration.

Advertising and fashion features in women's magazines still regularly present women in narcissistic poses, enthralled by their own mystery. Self-contemplation and self-absorption envelop the woman in a shrine of her own making, and poise the spectator uneasily between the contradictions of identification and voyeurism that Mulvey sees as characteristic of the 'male gaze' (1975, p. 10). Advertisements for women's perfumes typically zoom in on the facial close-up, but then partially obscure its features by means of tight framing, or the graininess or soft-focus of the image. Fantasy, not revelation, is the aim. As with 'Who is Giò?' (see Fig. 6), we are invited to impose on woman as an empty sign the fantasy stirred by the brand name. Male fragrances, on the other hand, typically give prominence to the phallic shape of the bottle, sometimes associating this directly with the muscular physique of the male. Connotations of power deprive such signs of mystery and allow little scope for variegated readings. The gender pattern in fragrance advertising is slowly beginning to change, with innovation marked particularly in Calvin Klein's unisex yet sensual advertisements for Obsession in the mid-1980s, but it is as yet far from broken.

In the fashion feature, as in the fashion-house advertisement, the more sophisticated the label, the more intense the sense of mystery. In teenage girls' magazines, clothes are associated with activity and having fun. Models in these publications participate actively in dancing, jump with joy, and generally look vibrant and alive. Prestigious publications such as *Vogue*, *Marie Claire* and *Elle*, on the other hand, employ exotic and atmospheric locations, and cast their models in sculpted and languorous poses. In between lie the more general glossy monthlies. By selling lifestyle rather than fashion specifically, magazines such as *Company*, *Cosmopolitan* and *19* combine the enigmatic and sensual quality of the models' poses and location with captions that add the spice of humour. In *Cosmopolitan*'s 21st birthday British edition (March 1993), a fashion feature urges its readers 'to discover the new freedom' of a

Fig. 6 1993 Armani Giò advertisement

fashion that 'is about free spirit', and about 'being able to flirt with different looks'. Urging its readers simultaneously to discover freedom and to 'flirt' with their appearance captures the postfeminist spirit.

Fashion spreads in young women's glossies often allow a gap to open up between image and text, extending the enigma of the construction, but preventing us from taking it too seriously. 'Rebellion' and 'revolution' appear menacingly in fashion features, location shoots are held in Vietnam, but the pouting models exploit the connotations to shock with their sexiness, not their guns. *19* uses 'Industrial Revolution' as the heading for its feature urging women to 'layer up – and cause a riot' in tough workwear mixed with 'military influences' (November 1993). Workers' boots, leather apron-dresses, 'vintage leather military purse belt' and leather flying hat with goggles are teamed with ribbed dresses, white silk scarves and soft woollen sweaters to accentuate the mismatch between the tough talk of the verbal text and the youth and fragility of the model.

Similarly, the 'little girl lost' look of 1990s' fashion is often accompanied by text invoking discourses of power and strength. A feature on new party dresses in *Company* (July 1994), with models in vulnerable and infantile poses, sports captions claiming that these 'itty-bitty dresses ... come with a great big *attitude*', 'show off your *character*' and demonstrate '*pale-skin power*' (magazine's emphasis). The lack of synchronization between image and text, pulling the reader in different directions, retains the essential mystery of femininity while paradoxically acknowledging women's claims to freedom. By combining echoes of young women's contemporary street discourse with images that would not look out of place in pornography, the aim may be to create shock impact, but the effect is to rewrite woman's enigma for a sophisticated postmodern age. By being invited to share the joke, however, we are also invited to perpetuate it.

The contrast between the image and the text renews interest in the riddle of femininity, posing sexuality against innocence, fragility against strength, and vulnerability against self-confident indifference. What are we to make of this postfeminist puzzle? Janice Winship argues that the combination of sensuality and streetwise bravado visible in fashion spreads in 1980s' teenage girls' magazines can be positively construed. The influence of feminism on the readers of these publications allows them, she suggests, to enjoy and even poke fun at images that older feminists might regard as indisputably pornographic or offensive (1987a, pp. 127–41). On the same side of the argument, it might be added that younger women's magazines often overlay the femininity of their models' poses with intertextual referencing to popular music in ways that unsettle simple gender associations. A 'Baroque'n'roll' feature in *Company* (November 1993) urges the reader on the contents page to 'strut your funky stuff in riotous rock-goddess glamour', and within the feature itself to 'dance to the beat of a different tune'. However extravagant the fashion images, the urging to participate, to indulge in fashion as a wacky form of self-expression denies the simplicity of the passive gazing invited by the high fashion magazines. Yet the teasing quality of some of these texts remains disturbing. If the way to show 'attitude' or to 'revolt' is to buy girlish frocks or cashmere sweaters, postfeminist discourse repeats rather than solves contradiction.

In the 'classic' fashion magazine, the desire to turn fashion into an object of aesthetic admiration produces a more timeless feel. Woman is reincarnated as a pure fantasy symbol, extrapolated from reality by the absence of location or its exotic mysteriousness. Boundaries of class, time or place are easily crossed. Women can inhabit a post-industrial landscape in Baker Boy caps, military leather coats and gauntlets, or epitomize 1930s' middle-class sophistication in tweeds and cashmere (both from *Marie Claire*, November 1993). Within the same publication's fashion features, women move in quick succession from being 'Angels', evoking 'an ethereal feminine spirit' against an evanescent seascape; to a 'cool masculine look' sporting linens in the 'Tropical Heat' of Bali; to the 'schoolgirl' style of a small-town American set; to a final transformation into the mercurial and fragmented bodies of a moonscape setting, 'shimmering' in silver against its aridity (*Marie Claire*, March 1994). None of these locations, in their diversity, seems alien to the white young women photographed against them.

In men's style magazines, such as *GQ* and *Arena*, by contrast, fashion shoots in overseas locations tend to feature indigenous models. A 'tropical heat' feature on linen clothing in *GQ*, that directly parallels *Marie Claire*'s, differs from it in presenting an Indian model. 'Cuban Cigars', on shades of brown and check clothing for men, similarly features models who at least look Cuban (*GQ*, July 1994). A white man would appear out of place in either setting; an ethnic *faux pas* in an ethnically sensitive age. The white female model, on the other hand, raises no such questions in the mind of the white reader. So used are we to wax-like women symbolizing qualities of an unspecific kind, that issues of colour and ethnicity are suppressed. As Marina Warner puts it, in a different context: 'the female form tends to be perceived as generic and universal, with symbolic overtones; the male as individual, even when it is being used to express a generalized idea' (1987, p. 12). The fashion display in the male magazines typically depicts its models engaged in leisure activities, whether sporting or musical, guaranteed to retain their individualism. In the same issue of *GQ* as the 'Indian Summer' feature, black jazz musicians publicize clothes as well as music. Fashion is an adjunct to their success, not a drape to hang around limp bodies. These men are alive, have personalities and display active and vibrant poses. Their identifiable roles and personalities provide a sharp contrast to the archetypal quality of the female model.

From screen-goddesses to superstars

In the heyday of Hollywood, the female star's image as glamorous goddess was carefully cultivated. A controlled release of information about her private life surrounded her with an aura intended to enhance her screen characterization and the standing of the studio. Thomas Harris, in an article first published in 1957, comments that Grace Kelly's respectable family background was used to construct her as a 'lady', while Marilyn Monroe's chequered career as a model became the foundation for her 'playmate' image (1991, pp. 40–4). Star charisma depended partly on the individual's acting ability, and on the concealment (as far as the publicity machine was able) of awkward details about her life. Although the star image was a fabrication, it was still related to the star's acting performance and spectators' reactions to the roles played in film.

Glamour, in the era of the Hollywood studios, was the prerogative of the female film star. Now, it is arguably an outmoded concept, useful for selling nostalgia only. As the Pretty Polly tight and stocking advertisements of the 1990s proclaim, against the backdrop of screen goddesses of a past era, 'the glamour of yesterday, the fit of today'. In an era of phantasmagoric spectacle, designed to elicit a 'gee-whiz' reaction from the spectator, glamour is too tame for the adrenalin-inspired ecstasies produced by the technological wizardries now available to promoters. The stars no longer inhabit the studio, but strut the transnational stages of the popular music concert or the fashion runway. As stars transmogrify into superstars, and anonymous models reappear as supermodels, a new stage in the commodification of femininity is achieved. For audiences with jaded appetites, hype takes the place of publicity and the boundaries between publicity and performance come under increasing strain. While in the era of the screen goddess, the puzzle posed by the star lay in searching for the 'authentic' Bette Davis, Marilyn Monroe or Joan Crawford, in the contemporary period the enigma lies in unravelling which of the various versions of femininity on offer we wish to 'buy'. Issues of authenticity are on the agenda only to the degree that they are deliberately put there for us. Madonna, the prime superstar of the late twentieth century, excels at playing this game.

As a spectacular icon, carrying none of her own meaning, the supermodel is supremely postmodern. As part of a transitory spectacle which momentarily seizes our restless attention and then disappears, she no longer taunts us with the belief in an attainable essence of femininity, but teases us with the impossibility of its achievement. The excess and extravagance of her presentation tell us she is a simulacrum, not for emulating but for feasting our sated eyes on. Her bodily presentation is a sign that refers us to other signs of the supermodel body, but defies our attempts to seek meaning. What the 'essence' of the supermodel is we are not invited to ask. What we know of her is her commodity value, the extravagant fees she is paid for each appearance, and the ephemeral nature of her success. Unlike the actress, she has no control over her survival. Deracinated from her country of origin, she inhabits a transnational space. Despite our familiarity with her physical appearance, her voice is rarely heard. As Naomi Campbell puts it, 'In a way what we do is like acting, except that we don't speak. Because we don't speak, we don't have anything to say' (quoted in Craik, 1994, p. 87).

By displaying clothes that play with gender and ethnic boundaries and disrupt the divide between 'street' and 'high' fashion, the supermodel appears to open up the repertoire of late twentieth century femininities. From the extravagantly romantic, to the daringly sexual, to the boldly androgynous, femininity is continually being refashioned. The postmodern depthlessness of the signs, however, produces confusion in its wake. In the 1990s, fashion is reconstructing femininity from sexual power into waif-like innocence and insecurity. The 'little girl lost' look of the British supermodel Kate Moss revives the vulnerability that we might have imagined passed with the fading of Lillian Gish from the cinema screen. The 'big five' supermodels of the early 1990s, Linda Evangelista, Christy Turlington, Naomi Campbell, Cindy Crawford and Claudia Schiffer, exuded the confidence of the postfeminist woman: capable, in control, even if unknown. Now, in the pages of the fashion magazines, the waif connotes insecurity and a haunting vulnerability.

In *Vogue* (May 1993), Linda Evangelista is photographed with a new wistful look, her strength replaced by fragility.

In contemporary film criticism, the concept of 'the masquerade' has been applied as a critical tool to examine the play with codes of femininity that film often exhibits. This concept, developed by psychoanalyst Joan Riviere in an article in 1929, argues that since femaleness is denied cultural validity in its own right, women are obliged to don a series of masks both to act out conventional versions of femininity and disguise any personal rebellion against them. Feminist film critics of the 1970s and 1980s suggest that when femininity is displayed to excess (as, for example, in Mae West or Marilyn Monroe) its mask-like quality is drawn to our attention and we are encouraged to review, and thereby challenge, femininity as an artificial construction (Kuhn and Radstone, 1990, p. 257). Mary Ann Doane, in a 1982 essay, claims that 'masquerade, in flaunting femininity, holds it at a distance' (1991, p. 25). Self-conscious play with bodily image 'doubles representation' as, in Silvia Bovenschen's words, 'we are watching a woman demonstrate the representation of a woman's body' (ibid., p. 26).

The chimeric quality of the supermodel might seem to invite analysis in terms of the masquerade. In film, however, the narrative development allows the audience to attach meaning to the masking process. In the case of the supermodel, masks are lightly and playfully worn, replaced in whirlwind succession, and never endure long enough to suggest meaningfulness. Since the construction of the supermodel obliterates personality, the concept of the mask becomes difficult to sustain. Contrasting the images of the American photographer Cindy Sherman, known for photographing herself ironically in a variety of classic feminine poses, with those of Madonna, David Tetzlaff claims: 'A Cindy Sherman image says, "Interrogate me". A Madonna image says, "Buy Me!"' (1993, p. 256). Supermodels fit decisively in the latter category.

The supermodel is not, of course, confined to the catwalk, but appears also in various guises in advertising. In 1993, she was enlisted to sell Vauxhall Corsa cars. For the advertisers, this was an audacious move, flouting as it did the outdatedness of selling cars by draping models across their bonnets. The agency, Lowe Howard-Spink, tried to disrupt the cliché by exaggerating the drama. Fast-paced editing transports us from Linda Evangelista as cat-like *femme fatale*, through Naomi Campbell, dressed in bondage gear, sadistically torturing men, to Kate Moss as superstar literally bumped off the set by the Corsa. So excessive are the images, so fantastical the narrative mini-sketches, that the audience is not invited to take this seriously. Whether this amounts to pastiche or parody is another matter.

Pastiche, in the terms of postmodernist critic Fredric Jameson, is 'blank parody', using imitation and mimicry merely to play around with images that are already familiar to us. Parody, by contrast, has an ironic intent, seizing on the 'idiosyncracies and eccentricities' of the original in order to send it up (1983, pp. 113–14). Whereas parody could be deployed critically in a modernist age anxious to seek methods of improving the world, but unsure already of how this could best be accomplished, pastiche is all that is possible in a postmodern age lacking a common language, and fragmented culturally and socially. Whereas parody speaks from a particular point of view, pastiche plays with our fantasies, teases us and changes shape before we can pin any meaning on it. Ambiguity and ambivalence prevail.

The Corsa advertisement produced confused reactions. A lively controversy developed between those (such as the Campaign against Pornography) who thought it promoted pornographic images of women (their campaign succeeded in getting the advertisement removed to after the 9 p.m. watershed on British television), and those who argued that its lack of seriousness undermined its potential offensiveness. An Independent Television Commission press officer responded to complaints by saying: 'We think the campaign's tone reverses the stereotype of the bimbo on the bonnet' (*Campaign*, 23 April 1993). In its surface texture, the Corsa advertisement resembles pastiche, playing to an audience assumed to be aware of well-worn and even threadbare feminine mythologies. By replaying them, however, it also helps to keep them alive, even if this is achieved with a knowing nod and a wink. The claim to *reverse* these myths implies a parodic role difficult to associate with the fast-moving jokiness of this advertisement.

If the supermodel commodifies different versions of femininity, without imposing a value on any of them, the stridency of Madonna's voice and performance proposes meaningfulness, however ambiguously. Much has already been written about Madonna as a postmodern icon, and about her equivocal use of the codes of religion, gay sexuality, androgyny and ethnicity (e.g. Frank and Smith, 1993; Lloyd, 1993; Schwichtenberg, 1993). Without rehearsing these arguments, what is significant for this discussion is that Madonna perpetuates her enigma by eliminating the gap between publicity and performance. Performing through her self-publicity, and publicizing herself through her performances, both equally become part of the commodification process.

Madonna's supposedly self-revelatory *In Bed with Madonna* (*Truth or Dare* in the United States), and her much-hyped frankness about her sexual fantasies in *Sex* break new ground in a star's control over her own self-expression. Many questions, however, remain unanswered, reminding us that selling images of women (and Madonna is supremely talented at selling herself) depends on not solving the riddle of what woman wants, most particularly if the woman in question wishes to be classified as a superstar. In Glasgow, a store with the title 'What Every Woman Wants' used to be renowned for its cheap and cheerful clothes: its self-mocking title a clear index to the socio-economic grouping of its intended clientele. Commodifying femininity for a self-aware and sophisticated audience means ensuring that the magic enigma is *not* removed.

Madonna's antics as a supreme self-publicist guarantee automatic access to the media, but she severely rations and stage-manages the supply of information. Her self-presentation intensifies rather than destroys the conundrum of her life and attitudes. When, in December 1990, she appeared on the BBC television *Omnibus* programme, she stipulated that she be filmed in black and white. In contrast to her appearance on music video and stage, she sat stock still, framed consistently in a one-dimensional head-and-shoulders shot that denied visual exploration of her persona. Commenting on *In Bed with Madonna* in *Vanity Fair* in April 1991, Madonna herself admits that, while the film may be revealing, it is not necessarily accurate in a documentary sense: 'You could watch it and say, I still don't know Madonna, and *good*. Because you will never know the real me. Ever' (cited in Schwichtenberg, 1993, p. 312). Prevaricating that she may be 'acting' within the film, but that 'there's a truth in my acting', she makes the boundary between performance and documentary, marked out in the switch from colour to black-and-white noted by Deidre Pribram (1993, pp. 195–9), seem wholly artificial.

In *Sex*, Madonna similarly reveals all and nothing. Despite her borrowing of lesbian sexual images, and her previously much-discussed relationship with Sandra Bernhard, she remains enigmatically coy about her own sexual preferences. It is difficult to argue that this should be of no concern to us, when Madonna herself invites us to wonder. Heterosexual, bisexual or lesbian: sexuality becomes another guessing game; an avoidance of committed identity, politics and meaning. By shocking the moral majority, provoking diverse reactions from the gay community, and arousing the heterosexual population's interest in the book by its pre-sale hype, Madonna could at least guarantee that *Sex* would sell. Fantasy becomes the defence against solving the puzzle of her own persona. Nothing in the book is true, she claims; it is merely based on fantasies that she dreamed up. Adopting the persona of Dita Parlo, from Vigo's avant-garde film *L'Atalante* (1934), places a further distance between herself and the images.

Attacked by African-American critic, bell hooks, for occupying 'the space of the white cultural imperialist', moving through the colonies of gay sexuality or people of colour with curiosity, but without abandoning her 'white privilege' (1993a, p. 77), Madonna is also praised by other critics for breaking down boundaries between the taboo and the non-taboo. The ultimate clue to the enigma that is Madonna lies, as Simon Frith (1993) points out, in her failure to grow up, despite her consummate maturity as a performer and her outstanding skill in continually reinventing herself over a decade. Retaining adolescent playfulness in combination with the manipulative control of the shrewd financial operator prevents Madonna from having to declare too conclusively on her adult self.

Fatal women

The 1940s, dominated politically and socially by the Second World War, produced a psychotic cinema in terms of its representation of women. On the one side lay the 'women's film', with its waiting wives and its eventually resolved tensions between duty and passion; on the other, the 'film noir' with its stylistic confusions, its questioning of both male and female sexuality, and the deceptions and trickery of its plots. Each adopted contrasting attitudes to the dominant ideology of American family values: the women's film by unequivocally endorsing these; film noir by posing the family as the absent centre that destabilizes relationships and sexual identities (Harvey, 1980). In the women's film, woman is represented as torn between emotion and duty (e.g. *Since You Went Away*, 1944), or between love for different men (e.g. *Daisy Kenyon*, 1946). Her triumph is to overcome the challenge to her womanly virtues. In film noir, by contrast, woman is mysterious, sexually alluring, and manipulative. Siren-like, she tricks men into believing in her sincerity and affections, often using song as well as body language as a tool of seduction (e.g. *Gilda*, 1946, and *The Lady from Shanghai*, 1948).

Within the women's film, hearth and home feature as the natural location for women. In film noir, woman's dislocation from the fireside signals a wider disruption of normal expectations. Several noir heroines pose mystery about where they belong, and where they have come from. Kathie Moffett, in *Build My Gallows High* (RKO, 1947, titled *Out of the Past* in the United States), tracked down by Jeff Bailey in the exotic world of Acapulco, walks in 'out of the sun' or 'out of the moonlight', in sharp contrast to his sweetheart back home who blends comfortably into the small town environment where she has grown up. Like the mysterious woman in the contemporary perfume advertisement or fashion shoot, Kathie Moffett (Jane Greer) has no locatable environment: instead she roams the landscape of dreams, a wild and free spirit. Jeff (Robert Mitchum) describes her as living by night; the activities of gambling and smoking in which she indulges act as a thinly-veiled 1940s' code for her active sexuality. A similar pattern emerges in *The Lady from Shanghai* when Michael O'Hara (Orson Welles) enquires of Elsa Bannister (Rita Hayworth) where she comes from:

MO'H: I want to know – where does the princess come from?
EB: I don't know why she should tell you. Well, her parents were Russian – White Russian. You never heard of the place where she comes from.
MO'H: Would your highness care to gamble?
EB: Gamble? She's done it for a living.

The exotic quality of Elsa's origins and her previous life in China enhance the fairy-tale construction of Elsa as princess and Michael as roving sailor boy.

When the noir heroine does inhabit a domestic environment, her lack of ease within it is emphasized by the prison connotations of the *mise en scène*, by off-centre framing, by restless camera movement, and by acerbic dialogue. Far from being constructed as a peaceful haven, the domestic setting in these films is filled with menace and foreboding. The early encounters between insurance salesman Walter Neff (Fred MacMurray) and his scheming wife Phyllis Dietrichson (Barbara Stanwyck) in *Double Indemnity* (1944) illustrate several of these features. Initially separated from Neff by the barrier of the stair banisters, Phyllis's subsequent encounter with him in the comfort of her own living-room evokes an atmosphere of distinct unease as the camera tracks her restless pacing of the floor. Her verbal jousting match with Neff includes sardonic comment on the boredom of married life:

PD: Sometimes we sit here all evening, and never say a word to each other.
WN: Sounds pretty dull.
PD: So I just sit and knit.
WN: Is that what you married him for?
PD: Perhaps I like the way his thumbs hold up the wool.
WN: Any time his thumbs get tired ... Only with me around you wouldn't have to knit.

This exchange establishes Phyllis's alienation from the conventions of matrimonial life and domestic contentment. Its teasing suggestiveness results in part from the restrictions on overt sexual display imposed by the Hays Production Code, but it also establishes an equality in sexual nuances between the male and female protagonists. The woman's know-ingness, her ability to pick up and play with Neff's verbal advances and initiate several of her own, combine with lighting, framing and dress codes to establish Phyllis as a sexual being. Its playfulness also signals to the audience that access to this woman's 'reality' is going to be problematic. Like the sirens of ancient legend, the central female charac-ters in film noir pose a threat and danger because they lack the sexual innocence that ironically characterizes even the mother figure in the domestic film.

The instability of the woman's voice, and its eventually unmasked duplicity are recurring themes in film noir. Whereas the 'vamp' of the silent era had been clearly visually encoded as the 'spider-woman', trap-ping men within her sexual allure (often signified by bold motifs of webs or tentacles on her clothing), the danger of the *femme fatale* is more subtly suggested. The screenplay in film noir conspires with the musical soundtrack to signal disturbance by shifting from the easy verbal exchanges of classic Hollywood dialogue to the minor key of risqué and riddle-like banter. The absence of straightforward verbal contact between the *femme fatale* and the male character whom she is set to ensnare marks the beginning of his fall. While the early verbal exchanges between Phyllis Dietrichson and Walter Neff in *Double Indemnity* establish the fugue between them as one of complicit sexual innuendo, in *Gilda* (1946), tension between words and image disrupt the classical narrative synthesis from the first encounter between Johnny (Glenn Ford) and Gilda (Rita Hayworth). The exchange of polite greetings between them rises like steam from a bubbling cauldron, as Gilda's newly acquired husband, Ballen, orchestrates the dialogue from outside the frame, and former lovers Johnny and Gilda remain fixated in each other's desiring gaze. The acidity of the relationship that is set to evolve between these three characters is mapped out, and the audience given a foretaste of how subtext and *double entendre* reign supreme in this film.

In film noir, woman is, as Richard Dyer puts it, 'above all else unknowable' (1980, p. 92). The *femme fatale* unmistakably enacts and re-enacts 'the conception of womanliness as a mask, behind which man suspects some hidden danger' (Riviere, 1929, p. 313). In a variety of films, her aptitude at putting on a seductive show of her latent sexuality and her feminine charms makes her more memorable for her physical presence than for her role in the plot (Kaplan, 1980, p. 36). The puzzle of the *femme fatale*'s motivation is almost always unsolved at the end of the film. Instead of answers, the film noir director provides moral punishment for the woman's abuse of male trust. In an often sudden switch of narrative direction, she is either imprisoned, killed or (more unusually) re-incorporated into the 'norms' of family life.

The *femme fatale*, so visually central to these films, eludes our understanding to such an extent that we are invited ultimately to be more curious about the psychology of the male protagonist than about the interior psychodrama of the woman. Like the tease, who taunts us with the unattainability of the truth, the *femme fatale* encourages us not to search for answers but to enter into the spirit of the play. Frank Krutnik (1991) goes as far as to suggest that masculine identity and desire constitute a more crucial puzzle than femininity in film noir. The routine authority of masculinity is challenged in two ways: by men being duped by women, and by the latent homosexuality of films such as *Gilda* and *Double Indemnity* (Kaplan, 1980, pp. 93–5 and 102–3).

Despite this unsettling of dominant masculine discourse, it is the male voice-over that typically directs the narration of film noir. Through their confessional modes of address, the male protagonists invite the audience to identify with the mystery of how their behaviour has been so strangely affected by the power of the *femme fatale*. The voice is authoritative and earns respect because of its willingness to admit mistakes. Walter Neff in *Double Indemnity*, making his dictaphone confession to his boss, Barton Keyes, at the start of the film, comments: 'I killed Dietrichson . . . killed him for money and for a woman. I didn't get the money and I didn't get the woman. Funny, isn't it?' Michael O'Hara's initial words in *Lady from Shanghai* similarly take the form of an admission: 'When I start out to make a fool of myself, there's very little can stop me. If I'd known where it would end, I'd have never let anything start – if I'd been in my right mind, that is. But once I'd seen her – once I'd seen her – I was not in my right mind for quite some time . . . Some people can smell danger – not me'.

While the woman's voice rejoices in riddles and an appearance of openness that masks concealment, the male voice acquires the ring of sincerity. The division between masculine discourse (logical and verbally based) and female discourse (intuitive, emotional and of the body and the non-verbal sphere) has, as we saw in Chapter 2, cultural currency that is by no means unique to film noir, but it operates particularly sharply here. A possible exception to the rule is *Gilda*. This film establishes a rare equivalence of discourse between the leading male and female characters, in spite of the openly misogynistic characteristic of Johnny's perspective. Bitter about his loss of Gilda to Ballen, and ambiguously poised himself in relation to Ballen's patronage, his contempt for women is frequently articulated. Challenged by Gilda to reveal the sex of Ballen's 'friend' (his trusty walking-stick-cum-stiletto with which he rescues Johnny at the start of the film), Johnny comments that it must be feminine 'because it looks like one thing and right in front of your eyes it becomes another'. Later in the film, Johnny provocatively comforts Ballen, now worried about his wife's infidelity, by noting that 'statistics show that there are more women in the world than anything else, except insects'. His words are matched by his deeds. In revenge for Gilda's treachery (as he sees it) of marrying Ballen for money, Johnny uses his own eventual marriage to her as a form of psychological torture. Johnny's inventiveness in creating opportunities to humiliate Gilda turns this marriage into the antithesis of romantic bliss.

Yet isolating Johnny's role in this way distorts the nature of this complex film. Johnny's cynicism is matched in the dialogue by Gilda's taunting play with his metaphors. When Johnny, in his role as Ballen's protector, warns an unfaithful Gilda that he is going to monitor all her activities and pick her up and take her home 'exactly the way I'd . . . pick up his [Ballen's] laundry', Gilda sarcastically retorts that a psychiatrist would find his metaphor 'very revealing' and that he's 'kidding' himself if he thinks he's doing this purely for Ballen. In the following scene, she appears in the casino at five o'clock in the morning, baiting Johnny with the greeting 'Well, here's the laundry waiting to be picked up'. This verbal jousting between Gilda and Johnny continues throughout the film, preventing the masculine voice from taking control. As Richard Dyer (1980) points out, Johnny's voice is further undermined by the hints of homosexual desire between him and Ballen, and by the frequent visual construction of Johnny as the object of Gilda's desire. In addition, Rita Hayworth's exuberant star image acts against our ability to perceive her as a victim: a resistance that is strengthened by her defiant dancing, and her use of the song 'Put the Blame on Mame, Boys' to draw the audience's attention to the cultural tendency (of which noir is one element) to hold women responsible for all the ills of the world. By ironically foregrounding the narrative message of the typical noir plot, Gilda cuts across its misogynistic power.

Gilda's ability to put on a stunning and provocative performance, culminating in her bravado casino strip act, intensifies the see-saw battle between herself and Johnny to get 'fair and even'. By the end of the film, they have succeeded, as, unusually for the last scene of a film noir, they walk off arm in arm into a dubious sunset together. The police chief, traditionally a male voice of authority, tells Gilda that Johnny's behaviour has been 'just an act', a performance equivalent in persuasiveness to her own. The audience may question this, since Gilda's performance has manifestly been a masquerade while Johnny, we feel, has been playing for real. Yet both share other links, most especially in their relationship to Ballen. Both, as Richard Dyer points out, are picked up by him; both claim to have no past before they meet him, and both are implicitly or explicitly sexually linked to him.

The pathological feel of film noir leads some critics to seek a psychoanalytic explanation (see, for example, Claire Johnston's discussion of *Double Indemnity* in Kaplan, 1980). Others, such as Janey Place and Sylvia Harvey (ibid.), prefer to relate film noir to its historical and social origins at a time of deep angst and unease about male and female roles. More than most genres, its specificity to a particular period in film history favours this approach. Unlike the propaganda films of wartime, the relationship between film text and social conditions is complex, with noir imaginatively giving voice to 'structures of feeling', and trying, but not succeeding, to contain the miasma of fear. The enigma of the sexually alluring and manipulative woman seems, like a virus, to outlive the temporary 'cures' of these films' endings. By the 1980s and 1990s, the virus reappears in a new strain, both in the reworking of film noir and in the moral-monster or she-devil film. Why, at this stage of our knowledge about female sexuality and women's ambitions, these should revive latent fears about women, is another question for the historical pathologist.

Rewriting film noir

There have been several attempts to refashion the noir film in line with changing gender roles. In *Jagged Edge* (1985), the conventional positions of male and female are reversed, with the female investigator, played by Glenn Close, struggling to overcome the wiles of the deceptively charming Jake Forrester (Jeff Bridges). Role reversal here, as in other areas of cultural representation, only partially subverts ideological norms. Putting a man in the shoes of a woman or vice versa may question the naturalness of their habitual roles, but it does not overturn our expectations of femininity and masculinity. A female 'chump' cannot be read in the same way as a male 'chump' because the audience's expectations of male and female foolishness start from a different base. Women, we have been led to believe, by cultural forms as varied as popular romantic fiction and newspaper discussions of 'women who love too much', have a 'natural' tendency to foolishness over men, whereas men, more worldly-wise and hardbitten, have to be seriously duped before they turn into dopes. Investigator, Teddy Barnes retains the audience's sympathy not by virtue of her confessional discourse, but by her impressive hard work, persuasive argumentative skills, and her guilt-ridden desire to atone for a previous miscarriage of justice. All of this feminizes the characteristics of the typical private eye.

Other recastings of film noir in the 1980s and 1990s remove women's sexual mysteriousness, and replace it with the enigma of their moral treachery. Women such as Matty Walker in *Body Heat* (1981), Rebecca Carlson in *Body of Evidence* (1992), and Catherine Tramell in *Basic Instinct* (1992) are all openly adventurous in their sexual tastes and behaviour. Women's sexuality in these films enters the designer age, bringing the manipulativeness of their sexual technique into line with the sophistication of their wardrobes and their living spaces, none of which exudes the cosy romanticism of 'home' in traditional Hollywood visual discourse. These erotic heroines are dangerous new women, professional as much in their sexual scheming as in their shadowy lives as art gallery owners (Rebecca Carlson) or best-selling authors (Catherine Tramell). In rewriting the mythology of the she-devil or moral monster of ancient legend in terms of women's liberated sexuality and their professionalism, the noir legacy in mainstream erotic thrillers cocks a snook at feminism. These women may be in control in the bedroom, but they have no more control than their 1940s' counterparts over the filmic discourse.

In ancient mythology, the dangerous aspect of femininity appears in various physical guises. The Harpies, part bird and part woman, swooped down and carried off their victims; the Sirens lured men to their deaths, and the snake-haired Medusa turned anyone who looked at her to stone. Deviousness was often part of the act. In more recent times, women who were regarded as beyond the moral pale were demonized as witches, female vampires or she-devils. This association between the feminine and evil extends well beyond fictional representations to influence media coverage of female criminals (Birch, 1993). The 1960s' 'moors murderer' Myra Hindley has been persistently characterized in Britain as an evil monster, while her lover, Ian Brady, has faded from public view. Barrister Helena Kennedy (1992) has also indicated how the power of such myths extends even into sentencing decisions. The myth of the man-eating vagina (*vagina dentata*) resurfaces, as Barbara Creed (1993) points out in a fascinating recent study, in the horror film. Creed suggests that the Freudian notion of the terror invoked by the castrated woman needs in this case to be rewritten in terms of her castra*ting* threat. Labelling this phenomenon the 'monstrous-feminine', she comments that it 'speaks to us more about male fears than about female desire or feminine subjectivity' (1993, p. 7). This applies also when the 'monstrous-feminine' takes moral rather than physical shape.

In *Body of Evidence*, DA Robert Garrett (Joe Mantegna) introduces the case for the prosecution against Rebecca Carlson (Madonna) in the following terms: 'she is a beautiful woman, but when this trial is over you will see her no differently than a gun or a knife or any other instrument used as a weapon'. The description would also fit the eventual definition of Matty Walker (Kathleen Turner) in *Body Heat* and Catherine Tramell (Sharon Stone) in *Basic Instinct*. All use their bodies to manipulate men into doing what they want them to. The sexual encounters are raunchy, sometimes sado-masochistic, occur in varied locations, and routinely position the woman as controlling or at least initiating the encounter. If this is postfeminist sex, it is about playing games, not about female desire.

None of these films engages our sympathy with the motives of the women. At best dimly sketched, these relate to dishonourable desires such as 'greed' or 'jealousy'. Matty Walker, Rebecca Carlson and Catharine (the 'black widow' in Bob Rafelson's film of that title) want money, although their lifestyles suggest this has become an obsession rather than a need. Catherine Tramell wants the power of playing out

Fig. 7 The four faces of the 'black widow'. *Black Widow* © 1987 Twentieth Century-Fox Film Corporation.

her authorial fantasies in real life. What all these women share is a compulsive professionalism. In playing the game of beguiling femininity, they are fastidious in their planning and execution.

Catharine, in *Black Widow* (1987), says to Alex (Debra Winger), the female private eye who is tracking her down: 'I used to think of it as my job: making myself appealing. I was a professional'. Her cultivation of the four different disguises she needs in order to carry out her plan to kill four different husbands involves far more than changing dress and hairstyle, although this feminine manoeuvring is an important part of her strategy (*see* Fig. 7). Each new role follows an intensive period of research and preparation before she can gain the trust of the men she wishes to deceive. The guises of femininity she cultivates are all equally plausible, all equally inauthentic. As we saw with the super-model, femininity has a wider selection of masks to choose from in the 1980s than in the era of romanticized seductions. Matty Walker also assumes a 'false' persona, that of her classmate, described in her college profile as 'the vamp' whose schoolgirl ambitions were 'to be rich and live in an exotic land'. Since this is the fate that Matty works out for herself, fantasy and actuality blur into each other. The spectator is also exposed to the actress within the frame, when Matty, established as the sultry seducer in the earlier scenes of the film, plays the devoted wife and lady during a chance dinner encounter that places her tensely between her husband and her lover. While in the 1940s, Elsa Bannister or Phyllis Dietrichson could retain a consistent persona in the joint presence of possessive husband and lustful lover, the conflict between the differing masks of femininity is more pronounced by the 1980s.

Although the central female characters in *Basic Instinct* and *Body of Evidence* have careers of their own, these appear filmically as means to an expensive lifestyle rather than as jobs requiring talent and dedication. 'Work' in these latter-day films noirs, is reincarnated as sex, with Catherine Tramell's much-practised 'fuck of the century' echoing Rebecca Carlson's accurate (from the point of view of the audience) definition of her own job towards the end of *Body of Evidence*: 'That's what I do. I fuck. And it made me $8 million'.

These films exploit the commercial advantages of their 'scorching' sex scenes while still branding as dangerous the female sexual passions that enable them. By turning two of the key planks of postfeminism – liberated sexuality and a lifestyle based on independent and plentiful financial resources – into the markers of the monstrous-feminine, they undermine postfeminism's credibility. If in the 1980s, some women at least appeared to get away with their perfidy (Matty Walker, for example), the norm remains that there is a price to be paid, through imprisonment (*Black Widow*) or through death (*Body of Evidence*). By wrenching the women sharply out of anything approximating a 'normal' domestic environment, and out of any meaningful relationship with other women, these films also give narrative substance to the impressionistic hint of advertisers and fashion photographers that the 'new woman' of the postfeminist age is a social failure. Men are her prey, not her companions, whatever her protestations of love. These women live richly on the edge of society, in beach houses or boat houses, affluent but isolated. In *Black Widow*, Bob Rafelson allows the issue of female friendship and the fascination that women have for each other to intrude, but at the end of the film the *femme fatale* is consigned again to the social wilderness.

By casting a woman in the role of investigator, the balance of power that was automatically loaded in favour of the male in the 1940s is more unpredictably weighted in *Black Widow*, as Alex and her prey engage in the cat-and-mouse parrying that reaches a dramatic climax in the double-bluff of the final sequence. Catharine's hostile kiss after Alex has given her the revealing wedding present of a 'black widow' spider brooch ('she mates and she kills') epitomizes the tension in this film between female fascination and competitive hostility. Well established also in other areas of the media, most notably in girls' magazine stories where rivalry and fascination between female friends often provide the key sources of narrative tension, it is also the spark that ignites the 1992 film *Single White Female*.

Black Widow enables both masculine and feminine points of identification. Seen as a reworked film noir, with Alex as a male substitute (her name, dress and integration with her male colleagues encourage this reading), she becomes the surrogate male private eye. This would make the film compatible, if paradoxically so, with Mulvey's thesis of the dominance of the masculine gaze. On the other hand, the film also foregrounds the fascination between Alex and Catharine, in terms akin to the female spectating positions offered by fashion photography and advertisements in women's magazines. Although this fascinated looking may be sexually and erotically inflected for lesbians, it is not intrinsically so. After both women have indulged in a strenuous practice diving session, Alex gazes admiringly at Catharine, and comments: 'we spent most of the day in the pool and you come out looking like that, and I look like this – and I just wondered why that is'. Catharine's answer is to suggest a change of swimsuit. Consumption, here as in the magazine features and advertisements, is the answer to woman's sense of personal inferiority.

Some critics have seen the feminization of Alex as a central theme in the film. From carelessness about her appearance, Alex is transformed into chic model, aware of her need to compete through dress and image for male attention. But this aspect of the film remains ambiguous. We are never entirely clear whether Alex is merely playing out the game of thinking and behaving as Catharine does, in order better to understand and outwit her opponent, or whether she is rejecting her own more 'masculine' side. At the end of the film, the ambiguity remains unsolved. Although Marina Heung sees the final scene of Alex walking triumphantly out of the court house dressed in a colourful sundress as a sign of her accomplished feminization (1987a, p. 58), I would agree more with Teresa de Lauretis that the feminization theme is quietly dropped, or left hanging at the end of the film (1990, p. 21). It is Alex's professional skill that leads to her success in her final showdown with Catharine, and her exit into the sunset is on her own. Had it been with Catharine's last intended victim, with whom Alex had a brief affair, Heung's argument would be more convincing.

Moral monsters and she-devils

Casting the postfeminist woman as pathologically disturbed turns her from moral monster into she-devil. In the 1970s, a number of films, such as *Klute* in 1971 and *Looking for Mr Goodbar* in 1977, scraped the gloss off the single working woman's life and revealed the vulnerability and misery underneath. Bree Daniels (Jane Fonda) in *Klute* works as a prostitute, smokes cannabis and dabbles in the occult: her private moments of pleasure are undercut by threatening camera angles, voyeuristically putting the audience in the place of the psychotic killer who stalks her. This reaction to feminism in mainstream Hollywood films of the 1970s was to develop into something even more sinister in the 1980s and 1990s. *Fatal Attraction* (1987) is not the only film of these decades to suggest that independence and derangement are strangely akin (*Single White Female*, for example, is another), but the publicity surrounding its change of ending and audience reactions makes it the best known.

As a successful career woman, Alex (Glenn Close), the anti-heroine of *Fatal Attraction*, already has money, influence and sexual satisfaction. What she cannot come to terms with is her exclusion from the romanticized world of family life, shot in this film with all the gloss and warm lighting of the commercials which form the other part of director, Adrian Lyne's, career. Her kidnapping of Beth and Dan's daughter, Ellen, and her savage attack on the child's adored pet rabbit, confirm her position on the outside that has already been signalled as she prowls round the house, looking in enviously on the cosy sentimentality within.

In the early stages of the film, this golden-haired Medusa (William-son, 1988b, p. 28) takes the initiative in her relationship with Dan (Michael Douglas). But this image of a sexually libidinous and sophis-ticated career woman, already established in the scenes at an office social function and a business meeting, quickly tarnishes as we are invited to doubt her sincerity and her stability. From rampageous sex, it is but a short step to severe and manipulative neurosis. As Alex fails to play by the rules of the one-night stand, Dan's happy home life, com-plete with idealized child and tail-thumping dog, is given added pro-minence. Alex's insistence that she have Dan's child, and that he face up to his responsibilities as its father, intrude stridently into this space.

In contrast to Alex, Dan's wife, Beth (Anne Archer), in the man-ner of the 'good' woman of 1940s' noir films, is unmysterious and unproblematic. Schematically indexed in the warmth of a domestic environment that contrasts sharply with the cold minimalism of Alex's living-space, this opposition might have functioned less sentimentally and more questioningly if Lyne's original ending had been preserved for mainstream release. In the original version Alex commits suicide, using the knife that has Dan's fingerprints on it. He had seized it from her grasp after breaking into her apartment and (in a burlesque reprise of their boisterous love-making early in the film) roughing her up. Dan is implicated in her death, and both have to pay the price. The restora-tion of the family as the haven of normality, achieved in the screened version by Beth killing Alex to protect her husband, is pre-empted in the director's cut.

The original ending found no favour with the preview audience. Even with the revised conclusion, shouts of 'kill the bitch' reputedly accom-panied screenings in some areas. Alex's actions in this film against the sanctity of the family were sufficient to unleash a tirade of misogyny. With its remade ending, *Fatal Attraction* risks degenerating at its end into a farcical postfeminist parody of *Psycho*. This woman, who has asserted her presence throughout the film, will not, experience tells us, lie quietly at the bottom of the bath. Her lurching attempt at a second life, and a final destruction of the family, invites the audience to feel happy with her killing. Like the obliteration of the mad Mrs Rochester in *Jane Eyre*, her death extirpates the threat that lurks over all romantic attachments in a non-romantic world. Sherry Lansing, the co-producer of the film with Stanley Jaffe, claims that 'we chose to make the Glenn Close character a woman, but her problems are not gender-related. We could just as easily have made her a man' (interview by Sue Summers in *The Independent*, 15 January 1988). This is at best disingenuous. In a culture that perceives men's sexuality as unproblematic, their sexual rights as questionable only when they overstep legal boundaries, and their female partner as probably implicated in any blame that can attach to their actions, this rewriting would have drained the film of its tension and drama.

The original version, had it been screened (it is now available in video version), would have allowed more credibility for Alex's point of view, even although her actions would still have placed her in the she-devil category. One of the most disturbing aspects of this film is its use of the anti-heroine's voice to give expression to feminist-inspired sentiments. Alex accuses Dan of not considering her feelings, of thinking he can trample all over her: 'I won't allow you to treat me like some shit you can just bang a couple of times and throw in the garbage', but the validity of this point of view is sharply undercut by the excesses of her actions. A similar problem occurs in *Single White Female*. The psychotic flat-sharer, Hedy (Jennifer Jason Leigh), has the feminist lines. It is she who warns Allie (Bridget Fonda) about trusting men too far, she who insists that Allie's boss needs a serious fright after he has attempted to rape her, and she who takes the necessary action. Her extravagant and uncontrolled behaviour at the same time establishes her insanity. When feminism becomes identified with madness, even post-feminism seems dangerous.

In conclusion

The question 'What do women want?' is not easily answered, any more than the question of what men want would be. Women, like men, are too diverse and multifaceted to possess some unified and unitary set of desires and needs. Yet when women ask the question, it is inflected differently from the male conundrum. Women pose the problem to seek a solution, and to explore new possibilities. The utopian belief of early second-wave feminism that all women's desires could be melted in the same pot has evaporated under pressure from women anxious to declare their difference as strongly as their sisterhood. But the project, now more subdued and less romantic, still survives. As one feminist put it, we can entertain the question 'What do women want? . . . now that it is *we* who are asking it' (Vance, 1984, p. 444).

In media representations and in historical myth, women rarely have the opportunity to pose the question. Pandora, like Eve, as Marina

Warner points out, becomes the 'agent of fatality through the desire she inspires, not experiences' (1987, p. 222). Equally significantly, both women were punished for their overbearing curiosity. Pandora, forbidden from opening her box (or pitcher), and Eve, forbidden from tasting the fruit of the tree of knowledge, both broke the rules. As a result, their deceptive beauty and desirability were to be blamed in mythology for the downfall of humankind and the introduction of misery, pain and hard toil into the world. As barrister Helena Kennedy wittily puts it, commenting on the continuing tendency even in the late twentieth century to perceive women criminals as more culpable than men, 'Eve was framed' (1992). Similarly, in 1940s' film noir, woman is the beguiling and untrustworthy seductress punished for her incitement of desire, not its expression. Fashion features still conjure up fantasy landscapes where women appear enticing as in dreams, but voiceless to articulate their own demands.

This chapter suggests that, in some respects, this pattern has changed, as the media have begun to acknowledge the existence of female desire. Madonna especially bases her appeal on her confrontational approach to the silencing of what women want. The new women of 1980s' and 1990s' film noir remakes know what they desire, and are willing to pursue it. Yet, there are limits here, too. Madonna, by locating desire solely in sexual fantasy, severely restricts the menu of what desire means, at the same time as she gives the impression of daring to break the taboos and speak the unspeakable. Judith Williamson's comment on film noir remakes such as *Body Heat* could apply equally to Madonna. There is, she says, something ridiculous about simultaneously suggesting 'that something is *out of bounds*, while flaunting its explicit *inclusion*' (1986a, p. 177). Madonna's teasing approach, her multifaceted, but never stable, answer to the question of what women want, like the contrast between the captions and the image of the fashion features in young women's magazines, recreate a mystery around female desire that allows it, too, to be commodified and sold back to us.

More perniciously, as feminism has opened up debate about a wide range of women's sexual, social and political desires, and demanded that they be listened to, popular media representations have reasserted masculine control. The dangers of the feminine enigma have been reinvoked in 1980s' and 1990s' narratives in the threat that women pose, especially when they express their own desires. While the seductive glamour of the 1940s' *femme fatale* did not save her from her fate, it offered a much softer version of misogyny than the more recent spate of monstrous-women films. In the reworking of film noir, and the she-devil films, the *vagina dentata* may be ironically metaphoric, but it is potent nevertheless. Madonna in her stage performances may be positively articulating the varied desires of the female body, but in *Body of Evidence* that same body is recuperated as the deadly weapon. Locating desire solely in the female sexual organs always leaves it vulnerable to reclamation by male fantasy.

5

Caring and sharing

I'm not the tiger-lady any more. I have a crib in my office and a
baby-mobile over my desk and I really like that.
(J. C. Wiatt, in *Baby Boom*, 1987)

I'm an actor: I can do the father.
(Jack, in *Three Men and a Baby*, 1988)

Femininity, denigrated in many other respects, has long been cherished
for its caring qualities. Women supposedly have a 'natural' talent for
looking after others. This chapter explores the role of the media in sustaining this mythology. In the modern period, motherhood, as the
archetypal symbol of women's nurturing qualities, cropped up in a
variety of guises, often a site of unease in an era wrestling with changing
social roles and a growing awareness of psychoanalysis. As the century
draws to its close, the 'new traditionalism' of family values juggles the
value of motherhood against a surface recognition that caring has a new
fluidity: mothers are now permitted to be unruly, or carry filofaxes;
fathers, and even single men, can be nurturing and loving. Friendships
between women, given novel expression in the 'female buddy' films,
induce the acts of sacrifice and devotion previously imagined only in
the sanctity of the hearth and home. This chapter will consider how far
these changes have altered the ideological association between women
and caring.

The ready association between caring and femininity in the western
world stems from a number of factors. The most enduring of these is
the responsibility for moral leadership placed on women within the
family and the wider community by religions of Judaic descent.
Secondly, as indicated in Chapter 2, the split between public and private
spheres confirmed women's supportive role within the home. As
women's employment has grown, it has replicated this pattern by
locating most women in the service sector of the economy. Both in the
home and in the public sphere, women have been cast as smiling
servants. The third factor that has encouraged women to be seen as
'natural' carers is the essentialist belief in their biological predisposition

towards nurturing. Even if a 'maternal instinct' could be proved, using this as a touchstone for women's aptitude for caring in general sweeps a number of problems of logic under the carpet. Psychoanalysis, in the early decades of the twentieth century, propped up the significance of the maternal nurturing role in the development of the individual. As with the religious adoration of the mother, the compliment was double-edged. If women were capable of being 'good mothers', they were to carry a heavy burden of guilt if they failed.

Motherly love

The central icon of the caring person within western culture is the figure of the mother. Advertisers know this, as we saw in Chapter 3, when they use the image of the mother to invite us to buy not for ourselves but for the well-being of our families. Within Roman Catholicism, the dominant image of holy mother and child, reproduced in multitudinous statues, stained glass windows and other art forms, invites our admiration for what she symbolizes, not for who she is. Impregnated without sexual contact, she teaches us that nurturing is a spiritual experience untouched by either the complications of physical passion or our own desires. Mary, significantly, has also been cast as the 'second Eve', compensating through her virginal purity for the sins of the woman held responsible for the fall of humanity (Warner, 1985, pp. 50–67). In this polarity between sin and saintliness, the whore/madonna dichotomy that underlies so much of western culture's thinking about women takes root.

Society's confused reactions to the appearance of a sexualized maternal body remind us that this dichotomy still flourishes. In 1991 a photograph on the cover of *Vanity Fair* of a naked Demi Moore, in an advanced stage of pregnancy, provoked a hostile response from many readers. Breast-feeding in public is still, according to a 1993 survey carried out for the Royal College of Midwives in Britain, regarded as in bad taste by substantial numbers of British men. Happy with the frequent displays of female breasts in the popular tabloid press and on the cinema screen offered primarily for their titillation, they become paradoxically prudish when confronted with the combination of sexuality and maternalism that the nursing breast implies. The hypocrisy of public responses is piquantly captured in Posy Simmond's cartoon, *Public View* (*see* Fig. 8).

The spiritual reverence for motherhood intensifies whenever socio-economic conditions require it. After both World Wars, the ideological

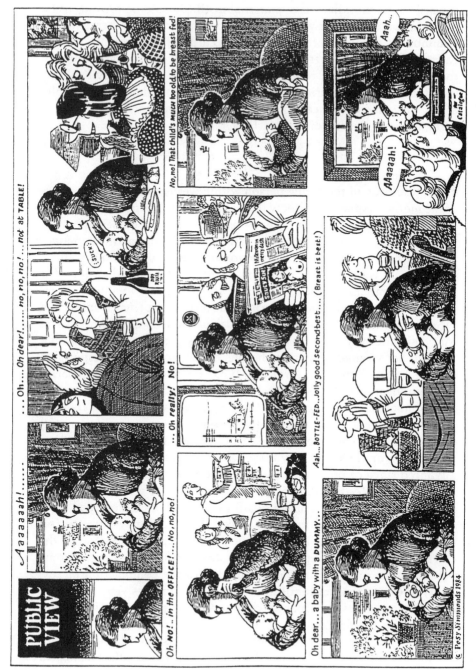

Fig. 8 Reprinted by permission of the Peters Fraser & Dunlop Group Ltd.

rating of motherhood shot dramatically upwards, as women were enticed back into the home. The help of women's magazines was enlisted after World War II. Whatever reluctance they might have felt about becoming political accomplices vanished before a consumer boom in the 1950s and 1960s that supplied them with a ready subsidy of plentiful advertising provided they idealized domestic life (Winship, 1987b, pp. 30–6). As with homecare in the interwar period (see Chapter 3), an injection of science, this time in the guise of psychology and psychoanalysis, helped to upgrade motherhood's status. During the interwar period, behaviourism was the dominant philosophy, but shortly after World War II parents were urged to encourage their children's self-expression (Ehrenreich and English, 1979, pp. 165–239). Manuals, such as those produced by Dr Spock from 1948, underlined the rewards as well as the difficult psychological skills of mothering (Phoenix *et al.*, 1991, pp. 66–85).

In the wake of the childcare manuals, a range of mother-and-baby magazines developed in the post-war period to first create a mystique, and then dispel it, around the art of mothering. In the 1990s, these publications have to a large extent transformed themselves into the more politically correct 'parenting' magazines, but the modes of address still imply a distinctly female readership. From advice on what foods to eat during pregnancy, to ways of ensuring a successful toddlers' party, these magazines hold out an ideal of how to be a perfect mother. Financially, they are supported by advertisements and inserts that target the new parent as a uniquely susceptible consumer, poised on the cusp of self-sacrificial rather than self-indulgent spending habits.

Psychoanalysis boosted anxieties about mothering. As we saw in Chapter 1, the child's early relationship with the mother played a significant part in the formation of subjectivity in both Freudian and Lacanian theories. Additionally, object-relations theorists such as Nancy Chodorow focused on the consequences for girls of the early bonding with the mother. These ideas filtered through into the advice of the specialists, and breathed fresh life into discourses of 'good' and 'bad' mothers. 'Good' mothers are self-sacrificing and selfless; 'bad' mothers are either overbearing or neglectful. As Ann Kaplan points out, these categories are frequently deployed to serve the interests of the state and the economy (1992, p. 45).

Support for this thesis comes from discourses of the family in Britain in the early 1990s. Spurred by worries about moral decline, increasing crime, and the reliance on a shrinking welfare purse of a growing number of young families, politicians constructed a moral rhetoric of 'family values' that was amplified by the media into a panic about young single mothers 'choosing' to bring up children alone. Fuelled by occasional reports of single women leaving their children on their own, this discourse demonized mothers who, in the notorious terms of a 1993 BBC *Panorama* investigation, were producing 'babies on benefit'. Widely available statistics, on the other hand, revealed that only a third of lone parents in 1993 consisted of single women who had never been married. Freudianism was invoked to support the thesis that children brought up without fathers, including children of lesbian mothers, would be psychologically scarred for life. The spectre of the 'bitch', evoked by a *Daily Mirror* headline on a 1993 report of a mother who allegedly left her child alone while she went on holiday, haunted the coverage of all single mothers, regardless of status.

Modernism and maternalism

In the modern period, ideal mums or moms appeared most frequently in advertisements, in women's magazines, in the emerging radio soaps or on the women's pages of newspapers. Here, in the fake intimacy of the modes of address, women could be given role models to follow, step by imitative step. At the same time, women were increasingly experiencing the attraction of employment and of increased leisure opportunities. While those media funded partly by advertising gained commercial advantage from focusing on the joys and skills of motherhood, the cultural anxieties about white women's restlessness in their domestic place began to be expressed in film. Black women were still represented within Hollywood as instinctive 'mammies', finding a satisfaction in caring that compensated for their lowly social status. The second version of *Imitation of Life*, directed by Douglas Sirk in 1959, changes the motivation of the white woman from that of the earlier version, directed by John Stahl in 1934. Whereas in 1934, widowed Bea works out of necessity, in 1959 Lora has ambitions and aspirations to dazzle on the stage. The black woman's role, on the other hand, remains static, content in her servicing of others' needs (Kaplan, 1992, pp. 163–79). Marina Heung (1987b) goes further in suggesting that the construction of the mammy in the later film takes a step backwards. She points out that at least in the earlier version Delilah had a role in the white woman's career, helping Bea run a restaurant. Linked historically to slavery and contemporaneously to the restricted employment prospects of African-American women, the image of the 'mammy' was to have a long survival record in the American media (Jewell, 1993, pp. 37–44).

For white women, the role of the mother, influenced increasingly as the century evolved by psychoanalytic thinking, produced greater narrative dilemmas. Two films of the 1930s that explored aspects of that angst were *Blonde Venus* (1932) and *Stella Dallas* (1937). Both have drawn extensive critical interest (e.g. Kaplan, 1983, 1992; Gledhill, 1987), because of the tension between their overt support for maternal sacrifice and their differing hints that, in the modern world, femininity cannot be so easily contained.

In *Blonde Venus* Marlene Dietrich plays the, for her, unusual role of a mother, forced temporarily through poverty and humiliation to give her son over to his father's care. The director, Von Sternberg, was reputedly reluctant to cast this 'sex goddess' in this uncustomary role (Kaplan, 1983, p. 53). The clash that he perceived between Marlene Dietrich's star image and her narrative role is one that refuses the viewer a uniform spectating position. Repeatedly, Helen Faraday (Dietrich) embodies the tension between the sexual woman and the 'good' mother. In the opening scene, she is the object of male voyeurism as she bathes nude in a pool. Within a short sequence of shots Helen, now married to Edward Faraday, reappears as a caring mother. Despite the sobriety of her clothing in the early domestic scenes, and her engagement with the 'feminine' art of tapestry while her husband works at his instrument-laden desk, the enactment of the bedtime story she and her husband relate to Johnny dislocates our expectations of the family melodrama. It is the child who demands to hear again the story of how his mother and father met, and he who provocatively prods the tellers to reveal details of the sexual development of their relationship. This shifts the spoken discourse onto a plane of sexual knowingness that is strangely at odds with the sentimental cosiness of the *mise en scène*.

As the narrative develops, Helen fails to resolve this tension. She is frequently framed as the caring mother; bathing her child, feeding him or even, once they have become fugitives from Johnny's father, teaching him to write by paradoxically making him repeatedly copy the word 'father'. Defined by Edward Faraday as a 'rotten mother', Helen's actions and non-verbal behaviour belie this. Narratively, we are also led to believe that it is the desire to see Johnny that bribes Helen back to New York rather than her desire to be with Nick Townsend (Cary Grant).

Helen's motivation as carer of her husband is also ambiguously presented. Her decision to return to the stage in order to raise the money for his medical treatment is both potentially an act of self-sacrificial love and a self-enhancing move. As she becomes involved with Townsend, whose charms clearly outstrip those of the dour and self-regarding Faraday, our doubts about her motivation increase. Yet, although she is capable of exploiting her sexuality to get her own way, Helen never articulates any clear personal sexual ambition, even in relation to Nick. As the film draws to a close, both men are excluded from the close bonding between mother and son, but it is Edward who is finally drawn back into the frame to reassert the primacy of the family.

Marlene Dietrich throughout much of this film acts as a fetishized object of the audience's gaze, especially once Nick's money enables her to dress like a couturier's model. In the final scene, Helen wears a daring creation in black satin that contrasts dramatically with her dowdy dress in her maternal role at the beginning of the film. As she re-establishes her place within the family, abetted by Johnny's insistence that both parents again recite the story of their meeting, her appearance is still that of 'blonde Venus' rather than asexual mother. *Blonde Venus* collides signifiers of sexuality and motherhood in a way that refuses comfortable endorsement of the maternal role. In narrative terms, Helen Faraday is punished and humiliated for breaking out of her proper domestic role, and her reinstatement is achieved only at the expense of abandoning any hope of sexual fulfilment with Nick. At the same time, as several critics have recognized, this simple message is not supported by the visual presentation of the star.

If sexuality is the signifier that troubled conventional discourses of motherhood in *Blonde Venus*, in *Stella Dallas* the offender is class. King Vidor, the director of the 1937 version of this film, casts doubt on the mother's fitness to care for her daughter by emphasizing her lowly status. In order to become the 'good' mother, Stella has to make the ultimate sacrifice of giving her daughter up to a more affluent home. Yet, at the same time as the film invites us to view Stella as working-class and unrefined, it endows her with a warmth and sensuality that make her appear more endearing than the sophisticated Helen Morrison who eventually wins the affection of both her husband and her daughter.

Linda Williams, in an article that sparked off a protracted debate in the columns of the *Cinema Journal*, pointed to the varying and even contradictory discourses that are aired in this film. The famous ending, with the mother excluded from her daughter's wedding, but gazing wistfully at it through the uncurtained window, has been seen by some critics as a typical Hollywood ending that strips the woman of her rights and feelings in order to exalt the state of motherhood and maternal self-sacrifice. Linda Williams, on the other hand, argues that the rest of the film resists this reading by inviting the audience to identify with 'the contradiction of Stella's attempt to be a woman *and* a mother' (Gledhill, 1987, p. 314). Although, as Ann Kaplan (1985) suggests, our reading of this film now may be inflected by a feminist awareness not available to the 1930s' audience, its attitude to the mother's sacrifice is not simplistic. The central conflict is, as Mary Ann Doane puts it, that 'although her [Stella's] behavior toward Laurel is that of the "good mother", her image is not' (1987, p. 77). What *Stella Dallas* threatens to open up, even if the closure of the ending papers over the cracks, is that motherhood is shaped by socio-economic factors as well as moral will.

Both these films follow in the tradition of the nineteenth-century maternal sacrifice narratives. As Maria La Place points out, the constraints of the Depression, coupled with the restrictions of the Hays Code, gave these renewed viability in the 1930s (Gledhill, 1987, p. 153). Yet the obstacles to 'proper' caring are depicted in terms of dangerous forays outside the domestic sphere. Significantly, these escapades take the woman into the realm of collective pleasures (drinking, dancing and singing) more customarily associated with the dangers of the modernist city. While this removal of the mother from the home serves metaphorically to warn us of her departure from her natural caring role, it also establishes a positive iconography of woman's independence and potential pleasure that conflicts with the simple moral message of the narrative resolution. As in film noir, the woman's desires may not prevail as a dominant discourse, but their appearance on the agenda stirs a problem that the uniformly glowing accounts of motherhood in the instructional literature ignored.

By the 1940s, the propagandist maternal melodrama sat alongside the film noir, offering competing versions of femininity. *Mildred Pierce* (1945), a film exploring the problem of mother–daughter relations, given popular currency by the growing interest in Freudian thinking, sits uneasily between the two. Employing film noir visual rhetoric for the contemporary scenes and melodrama discourses in the flashback sequences, this film both articulates and suppresses the voice of the mother (strongly played by Joan Crawford). Critics diverge in their explanations for this. Pam Cook (1980, pp. 68–82) applies a timeless psychoanalytic model, seeing Mildred's elision as symptomatic of the

Oedipal repression of the feminine, whereas Linda Williams (1988, pp. 12–30) prefers a social and historical analysis. She regards World War II as the absent centre of the film, with Mildred's temporary triumph as a working woman being sharply repressed in line with the real events of the year when the film was released. Williams also makes the interesting observation that the shift from female to male discourse might be materially related to the replacement of the initial female screenwriter, Catherine Turney, by Ranald MacDougall (1988, p. 13).

Within the flashback sequences, Mildred progresses from being 'always in the kitchen' to launch her career as a restaurant entrepreneur. This shifts the dominant *mise en scène* of the film from the home to the world outside, where glamour and success predominate. But a film of 1945 can scarcely give its blessing to such a choice, any more than it can endorse even an isolated sexual adventure on Mildred's part. Following a passionate night with playboy Monty Beragon (Zachary Scott), Mildred returns home to find her daughter Kay dying of pneumonia. Having failed Kay by being insufficiently caring, she fails her remaining daughter, Veda, by imagining that buying expensive gifts for her can be a substitute for personal attention. In return, Veda rejects her, treats her with contempt for being a working woman, and finally betrays her by having an affair with Monty. Ida (Eve Arden), Mildred's more independent and androgynous business partner, acts as touchstone to Mildred's romanticism. When Mildred says she cannot put Veda out of her mind, Ida's acerbic reply, 'Personally, Veda's convinced me that alligators have the right idea: they eat their young', injects an uncharacteristically discordant note into the film's melodramatic discourse.

Although none of these films addresses directly the emergent conflicts between maternalism and sexuality, or between the aspirations of ideal motherhood and personal success in the workplace, their suggestion of the latent tensions is palpable. Significantly, too, the obstacles to 'good' motherhood in these films originate in economic difficulty. This is most clearly articulated in *Stella Dallas*, but the shadow of financial problems extends also over the other films. In *Blonde Venus*, it is the need to raise money to pay for her husband's cure that sets Helen Faraday on the course that leads to her downfall; in *Mildred Pierce*, the necessity of earning an income after her husband has left her stirs the ambitions that are to overwhelm her. All of these films also suggest a disjunction between 'normal' motherhood, contained within the home and fulfilling an integrative function, and 'good' or sacrificial motherhood. Helen has to give up her son temporarily; Stella has to give up her daughter permanently in order to ensure her well-being; Mildred Pierce tries to confound the processes of the law by persuading the authorities that it was she, not Veda, who killed Monty. The happy framing of family relations in the advertising of the period is absent in these films.

Feminism rocks the cradle

Feminism had two effects on discourses of caring. First, as we saw in Chapter 3, it challenged the burden of care that society placed on women, without recognition or state help. Highlighting the inadequacies of childcare provision, the injustice of a career structure that expected women as well as men to reach their peak during their childbearing years, and the reluctance of employers to introduce schemes such as flexi-time or job-sharing, feminists condemned the hypocrisy of a dominant ideology that valued care in moral but not in material terms. At a personal level, feminism invited men to acknowledge that caring involved a set of demanding practices, and could only fancifully be reduced to a matter of sentiment. Feminism also extended the concept of caring to include political and social action through the international development of its movement, and its links with other alternative political, social and environmental groupings. The difficult issue of sisterhood was also addressed.

The media picked up on some of these discourses, but neglected others. The invention of the 'new man' and the 'new father' in the 1980s incorporated men within discourses of caring. During the 1980s, also, female friendships became popular subjects of treatment in television genres such as the situation comedy and the crime series, and in a variety of films. The media were less enthusiastic about exploring the material circumstances within which caring occurred, or about extending representations of women's caring talents in political directions. In a society where psychiatry and psychotherapy were big business, it was the psychodrama of caring that still held particular attractions for Hollywood.

Family relationships continued to be the favoured context for exploring caring in film. *Ordinary People* (1980) focuses on a middle-class family trying to come to terms with the death of the elder son in a boating accident. The mother, Beth (Mary Tyler Moore), is unwaveringly represented as the antithesis of the generous and expansive American mom. Tidy and impeccable in appearance, even on the golf course, her emotional life is colour co-ordinated: bleached and drained of life and vitality, except when appearances at neighbourhood social events require a sparkling performance. The starched white napkins which lie neatly rolled up on the dining-room table serve as an apt and recurring index of order in this emotionally sterile household. The film reverses the normal expectations of male and female discourse. It is the mother who is unable to communicate with her other son, and the father who eventually succeeds in establishing a relationship with him and confronting his own feelings. As Conrad embraces his mother on her return from holiday, a lingering shot reveals to the audience her frozen and bemused expression. Like a tailor's dummy, her face remains totally impassive and her arms immobile. By the end of the film, Beth, unable to cope any more with the trauma, has left the family home.

If *Ordinary People* questioned the naturalness of women's capacity for caring, it granted little insight into the mother's own perspectives. Other films of the same period or slightly earlier were content to replay the romantic conceptualization of women as carers, even if the context increasingly moved beyond the confines of the maternal relationship. *Coming Home* (1978) is set topically in the aftermath of the Vietnam war. Housewife Sally Hyde (Jane Fonda) deals with her anxieties about her husband's term of duty in Vietnam by going to help in the local hospital where veterans are being rehabilitated. This act of caring, which meets with opposition from her husband Bob (Bruce Dern), quickly mutates into sexual desire for one of the patients, Luke Martin (Jon Voight). Her evolving relationship with him prevents her from being able to offer her husband similar support when he returns from the war, anguished, moody and abrasive. The film ends with Bob vanishing into the waves in an act of suicide, symbolically marking Sally's failure to care adequately for him at the same time as it frees her to develop her attachment to Luke.

The film romantically endorses Sally's rights to her new life, by contrasting Luke's progression from cynicism and despair to thoughtfulness and sensitivity with Bob's downward spiral into brutishness, anger and vindictiveness. In addition, Sally's relationship with Luke is legitimated by its growth out of an act of caring. Sally's emergence in the film from self-doubting, awkward small-town wife into a confident woman sure of her own mind is a transformation wrought by the discovery of her feminine, not her feminist, self. Despite its generic relationship to the Vietnam films of that period, *Coming Home* confines its interest in the war to the fall-out on personal relationships.

A rare attempt in the 1970s to extend the discourse of caring beyond the network of personal interaction was *Norma Rae* (1979). The heroine (Sally Field), a cotton-mill worker, becomes politically involved in setting up a union to fight for basic rights for the workers. Although Norma's politicization depends in part on her attraction to Ruben, the union organizer who masterminds developments, there are moments when her readiness to care is powerfully transformed into determined political action. It is she who succeeds in bringing the cotton-mill to a standstill in an act of defiant leadership that wins over her fellow workers. Her struggle to combine her political and domestic responsibilities, in contrast to postfeminist narratives, is not easily won. In set-piece cameos, the cost to Norma's personal life is represented, most graphically in a scene where an exasperated Sonny accuses his wife of deserting her domestic duties to devote her energies to union business. She retaliates by aggressively sending up his demands in a series of mocking actions that ambiguously invite us to read them either as feminine hysterical excess or as a feminist challenge to male expectations. Although the conflict between political and personal caring is firmly on the agenda, it is sidelined by the romantic interest of the evolving relationship between Norma and Ruben. Norma's consciousness of her own ignorance and inferiority to him runs like a sore throughout the film. *Norma Rae* does, however, avoid a traditional romantic ending. Norma and Ruben part amicably, their mission to establish a union complete. The conclusion leaves unresolved the tensions between domestic responsibilities, personal satisfaction and caring for the wider community that the film puts on the agenda, but then seems reluctant to handle.

The media became more fully aware of the effects of feminism in the era of postmodernism. This produces a strange mix. While soap operas did begin, in Britain at least, to explore the tensions for women of combining caring for others with caring for themselves and developing their own potential, this was not a popular source of dramatic conflict elsewhere. Occasionally, as in *The Good Mother* (1988), the incompatibility between the mother's sexuality and her maternal commitment surfaces as a central interest, but even in this film, the narrative centrality of the custody case shifts the focus onto the well-being of the child rather than the mother. Anna (played by Diane Keaton) refuses to give up her lover in order to vindicate her entitlement (in the eyes of the law and the jury) to care for her own daughter, but, despite this faithfulness to her own principles, she is by the end of the film left on her own, bereft and inconsolable. The parallel between her fate and that of her liberated aunt, who mothered an illegitimate child but drowned in an accident caused by drink, is sufficiently clear to suggest that this film is in part a retraction of liberal values.

In the 1980s and 1990s more generally, caring became detached from its conventional narrative association with angst-ridden mothers, to appear in a number of different guises. Fathers took on the mantle of carers, and children became the sentimental focus of films, dislodging women to the margins. The split between women's role as carers and their own desires became a matter for comedy and fun, the tone one of frustrated resignation that killed the feminist agenda with a lethal injection of 'new realism'. Battles between 'good' and 'bad' mothers were still played out, and reached the same conclusions as earlier decades, but the stories became more fantastical or more metaphorical. If postmodernism successfully uncoupled the 'grand narrative' of caring from its most obvious maternal associations, it could not topple the edifice entirely.

Fun mums

In the 1980s and 1990s the angst of mothering, obvious in the modern period, has given way to the light-hearted approach, visible also in the advertising strategies discussed in Chapter 3. Even the social realism of soap opera has never sustained for long the dilemmas of motherhood, before it lightens its tone and shifts its narrative attention elsewhere. The American comedy series *Grace Under Fire* depicts a single mother struggling to combine work in an oil refinery, care of three small children and her own personal life. Her 'new realism', wittily articulated, sets her apart from the earnest politically correct feminist who is her only female colleague at work. Maternal anxieties are dispelled by Grace's sense of humour, but so, too, is feminism. *Roseanne* also captures the gap between personal aspirations and domestic realities, but Roseanne toys with freedom in the manner of the mouse sniffing the cheese. While Edina in the British comedy, *Absolutely Fabulous*, is the 'unruly' mother, breaking all the rules in the book, Roseanne, despite her transgression of the codes of feminine behaviour and appearance, is still the ideal mom, but with the sentimentality removed. The series format of the show, requiring crises to have immediate resolutions, prevents *Roseanne* from developing the tensions it raises. When, in a 1994 episode, Roseanne, still, as she puts it, with *some* skin left on her hands, regrets that Dan does not match the romantic hunks of television soaps, his feeble attempts to live up to this image are reduced to buying his wife a second-hand dishwasher.

Roseanne frequently articulates desires for sexual fulfilment, or for personal achievement, that challenge the status quo of the traditional mom. None of these does more than crack the surface of her caring role. In a 1990 episode, on the brink of her thirty-seventh birthday, Roseanne regrets that her domestic responsibilities have prevented her from fulfilling her ambition to become a writer. In response, Dan constructs a den for her in the basement, and the family leaves her there on her birthday in splendid isolation to compose her manuscript. Quickly surrounded by crumpled sheets of paper, Roseanne ends up dusting the shelves and reverting to domestic type. In this episode, the tensions between self-fulfilment and caring for others is magically resolved. Roseanne finds her creativity restored by her son's suggestion that she write down the stories she makes up for him at bedtime. In this way, her frustrated complaint that 'I'm 37 years old. I'm a mom. That's what I am' is transformed from an impediment to personal fulfilment to its solution.

This phase can, however, only be temporary. The show depends on the gap beween Roseanne's dreams and the actuality of her domestic situation for its humour and the sharpness of her one-line comments. By 1993, Roseanne continues to reflect that marriage and family life have prevented her from fulfilling her own potential as a writer, as she urges daughter Darlene to leave the home nest to develop her artistic talents at college. While Roseanne's failure to contain herself within the saintly paradigm of the motherly ideal strains at the feminine conventions, and puts her own desires (including her un-maternal sexual appetite) into play, the conventions of the series prevent them ever spilling over into misrule and subversion.

Designer parenting

Another way of fending off the material problems of caring in the postmodern era was to commodify the child and invent a new discourse of designer parenting. With toddlers and babies widely used for their cuteness value by advertisers, it did not take long for film-makers, anxious to tap emotions in a cynical age, to catch up. Parenting magazines regularly mix features on the emotional and physical needs of young children with advertising-led copy that presents the child as the latest status symbol. An insert for British Telecom answering machines and

Fig. 9 Initiation in designer mothering. *Baby Boom* © 1987 United Artists Pictures Inc.

cordless phones in the August 1993 issue of *Practical Parenting* makes the association between child and lifestyle explicit. Featuring a triptych of happy images: mother cradling baby; mother cradling phone; and mother caressing her own skin, it promises: 'The Response 50, the Freestyle 300 and free Vichy body care. Now you'll love picking those up as much as you do your baby'.

Baby Boom (1987) revolves around the designer child. The central character and voice in the film is that of J. C. Wiatt (Diane Keaton), who discovers a talent for maternal enjoyment submerged under her ambitious executive exterior when she unexpectedly inherits a daughter. Forced eventually to give up her high-powered job in the interests of caring for Elizabeth, she assumes a new life in idyllic Vermont, and, after some initial tussles with the trials of rural living, magically finds her *métier* in making and selling gourmet baby food from the abundant supplies of natural products on her doorstep. Transformed from 'tiger-lady' to doting mother-cum-businessperson with 'a crib in my office and a baby-mobile over my desk', J. C. eventually rejects the offer of her former employers to take over her company in return for lavish rewards and a top-salaried executive position. Although the excesses of this film can be seen to mock the codification of 'superwoman' as able to combine motherhood, career, leisure and sex-life, they also conspire to promote this stereotype. The film starts with statistics of women's success in the American workforce, and with J. C.'s personal credentials, commenting 'one would take it for granted that a woman like this has it all. One must never take anything for granted'. Like Alex in *Black Widow*, and Alex in *Fatal Attraction*, even J. C.'s name hints that femininity is the missing asset.

Baby Boom is responsive on one level to feminism's exploration of how job satisfaction and mothering can be combined, but its solution is self-mockingly naïve, fantastical and utopian. The film transforms the caring role of motherhood into pure fun, a matter of appropriate consumption with success as a mother depending on successfully targeting baby's needs. That J. C. worked in marketing is not accidental. In contrast with the 1930s' and 1940s' films, money poses no problems for J. C., and the cuteness of her adopted daughter, enhanced by appropriate consumption, turns her into an ideal accessory. Since Elizabeth is not J. C.'s biological offspring, there is no space in this film for the psychic tensions that psychoanalysis proposes between mother and daughter.

The advent of the child prepares J. C. for discovering her feminine side. From second-regulated love-making to order, squeezed in between business commitments in New York, J. C. dissolves into romantic incompetence and girlish coyness in her evolving relationship with the local Vermont vet (Sam Shepard). Femininity, the film more insidiously implies, involves abandoning feminism. In a scene that is meant to be humorous, but ends up being disturbing for many women, J. C. resists the advances of Dr Cooper as he offers to help her mend her punctured tyre, declaring her desire to be an independent woman. Ignoring her wishes, he clutches her in his arms and kisses her. Her reaction, straight out of Mills and Boon, is to swoon helplessly and utter 'Wow!' to camera. If this is meant to be a take-off of the romance of the women's film, it misses its mark. *Baby Boom* replays the contrast between a life-enhancing country life and a dehumanizing urban one (familiar from many American narratives) in terms of the contrast between femininity and the career woman. Postfeminism wins, even if it is also gently sent up.

New men and caring fathers

Those who think the postmodern habit of uncoupling signifiers from their familiar signifieds is liberating will have cheered the advent in popular culture of the caring man. This sensitive and nurturing 'new man' of the 1980s struggled to break out of his shell all over *Thirtysomething*; appeared regularly in advertisements; and became a popular hit in the cinema, with films such as *Kramer vs Kramer* (1979), *Three Men and a Baby* (1987), *Rain Man* (1988) and *Awakenings* (1990). Unlike the archetypal woman, men in these representations are seen as having no natural aptitude for caring, as needing to learn the appropriate skills, and as being amusing when they fail. A television advertisement for the Scottish Amicable life assurance company depicts a father so exhausted by a short period of play with the toddlers left in his care while the mother goes shopping that he falls asleep beside them on the bed. This would have no appeal if the parents changed places. The woman who fails at motherhood is, as we have seen, many things, but never amusing.

In Penny Marshall's *Awakenings*, the doctor (Robin Williams) is clearly established as a social isolate. His development into a 'kind man' who 'cares very much for people' depends both on his characterization as an amiable eccentric, and on the encouragement he receives from the nurse, Eleanor Costello (Julie Kavner). Even more tellingly, although Dr Sayer receives all the public credit, the awakening of Leonard Lowe (Robert De Niro) from his catatonic illness is crucially dependent on the perceptiveness of the women in the film. It is Eleanor who makes the important discovery that moving along with the patients appears to transmit will-power to them, and Paula (Leonard's girlfriend) who calms Leonard's uncontrollable spasms, once he begins to regress, by dancing with him. In this sense *Awakenings* reinforces gender norms, with the female characters providing the intuitive insights and the male doctor the scientific understanding to make sense of them.

Kramer vs Kramer presents fatherhood as a rewarding learning process for Ted Kramer (Dustin Hoffman). The film opens with a rare close-up shot of Joanna Kramer (Meryl Streep) fondly surveying the son she is about to leave. Lit and framed to connote a Madonna image, this sequence of shots invites our identification with the mother's dilemma.

When she leaves home, however, she vacates the discursive centre of the film. Thereafter, like the shadowy presence we glimpse occasionally behind a café window as she watches Ted delivering Billy to school, the woman who makes up half the title of this film is either absent when her point of view is articulated, or shot in such a way as to prevent identification.

Joanna's first account in her own words of her reasons for abandoning her child are given in a letter to Billy, read to him by his father as both choke back their emotions. 'I have gone away', she writes, 'because I must find something interesting to do for myself in the world. Everybody has to, and so do I. Being your mommy was one thing, but there are other things, too'. Just as Billy drowns out the end of the letter by switching on the television, so the *mise en scène* of this scene establishes the pathos of the abandoned father and son as the central focus of our interest, pushing into the background the woman's voice as she articulates the tensions between caring and self-fulfilment.

This dialectic surfaces briefly again both as Joanna meets Ted in a New York restaurant to explain to him that she wants Billy back, and, later, as they fight out their corners in the court case. Joanna informs us that she needed to establish an independent identity: 'All my life I've felt like somebody's wife, or somebody's mother, or somebody's daughter. Even all the time we were together, I never knew who I was. And that's why I had to go away'. Her aim has been to establish her own career, an ambition for which her husband originally showed little sympathy. Yet on both occasions, this explanation is narrated without passion, and with flat lighting and a directorial avoidance of close-up shots that encourage little audience identification with Joanna's point of view.

The voice that we are asked to identify with in *Kramer vs Kramer* is, emphatically, that of the husband and father. It is his plea in court for gender equality that resounds with most passion and conviction: 'My wife used always to say to me "Why can't a woman have the same ambitions as a man?" I think you're right and maybe I've learned that much. But by the same token I'd like to know what law is it that says that a woman is a better parent, simply by virtue of her sex?'. *Kramer vs Kramer*'s denial of the issues it places on its own agenda is strongest in relation to the conflicts between 'mommying' and self-fulfilment. The film's failure to grant Meryl Streep the kind of role that was to produce her star status in other films is symptomatic of the muting of feminist discourses at the heart of the narrative. Joanna, morally although not legally defined as an unsatisfactory mother, pays the penalty of being deprived of living with the child she loves.

What Joanna is giving up is underlined within the film by the construction of parenting as life-enhancing fun, despite its occasional spats and traumas. *Kramer vs Kramer* concentrates on vignettes of idyllic father/son bonding at bedtime, or during bicycling lessons in the park. There is a sequence in this film that tellingly contrasts the material and emotional aspects of caring. Advised by his lawyer to calculate the 'pros' and 'cons' of pursuing the custody case for care of Billy, Ted finds his 'con' column filling up speedily while the 'pro' side of the sheet remains blank. Allowed a glimpse of what he is writing, we read: 'No privacy; work affected; no social life; **no let up**'. This realistic evaluation of the balance sheet of caring is quickly undermined by the director cutting immediately to a scene of Ted fondly hugging a sleepy Billy.

While mothering has been constructed as sacred, self-sacrificing and asexual, fathering in 1980s' popular media discourse is represented as trendy, fun and physical. Athena posters reveal naked men holding babies aloft; advertisements place infants on shoulders and backs. Images of men cradling babies passively in the manner of the Madonna figure are still rare. Calvin Klein's print advertisements for the fragrance Eternity depict a mother gazing lovingly into the eyes of her daughter, while an equivalent image for men shows a father carrying his son on his shoulders. Even *Baby Boom* which, as critics have pointed out, shares many qualities with the *Three Men* films (see, for example, Williamson, 1988a), makes J. C.'s conversion to motherhood both more smooth and less hilarious than the three men's erratic and comic acquisition of fathering skills (Kaplan, 1992, pp. 196–8).

The construction of fatherhood as fun depends in part on the 1980s' consumerist tendency to depict babies as the latest fashion accessory. The fashionable appendage for the new man used to be the cat; now it is a baby. It is difficult to resist the conclusion that both serve identical roles, stressing the man's intrinsically loving and caring nature without putting him to the test of adult human relationships. In a world of minimalist design, hi-tech sophistication and regulated lifestyles, the baby injects chaos, warmth and vitality. As Judith Williamson puts it, 'Babies become the signifiers of emotional life, in representation, now that women are no longer available for that task' (1988a, p. 45).

In *Three Men and a Little Lady* (1990), the sequel to *Three Men and a Baby*, there is a moment when the contradiction between adult needs and the responsibilities of childcare threatens to break through the light-hearted comedy. Deprived of sex and fulfilling adult relationships, the three 'fathers' are asked by Sylvia (Mary's biological mother) to confront the demands of caring for a school-age child. The seriousness of the conflict between their sexual needs and the demands of surrogate mothering is quickly undermined by the men's jocular ripostes, and more extensively by the plot's development. Sylvia's solution, to marry the cold and hypocritical English actor, Edward, cast increasingly as the 'evil' father, is eventually overturned, after a series of fantastical and improbable events. In a fairy-tale ending, Peter, one of the original three fathers, stimulated by Edward's reference to Mary as a 'little shit', finally declares his love for Sylvia and carries her off to the altar. The material problem of caring is answered by the most traditional of endings.

Consumerism is a stronger influence in these films than feminism. Although they break the mythology of women's natural talent for caring (in both *Kramer vs Kramer* and *Three Men and a Baby* the mothers themselves renounce this expectation), what they offer in its place is a new lifestyle fantasy. It is significant that none of these male parents has yet had to deal with an awkward adolescent (*Three Men and a Tearaway?*), or make any major sacrifice in order to balance childcare and career fulfilment. Relating to babies, despite its self-evident frustrations, poses none of the tests of caring most commonly raised by women and feminism, such as the ability to listen and respond; the ability to empathize; and the struggle to balance one's own priorities with those of others. Although Ted Kramer loses his high-profile job in advertising, the rewards, the film suggests, outweigh the disadvantages by turning him from a career-obsessed selfish person into a rounded human being. The daily problems of combining work and care seem in this film to amount to no more than running for taxis. In *Three Men and a Baby*, not even this degree of difficulty is suggested. Baby as appendage can be slung on actor Jack's back during rehearsals, or carried round wearing her own miniature hard-hat by Peter, the architect. The versions of caring linked on the screen to male parents do little to question basic gender roles.

A different version of the caring man has appeared in recent years in films about AIDS. Built in part around the stereotype of gay men as 'naturally' more caring, because supposedly more 'effeminate' than heterosexual men, the paradigm of caring that emerges in the film *Longtime Companion* (1990), a low-budget film distributed to a wider audience through television, is nevertheless one drawn from masculine

genres such as the western. The one death-bed scene in this film is between David (Bruce Davidson) and his partner Sean (Mark Lamos).
David emerges as the 'hero' of the film, becoming the leader and adviser
to the increasingly alarmed and besieged group of friends. His parting
from Sean is filmed, despite the markedly different context, in the style
of the western hero reassuring his partner as he faces death. Urging Sean
repeatedly to 'let go', he provides the solidity of masculine companion-
ship, not the tearful emotionalism of female partings in films such as
Terms of Endearment, *Fried Green Tomatoes* or *Steel Magnolias*.

What is hinted at in *Longtime Companion*, although it never becomes
a pivotal centre of narrative interest, is the transference of private
values of caring into the public arena of AIDS campaigning. Alan, alias
Fuzzy the lawyer, is by the end of the film fully involved in AIDS work
despite his earlier refusal to participate, and Willie has overcome his
fear of catching the HIV virus to act as a 'buddy'. Constructed for much
of the film, in true postmodern fashion, as a lifestyle grouping, the 'gay
community's' capacity to function also as a network for practical support and political solidarity is less forcibly enunciated in this film, but
the connection is implied, especially in scenes in the latter stages of the
film set in the support offices. *Longtime Companion* in this sense
establishes, however tentatively, a link between the personal and the
political absent from many of the women's films of the 1980s and 1990s.

Monstrous mothers

The aberrant mother-figure is the most dreaded of all the monstrous-
feminine symbols. Since maternal instincts are supposedly innate, the
mother who reverses the caring paradigm to assail and kill her victims
earns a special place in the gallery of horrors. In the 1980s and 1990s,
films sought graphic situations in which to depict this treachery. The
monstrous feminine appeared in the guise of the 'alien' of the horror
film, willing to rip bodies apart, or crept surreptitiously into the sanctity
of the happy family home, invited in as the trusted nanny, in *The Hand
that Rocks the Cradle* (1992). Both this film and *Aliens* (1986) end with
a fight to the death between two women, each of whom claims her
maternal rights.

In *Aliens*, James Cameron presents Ripley (Sigourney Weaver) as the
intelligent, androgynous leader pitting her wits against the monster. Her
masculine appearance is softened by her caring adoption of the child,
Newt, found alive on the base. Ripley becomes the armed maiden of

Fig. 10 Sigourney Weaver as armed 'mother'. *Aliens* © 1986 Twentieth Century-Fox Film Corporation. All rights reserved

legend, but now with additional maternal responsibilities. The image of her bearing child and arms (*see* Fig. 10), taken out of the context of the film, suggests a paradigm clash between the mother and the warrior. Within the film, the rescue of the child, which endangers Ripley's own safety, personalizes her campaign, as the tussle begins between two 'mothers'. Kitted out in the protective shell of the mechanical loader, her challenge to the alien to leave Newt alone: 'Get away from her, you bitch!', leaves no doubt about the nature of this battle.

Despite the generic differences, the final struggles in *The Hand that Rocks the Cradle* bear the same characteristics, as Claire (Annabella Sciorra), the natural mother of Emma and Joe, battles for survival and possession of her family against the invading nanny (Rebecca de Mornay). The nanny has abused the family's trust and taken on the role of surrogate mother, breast-feeding the baby, and turning Emma against her real mother. The publicity still for this film graphically depicts Rebecca de Mornay highlighted in colour, rending apart the happy family scene (in black-and-white). Both the alien and the nanny are perverse mother-figures, the alien in her destructive reproduction and the nanny in her attempt to compensate for the loss of her own baby, following the shock of her husband's suicide. Claire, who initiated the abuse allegations against the husband which led to his death, becomes the focus of her revenge. The elemental nature of the struggle between two mothers acquires symbolic dimensions through the 'earth mother' connotations it provokes. With women cast as the fountains of life and givers of energy to the planet, the battle between them becomes rudimental and raw in a way unfamiliar in struggles between two male figures. Men struggle for power and supremacy, with no equivalent mythological representation of a battle for paternity.

Sisterhood and caring

The 1980s and 1990s have produced a number of films dealing with the relations between women. Following the success of television shows such as *Kate and Allie* and *The Golden Girls*, and the popularity of *Cagney and Lacey*, Hollywood has taken the commercial risk of reinventing the women's film. While many of these films exude sentimentality, particularly through the mechanism of the death-bed scene that injects pathos into the narrative, they have also been touched by feminism in their presentation of the strength that women derive from each other.

Claudia Weill's low-budget *Girlfriends* (1978) was an early exploration of female friendship from an overtly feminist perspective. This film investigates what happens to a close relationship between two young women who have shared a flat and much more besides when one of them gets married. Susan (Melanie Mayron), arriving late for a planned visit to Anne (Anita Skinner), accuses her friend of having betrayed her by getting married: 'Marriage means the only time I get to see you alone is if Martin [Anne's husband] is busy. I wanted a friend'. Anne, on the other hand, calls Susan selfish and clearly envies her independence: 'You have your own place . . . a job, a show even [Susan is becoming a professional photographer], a new boyfriend, and you're still free'. Neither woman's relationship with her man is shown to be ideal, and each has to struggle for her independence. At the end of the film, they are reunited, as Susan abandons her boyfriend to visit Anne, alone in the country after a secret abortion. Yet *Girlfriends* gives no guarantee of blissful sisterly permanence, as Martin's car draws up and Anne rises to meet him. The open ending of this film, as Annette Kuhn comments, suggests that 'the women's relationship continues to be problematic and contradictory, and yet important enough to be continued' (1982, p. 137).

Claudia Weill's experience as a documentary film-maker influences the naturalism of *Girlfriends*. Its narrative development endorses sociological research which indicates that marriage can both cause problems for the maintenance of women-to-women relationships and strengthen the importance of these (see O'Connor, 1992, pp. 56–89). While romantic fiction suggests that heterosexual love fulfils all a woman's emotional needs, evidence has been mounting over the last two decades that this mythology is rarely borne out in practice (see, for example, Hite, 1987, discussed in Chapter 2).

Girlfriends was atypical of its generation both in style and narrative development. Relationships between women were not yet popular material for fictional treatment. As Julie d'Acci (1987) has explained, *Cagney and Lacey* had to overcome an obstacle course to get onto the networks and survived there only against repeated, and ultimately successful, institutional pressures to destroy it. First conceived in 1974 by writers Barbara Avedon and Barbara Corday, apparently in reaction to Molly Haskell's pessimistic comments on the roles of women in film at that time, it took until 1982 to get this crime series accepted by CBS. Even then, controversy surrounded the casting of Meg Foster as Cagney. Felt to be insufficiently feminine and glamorous, she was replaced after six months by Sharon Gless. Although perceived by the CBS managers as a potentially dangerous programme, its feminism was a veneer that eventually showed a number of cracks. The value of home life was endorsed through the character of Mary Beth Lacey who, as a married and caring mother, was presented as the more stable and positive of the two women. As the series progressed, Cagney descended from independent, opinionated and self-reliant single woman to an unhappy, tormented individual, broken by her father's death and her own alcoholism. In addition, the plots often centred on children, or on the softer crimes, bringing the programme within a paradigm of femininity that was also connoted by Cagney's glamorous appearance.

Described by some critics (e.g. Alcock and Robson, 1990) as 'a fundamentally reactionary text consistent with the mood of the late eighties', *Cagney and Lacey* was welcomed by others as establishing a subversive 'female gaze' (e.g. Gamman, 1988). What this series did achieve was the construction of a strong female relationship based on work rather than family or friendship networks. It also succeeded in keeping sentimentality at bay despite the soap-style interest in the characters' private lives. Their caring support for each other is strengthened by their tetchy quarrels and rivalries. When Mary Beth is awaiting results of tests on the suspected return of her breast cancer, the characters' shared anxiety produces sharp exchanges. When Cagney enquires if she's had the results, Lacey testily asks why she's suddenly so concerned. This leads to the following exchange:

C: You're my partner. I care about you.
L: Then why didn't you ever ask me how I was feeling when Alice had the colic and we was up all night for nine weeks straight ...?
C: How the hell was I supposed to know about that?
L: You could have asked ... Tell the truth, Christine. Would you want the details if all I had was a broken leg?
C: You can't die of a broken leg, Mary Beth.

This scene ends here, but later in the car Cagney accuses Mary Beth of keeping her worries to herself. The representation of caring as involving difficult negotiations around other people's protective shells makes this more convincing than an indulgence in shared emotional outbursts would be. The episode ends with Mary Beth reaching out to clasp Cagney's hand as she is about to receive her results. The solidarity between the two is reasserted non-verbally.

Cagney and Lacey was also significant in locating the two women in a contemporary downtown environment. In the women's films of the 1980s and 1990s, the tendency has been to set them in the historical past (e.g. *The Color Purple, Fried Green Tomatoes, A League of Their Own*), or in a small-town setting (e.g. *Steel Magnolias*). By removing the unease of the modern city, these films replay the romantic values of community and family that have been part of the American Dream. It is even questionable, at least from the perspective of a white viewer, whether the film version of *The Color Purple* allows the unease of racial tensions to creep too far onto its narrative agenda. Apart from the brief episode of Sofie's hitting of the mayor's wife, this is an all-black universe where issues of gender oppression are more clearly given narrative priority over racial oppression than they were in Alice Walker's novel. There, the African letters from Celie's sister, Nettie, with their own accounts of racial intolerance and tensions, project onto a wider canvas the racism that is also endemic in the American South.

The equation of sisterhood with timeless emotional bonding in this new generation of women's films is accentuated by the death of one of the central characters. *Beaches* (1988), *Steel Magnolias* (1989) and *Fried Green Tomatoes* (1991) all share this feature. In *Beaches* and *Fried Green Tomatoes* the effect is to complete the taming of the wilder woman: CC Bloom (Bette Midler) in *Beaches*, and the young Idgie Threadgoode (Mary Stuart Masterson) in *Fried Green Tomatoes*. Both are presented at the beginning of the films as tomboys, extroverts and exhibitionists who break various codes of feminine behaviour. The development of fierce and protective attachment to one specific friend in the course of the film signifies as much a journey towards femininity as an exploration of sisterhood. Although both Idgie and, especially, CC Bloom (in keeping with Bette Midler's star image) retain their fun-loving sparkle, the softening of each woman's image through her commitment to her dying friend is unmistakable.

Despite these limitations, the transfer of the narrative interest from heterosexual development of male/female interaction to sisterly bonding, articulates the transformative power of sisterhood, and confounds the dominance of the 'male gaze'. Indeed, it is a frequent criticism of this group of films that it reduces masculinity to the position of the caricature. The male characters are either weak or laughable, offering few possibilities of positive identification. Friendships between women, on the other hand, are represented as capable of working miracles on low self-esteem. In all the films, in keeping with theories of gender discourse, relations with husbands or male partners lack the intimacy and constancy of the relationship with the female 'best friend'. In *Fried Green Tomatoes*, *The Color Purple* and *A League of Their Own* a woman who lacks confidence in her own abilities is encouraged by her interaction with other women to find her inner strength and develop a more fulfilling life. Significantly, the low self-esteem of Evelyn (Kathy

Bates) in *Fried Green Tomatoes*, Celie (Whoopie Goldberg) in *The Color Purple* and Kit (Lori Petty) and Marla (Megan Cavanagh) in *A League of Their Own* is expressed partly in terms of dissatisfaction with their appearance. Discourses of the body, as we will see in Chapter 7, often act as vicarious indicators of women's sense of self-worth or lack of it.

Evelyn (*Fried Green Tomatoes*) is overweight and sexually repressed. By the end of the film, thanks to her relationship with the older woman Idgie (alias Ninny) Threadgoode (Jessica Tandy) she has become exuberantly lively, self-confident and assertive. In *The Color Purple*, Celie's characterization by others (Mister and, initially, Shug) as ugly, powerfully indexes her oppression. In a tender scene, which skirts the lesbian relationship between Shug and Celie that Alice Walker makes explicit in her novel, Shug (Margaret Avery) persuades Celie to look at herself in the mirror without coyness or self-criticism. While the novel suggests a more gradual development of self-confidence through Shug's tutorship, the film transforms this scene into the turning-point in Celie's life, giving her the courage to stand up to her brutal husband and eventually to leave him and develop her own life and talents. Kit, in *A League of Their Own* develops the confidence to beat her sister at her own game, while Marla becomes an outgoing, sexually alive woman thanks to the support of her sisters in the team.

While bitchiness forms part of the discourse of these films, particularly where, as in *Steel Magnolias* and *A League of Their Own*, they focus on a group of women, they transcend this with humour and solidarity. A film about the All-American Girls' Professional Baseball League (based on an actual development at the start of World War II) would be implausible without an element of competitiveness, but Penny Marshall, the director of *A League of Their Own*, has taken pains to modulate this throughout the film with scenes of sisterly co-operation. Bus journeys to matches become occasions for sharing confidences, with medium close-up shots framing pairs of women talking intimately to each other. The paradigm of rowdy group camaraderie which we would expect from an equivalent male scene is replaced with a paradigm of closeness and intimacy. In *Steel Magnolias*, the director, Herbert Ross, includes frequent shots of women rallying round each other, tightly knit within the frame, however different their outlooks and however incompatible their temperaments. After the death of Shelby (Julia Roberts), the female characters break away from their male partners at the funeral to form a supportive tableau with Shelby's mother M'lynn (Sally Field).

Thelma and Louise, in its depiction of a female relationship, is markedly different from the other films I have discussed in this section. Visual rhetoric and soundtrack take over from dialogue as the major bearers of the narrative. Relying on the action interest of the road movie and the spectacular quality of Ridley Scott's directing, and filmed in an environment more typically associated with the masculine genre of the western, this film invites association with the road movie or the 'male buddy' movie rather than the women's film. The song soundtrack in *Thelma and Louise*, beyond its commercial purpose, has a powerful narrative effect in strengthening our sense of these women's pleasure and developing power.

Caring, it is suggested in this film, is not the same thing as emotional intimacy. In those scenes where the two women share an interior space, as in the motel, they are frequently shot at the edge of the frame, with the distance between them emphasized rather than bridged. Despite the restraint in articulating their feelings to each other, their relationship grows from carefree vibrancy to a more solemn exchange of trust. One of the most poignant moments in the film comes when Thelma, now self-confident and sure of what she wants, suspects that Louise is going to do a deal with the police. Aware that Louise has a potentially satisfactory personal relationship to return to, she fears betrayal. Hesitatingly, at first, but with a growing assurance, she says 'Somethin's crossed over in me, and I can't go back. I mean I just couldn't live'. Louise replies, again without sentimentality, 'I know; I know what you mean'. The transition from heterosexual dependency to self-reliance and the freedom of their mutual understanding produces the final decision to drive over the edge of the canyon, their hands clasped defiantly in solidarity and determination.

What the 'something' is that has crossed over in Thelma is less clear. Her transformation into an independent woman, capable of executing a robbery at gunpoint and of locking a troublesome cop in the boot of his car, comes partly from imitation of male action. She carries out the store robbery using the exact words and actions described by J. D. (Brad Pitt), the man with whom she has spent a passionate night in the motel and who has robbed herself and Louise of all their money. The 'little woman' whom Darryl describes as incapable of handling a gun may be recast as a gun-toting strong woman, capable of controlling herself and others, but this is inspired by fantasy rather than feminism.

The pleasure that *Thelma and Louise* offers women is precisely that of an exhilarating fantasy. Despite the ambiguous ending, the revenge the women wreak on the police officer and on the sexist truck driver encourages women to identify with the triumph of the central characters, at the same time as it provokes the reaction 'if only it were so simple'. Unlike the convincing industrial setting of *Norma Rae*, where solidarity is hard won and any triumph expensive in personal costs, the frontier landscape of *Thelma and Louise* offers the opportunity of symbolic victory. Out there in the wilderness, strange alliances have long been wrought in American cultural texts. The topicality of *Thelma and Louise* lies in its upbeat celebration of woman's potential, its declaration in favour of a universe where signifiers of pleasure and vitality take over from those of struggle and contestation. *Norma Rae* is located in the feminist discourse of the 1970s; *Thelma and Louise* in the postfeminist universe of the 1990s.

In conclusion

This chapter has identified two potentially positive developments in the cultural history that has associated caring with femininity. The first is that motherhood is no longer the only paradigm for caring, with women's relations with each other acquiring increasing narrative interest. In fictional forms, representations of the 'good' and 'bad' mother continue, but in more extravagant plot constructions than before. The second gain of recent years has been the evolution of a link between masculinity and caring. Neither development is inconsequential, but neither is untroubled either.

While the polarity between 'good' and 'evil' mothers may have subsided in fictional forms, the mythology remains active in popular newspaper coverage of family relations. Women there still carry the burden of the health or disease of the family, which is in turn constructed as a microcosmic version of the wider social fabric. By extension, women, like Eve, carry humanity's future on their shoulders. Only rarely does the network of social and economic factors that make up the structural foundations of family life intrude into this 'factual' narrative. When in Britain one of the 'Home Alone' mothers of 1993 was discovered to be leaving her child alone during the day in order to earn enough money to prevent her being a burden to the British taxpayer, the tabloid press had difficulty steering a course between support for her intentions and moral condemnation for her unmotherly behaviour.

In opening up the construction of caring to give greater prominence to women's relations with each other, film and television programmes have helped to give a higher profile to women's friendships. At the same time, the manner in which these are represented has replayed some of the tired versions of womanliness that existed in nineteenth-century novels, even if there the object of the woman's attention was almost always men. While the change in focus is welcome, more narrative questioning of the reduction of caring to intimacy and to see-saw gyrations between tears and laughter would buckle the frame as well as the content of the picture that characterizes caring as part of the female genes. In the same decade as many of the film representations of strong and supportive sisterhoods, women anti-nuclear protesters in Britain fought for honest coverage from the British media. Running a peaceful protest against the siting of American cruise missiles in Britain at Greenham Common, this wide spectrum of women was reduced to a strident bunch of raving lesbians and woolly-hatted extremists by most of the media that bothered to cover them (see Hollingsworth, 1986; Young, 1990 for more details). The tabloid press diverted attention from the positive aspects of these women's caring by focusing instead on their abandonment of their 'proper' maternal and wifely roles. Women's roles in caring about the future of the planet, or in rectifying injustices committed in the workplace, or in campaigning for improved health provision for women or for rights for women in oppressive régimes, rarely filter through into news prominence, and have made little more than a scratch mark on the polished surfaces of television drama and film.

Curiously, it is advertisers who have recognized the link between women's caring and the future of the environment. When in the 1980s marketers woke up to the potential of the 'green consumer' as a new niche market, it was women who were primarily targeted. Luscious green landscapes and soft-focus images of mothers cradling babies were the most frequent images used to trigger associations of environmental concern. As the novelty of green consumerism faded, and caring for the planet became less fashionable than caring for one's body, these images disappeared from advertising, too. At the same time, men's caring natures were being discovered by a multitude of advertising agencies. The 'new man' and the 'caring father' were commercially motivated inventions as evidence mounted that supermarket shopping was attracting more male trolley-pushers and that the increasing range of male toiletries and male fashion was having difficulty making an impact on its target market. Adopted into fictional form, the cue of the link with consumerism was already set. Designer babies, designer toddlers and the paraphernalia that went with them were, it was hoped, to become the new status symbols of the post-AIDS man. Caring, newly detachable from its feminine roots, was, like other postmodern signs, only to be skin-deep. As journalist and writer Suzanne Moore succinctly put it: 'Caring has to mean more than caring about how one looks. Two decades of feminist demands that men should be more sensitive must surely result in something more than men with sensitive skin?' (1988, p. 58).

6

Sex 'n spice

I'm not going to confess all my secrets, Nick, just because I have an orgasm.
(Catherine Tramell to Nick Curran in *Basic Instinct*, 1992)

If what you want is total female sexuality, be honest. The beautiful sex
organ is between your ears, not between your legs.
(Nola Darling's psychiatrist in Spike Lee's film *She's Gotta Have It*, 1986)

Men still have everything to say about their sexuality.
(Hélène Cixous, *Laugh of the Medusa*, 1975)

It is a well-known joke in Britain that in the weeks before Christmas
the queues in Marks and Spencer consist of men buying their partners
or wives exotic underwear; and in the weeks after Christmas they
contain files of weary women exchanging these for cotton knickers or
thermal vests. However true or apocryphal this is, it encapsulates the
longstanding mismatch between men's fantasies about women's bodies,
and women's resistance to having their femininity and their sexuality
defined through masculine discourses. This chapter and the next will
investigate both the popular discourses of women's sexuality and
women's bodies in the media, and the extent to which these are now
becoming the site of a struggle against masculine definitions. Whether
media representations have kept pace with, or lagged behind, women's
practical struggles for possession of these colonized territories is a key
question underlying the discussion that follows.

This chapter concentrates on the representation of female sexuality;
the next on the body. Both are areas that women practise as well as
encounter daily in representational form. It is here, therefore, that the
sharpest mismatch potentially exists between women's experiences and
the constructions of these, often from a masculine perspective, in the
mainstream media. Michel Foucault (see Chapter 2) would argue that
both the practice and the representations are equally discursive. If we
assume that discourse is like a socially and ideologically constructed
palette from which we all select our colours, this makes considerable
sense, but it is equally clear that there is a difference between painting

our own pictures and looking at someone else's. This distinction acquires particular importance when what we construct from the palette is also a form of public communication. While sexuality is primarily expressed in private, presentation of the body and fashion are increasingly recognized as public languages.

In comparison with the myths of femininity that earlier chapters have considered, the mythology of female sexuality appears to have changed radically in the course of this century. We have moved a considerable distance from the view that only 'bad' girls enjoy their sexuality. Yet questions of who defines and controls the discourses of female sexuality remain. The issue of dominant voice is especially complex in this area, as the earlier discussion of fantasy (Chapter 3) began to explore. With fabricated first-person accounts of women's sexual desires and pleasures occupying the pages of men's pornographic magazines, and scenes of lesbian sexual encounters or women masturbating appearing as regular features in male pornographic films and videos, the battle for control in expressing women's sexuality offers more than usual opportunities for friendly fire.

As Foucault explains in the first volume of his *The History of Sexuality* (1981), it is a mistake to think that sex has only recently emerged into public discourse after a period of repression. Since the eighteenth century, a multifarious array of discourses has volubly competed for our attention, presenting sex as variously mysterious, dangerous, exciting, delightful and intensely significant. Far from being reticent about sex, he claims, we are never done talking about it, in discourses as apparently opposed as the Catholic confessional and scandalous literature. Foucault is surprisingly reticent about the different construction of female and male sexuality, encouraging some feminist theorists to detach female sexuality from discourse and present it as an essence directly suppressed by patriarchy. This implies some prior, submerged, female sexuality that needs to be excavated from underneath the rubble of male definitions, as if sexuality could float free of social and historical influences (McNay, 1992, pp. 32–8).

This chapter argues instead that we need to examine the discourses through which female sexuality has been constructed if we are to find ways of exploring what else, and alternatively, female sexuality might mean. In the ideological struggle so far this century, the major contestants for establishing the dominant discourse have been sexology, feminism, consumerism and postfeminism. These have impinged, too, on our thinking about male sexuality, but our cultural habit of constructing the feminine as problematic tends to ignore this fact. Although this chapter will not depart radically from this trend, it will argue that one of the key problems with current representations of female sexuality is that these have undergone more evident changes than the portrayal of male sexuality. In this way, the discourses articulated through film or advertising especially have cut free of the shifts in the balance of power that would accompany discursive change in the non-fictional world.

Sexology and sexual advice

Women's entitlement to sexual pleasure, at least within marriage, was beginning to be recognized by the early twentieth century. Marie Stopes was only one of a number of writers of the period to acknowledge that sexual pleasure for women did not have to be secondary to men's. The astonishing ability of her *Married Love* (1918) to reach sales of 400,000 in hardback over a five-year period (Melman, 1988, p. 3) indicated that advice on birth control and sexual matters attracted an eager audience. Writers such as Stopes, Dora Russell and Stella Browne located female sexual pleasure firmly within the 'maternal cycle' (Coote and Campbell, 1982, p. 217), and Stopes' interest in birth control was allied to her interest in eugenics, but the audacity of these writers in suggesting that women were entitled to equal pleasure to men was startling in an era that more generally construed motherhood as a sexless state.

Havelock Ellis's *The Erotic Rights of Women* (1918) agreed with the feminist view of the time that women were entitled to the fulfilment of their sexual desires, but his earlier *Studies in the Psychology of Sex* (1913) has drawn fire from later generations of radical feminists for endorsing a view of male sexuality as driven by uncontrollable urges and a need to dominate. Indeed, Margaret Jackson argues polemically that Ellis's work constitutes 'a counter-attack against feminism and women's increasing independence' (Coveney *et al.*, 1984, p. 53). Debate about the relation between sexological and feminist discourse also surrounds the discoveries of Kinsey *et al.* (1953) and of Masters and Johnson (1966).

Sexual Behavior in the Human Female (Kinsey *et al.*, 1953), based on interviews with almost 6,000 women from 1938 to 1952, presented a major challenge to Freudian definitions of female sexual pleasure and to women's dependence on penile penetration. It uncovered the existence of the clitoral rather than the vaginal orgasm and, more controversially for the time, found that many women preferred this form of stimulation. Masters and Johnson adopted a more physiological approach in their investigation into human sexual behaviour, relying on the evidence of a sample of 382 women aged 18 to 78 and of 312 men aged 21 to 89. What they established clearly was that men and women shared comparable sexual responses: 'Attempts to answer the challenge inherent in the question, "What do men and women do in response to effective sexual stimulation?", have emphasized the *similarities, not the differences*, in the anatomy and physiology of human sexual response' (1966, p. 8). This study also confirmed Kinsey's claims about the clitoris, and found that 'understandably', masturbation produced the greatest intensity of sensation for women (ibid., p. 133). Women's sexual pleasure was found to surpass men's in two respects: first, in their capacity to enjoy multiple sequential orgasms, and second, in their ability to experience a more protracted period of orgasmic pleasure (ibid., p. 131).

These studies challenged the residual Victorian mythologies that women endured rather than enjoyed their sexuality, and that, without men, women could experience no sexual pleasure. At the same time, they have been vehemently attacked by radical feminists who argue that the sexologists' research turned women into obligatory MOMS (multi-orgasmic monsters) and that they ignored the logic of their own findings by concentrating exclusively on heterosexual rather than lesbian sexual relations (Coveney *et al.*, 1984, p. 97, *passim*). While it is simplistic to see the writings of these sexologists as part of a patriarchal conspiracy to perpetuate male dominance, as *The Sexuality Papers* tends to do (Coveney *et al.*, 1984), it would be more naïve still to argue that they presented a quasi-feminist challenge to male fantasies and feelings of control. The perception that the woman is enjoying whatever the man is sexually doing to her, or with her, is intrinsic to male heterosexual discourse (extending to the most perverse interpretations of resistive behaviour on the part of women in acts of rape or other forms of sexual violence).

The sexologists helped to reaffirm that sexuality was principally a matter of physical performance and athletic technique. This discourse was widely disseminated in the following decades through a steady supply of best-selling sex manuals and sex advice videos, encouraged by the 'permissive' attitudes to sex in the 1960s and by new contraceptive methods such as the pill. As Rosalind Brunt points out, many of the early examples of these in the 1970s claimed to be responding to women's liberation, but were, more accurately, exploiting and falsifying feminist terminology to produce new versions of heterosexual romance. While in traditional romantic narratives, the woman searching for the ideal man relied on 'her virginity for barter', the new sensuous woman engaging on the same quest 'must display a wide repertoire of sexual technique as her best exchangeable commodity' (Brunt, 1982, p. 158). As the bedroom was transformed into a sexual gymnasium, these guides did their best to convince heterosexual couples that sex was both exhilarating work and a liberating game. That this game had nothing to do with power relations differentiated it sharply from the discourse of feminism.

Even when women began to speak publicly in their own voices about their sexual feelings and experiences, through, for example, the work of Shere Hite and Nancy Friday, the difficulty of thinking about sexuality in different terms was evident. The *Hite Report* on female sexuality did, nevertheless, extend the definitions of female sexuality, starting provocatively even for the 1970s with a section on masturbation, and relegating intercourse to a later section. As Shere Hite explained: 'researchers must stop telling women what they *should* feel sexually, and start asking them what they *do* feel sexually' (1977, p. 60). The women who responded to her questionnaire expressed delight in being able to explore their own feelings, and contribute to knowledge about women's sexuality from a woman's point of view. Their answers, however, often indicated how male-driven their own experiences still were. Nancy Friday's *Women on Top* (1991) exults in the diversity of the powerful sexual fantasies she uncovers, comparing them favourably with the more guilt-ridden accounts of her earlier *My Secret Garden* (1973). Yet, she partly attributes the development of this new exhibitionism among women to the growth of the video market: 'It isn't just that women can take home films like *9½ Weeks* and *Blue Velvet* for closer scrutiny and instant replay, but as the 1980s rolled into the 1990s, X-rated films became more explicit, more available, and increasingly aimed at the female market' (1991, p. 295). Given this source material, it is not too surprising that many of her contributors construct a narrative very similar to those of male pornographic magazines.

Feminist discourses

Feminist writers such as Simone de Beauvoir and Kate Millett argued that sexuality was one of a number of key areas where women had to struggle to gain rights and entitlements if they were ever to establish their freedom from male rule. Their argument was political and structural. Neither proposed that wresting control of the orgasm from men provided a solution to women's problems. As Kate Millett wrote, 'Coitus can scarcely be said to take place in a vacuum; although of itself it appears a biological and physical activity, it is set so deeply within the larger context of human affairs that it serves as a charged microcosm of the variety of attitudes and values to which culture subscribes' (1977, p. 23). Kate Millett also argued that the long tradition of associating women's sexuality with the root of society's ills pre-empted easy reversal of negative connotations.

While Kate Millett wanted to put women's sexuality into its political context, Betty Friedan, in her influential book, *The Feminine Mystique* (1963), had pointed out that sex had already acquired symbolic significance for women. Her comment that 'sex is the only frontier open to women who have always lived within the confines of the feminine mystique' drew attention to its role as a vicarious magnet for women's unfulfilled aspirations across a range of fields. Where feminists put the stress on the difficulties of changing the balance of power in sexual *relations* (encapsulated in the slogan 'the personal is political'), the majority of younger women were exploiting more accessible and reliable contraception to experiment with sexual pleasure and desire. Helen Gurley Brown's celebration of the single life, *Sex and the Single Girl* (1963), quickly became a bestseller and set the tone for her revamp of *Cosmopolitan* in 1964. The potential tension between feminist discourses of sexuality and women's experience intensified as female sexuality became increasingly commodified in the 1970s and 1980s. With consumerist discourses offering self-discovery, fulfilment and ecstasy, feminist arguments about power and patriarchal dominance cut less ice.

The 'broad church' that was the women's movement in the 1970s did, in any case, splinter into a variety of groupings, in a pattern familiar to all oppositional political forces faced with prolonged resistance or apathy. Unity was easier when there were practical objectives to fight for, more difficult when issues of subjectivity and personal desire were at stake. In the sphere of sexuality, feminism was most coherent when campaigning on issues such as contraception, abortion, violence against women, or rape. Issues around sexual desire and sexual behaviour produced more heat. As Cora Kaplan notes: 'The possible positions on this troubling issue that can be identified as feminist range from a pro-pleasure, polymorphously perverse sexual radicalism, through cautious permissiveness, to anti-porn activism and a political lesbianism that de-emphasises genital sexuality' (1986, pp. 32-3). Sharp divisions began to emerge, particularly over pornography, between the pro-censorship lobby (Andrea Dworkin and Catharine MacKinnon were and are the leaders in this campaign) and those, such as Linda Williams, who argue that the best counter to the existing character of pornography is to make erotic material more widely available, for women as well as men (a useful account of these debates is to be found in Segal and McIntosh, 1992).

The most vociferous voices within feminism in recent years have been those of the radical feminists (e.g. Sheila Jeffreys, Adrienne Rich). They urge separatism and the avoidance of sexual contact with men since heterosexual relations can only, in their view, reproduce a power structure hostile to women. For radical feminism to suggest that lesbianism enables a purer form of sexuality depends on an essentialist belief that women are inherently different from men in their attitudes and emotions. As I have already suggested, this is a difficult position for feminism, with its commitment to change and intervention, to sustain. Recent critiques of this position (e.g. bell hooks, 1993b) have preferred to focus criticism on heterosexuality *as an institution* and avoid the personal attacks on heterosexual women that have sometimes accompanied the radical feminist position.

Consumerism and postfeminism

The commodification of female sexuality occurred in tandem with the growing awareness of sexological discourses, and the greater sexual freedom of a post-pill, pre-AIDS age. The uncertainties of feminism, grappling with the complexities of this area, presented little resistance to a predatory market-place. When the sexologists placed female sexual desires on the public agenda, they released an opportunity that no creative advertising agency could resist. Under pressure from the feminist lobby to pay more attention to women's changing roles and aspirations, one of the advertisers' favourite tactics was to take 'desire' and depoliticize it, transforming a complex concept into a harmless signifier of lifestyle aspirations. One of Shere Hite's respondents summed up the mismatch between feminism and the market-place thus: 'It seems to me that the sexual revolution has just given the con men the chance to sell douches and razors, but that you don't see much in the way of real free expression and happiness, or joy in the body and in sex' (1977, pp. 455–6).

By the 1980s consumerist discourses were rewriting sexual desire in ways that promised a private heaven on earth. Issues of the social construction of sexuality were removed to sociological textbooks, and experimentation and fun took over. The young women's magazines caught the fever to perfection. While the freedom encouraged by the market-place had beneficial effects in encouraging women to explore their own sexual preferences, and wriggle free of the wire-netting of taboos that kept their mothers constrained, the advent of postfeminist discourses of sexuality produced problematic consequences, too.

These have surfaced recently in the controversy over 'date rape' between young feminists, led by Katie Roiphe, and the generation of feminists reared on Susan Brownmiller's view that rape 'is nothing more or less than a conscious process of intimidation by which *all* men keep *all* women in a state of fear' (1976, p. 15). Roiphe (1994) argues polemically against 'rape-crisis' feminism, particularly in the United States, where worries over 'date rape' have led to repressive policing strategies on campuses. Her thesis is that an extended definition of rape, to include what she would prefer to define as 'bad sex', has turned feminism into a rule-governed orthodoxy, rather than the liberating movement she had understood it to be. Its new effect, she argues, is to breed a victim culture among young women, turning them back into weak, vulnerable creatures, afraid of their own sexuality.

While Roiphe has a point about the negative effects of campus policing policies (more likely in any case to protect the universities from embarrassing lawsuits than their female students from harassment), she speaks a postfeminist language about rape. Taking a robust attitude to the battle-zone of sexual relations, she underplays the dividing line between consenting fun and non-consenting invasiveness. Reared, as she herself puts it, in a culture of Madonna videos, 'horror movies and glossy Hollywood sex scenes', her plea is understandably for freedom; but her argument ignores the continuing issue of uneven power relations between the sexes. While policing is not the answer, neither is pretending that date rape occurs only in the imagination. Roiphe, in company with many women's magazines, captures the positive spirit of women's new self-confidence in sexual relations. What she and they relatively ignore is that new rules will work only if men as well as women decide that they want to play by them.

Sexuality in women's magazines and advertising

The history of young women's magazines since the 1960s indicates the uneven struggle between the discourses of the sexologists, consumerism and feminism. Addressing an individualistically minded readership, attracted by the aspirational quality of the glossy magazine, feature articles have tended to construct women's sexuality in postfeminist terms, emphasizing pleasure and achievement over struggle and unfulfilled desire. This enables a consistent tone in the appeal to readers and advertisers. At the same time, problem pages have more pragmatically dealt with the downside of a revolution that has generated confusion as well as new possibilities. Although feminism has been an influence here, it has been prone to co-option.

Glossy monthlies of the 1960s and even 1970s such as *Honey*, *She* and then *Cosmopolitan* exhibited a growing frankness about sex in their feature articles, and gave it a priority over domestic material, but the terms in which women's sexuality were discussed were not primarily those of feminism. *She*, reputedly the first magazine in the 1950s to break the taboo on sex in women's publications, was guarded about how it broached the subject. As Cynthia White put it in the late 1970s: 'It deals frankly and humorously with topics formerly considered unmentionable in polite women's journals, e.g. it has unblushingly informed its readers exactly what a bidet is for' (1977, p. 12). The new openness may have demystified novel objects of consumption, from the bidet to the vibrator, but it skirted nervously around questions of female desire.

Nova, a new magazine launched by IPC in 1965 expressly to appeal to the 'new woman', pioneered articles on women's sexuality and associated topics such as contraception and childbirth in an informative way, using graphic illustration as well as verbal text to aid readers' understanding. Addressing, in its own words, the woman with 'an inquiring mind and an independent outlook' (White, 1977, p. 19), *Nova* failed commercially partly because it neglected to forge an alliance between consumerist and sexual discourses. Assuming its readers to be in their late 20s or 30s, relatively affluent, and (at least in its early years) not always female, it was over-optimistic about its ability to attract quality advertising without pandering to consumer interests. In the late 1960s, as Janice Winship points out, the 'new woman' was likely to be younger than the *Nova* profile, and more attracted to IPC's less expensive *Honey*, launched in 1960, and already aligning the fun of sex with the fun of fashion and attention to the body (1987b, pp. 49–50). *Nova* limped into the 1970s, squeezed from different directions by the earnestly feminist *Spare Rib* (1972–93), and the increasingly successful *Cosmopolitan* (published in Britain from 1972). It was *Cosmo* that most accurately detected the kind of discussion of female sexuality which would appeal to advertisers; stressing the young woman's aspiration to shine in the game of (hetero)sexual play as an index of her ability to handle all interpersonal and work relations with self-confidence and panache, and relying on a paradigm of independence based on economic self-sufficiency and individualism.

Cosmo took its discursive cue from the findings of the sexologists, however much it dressed this up to imply a feminist inspiration. Sexual fulfilment, readily achievable, it implied, by the *Cosmo* girl who paid sufficient attention to the magazine's (and advertisers') advice on beauty and fashion, had nothing to do with a collectivist assault on masculine versions of women's sexuality. While feminism encouraged women to form consciousness-raising groups and work through their problems together, *Cosmo* adopted the pose of a quasi-feminist cheerleader, urging women onwards and upwards towards greater achievements. Its view of feminism was recently rearticulated in a special feature on 'Feminism Now' (October 1993): 'It's not about dungarees and hating men. Feminism is . . . Relevant. Positive. Powerful. Sexy. Strong'. Struggle is out: sexiness and power are in. Despite the feminist claim, the tone is distinctly postfeminist.

The cover regularly exhorts young women to make the most of every aspect of their lives. Pride of place is given to SEX (routinely emphasized in capital letters), in jokey, conversational discourse that establishes both complicity and intimacy between magazine and reader:

Could you handle SEX with
A boomerang penis
The man who has two
A thingy that grew from his thigh?
(*Cosmopolitan* cover, March 1993)

The world of work is equally a contest where the rules have to be learned if success is to be achieved. The analogy with sex is often made directly: 'Does SEX appeal rule? How *they* want you to dress at work' (ibid.). 'They' are the mysterious other sex whose power is implied in the attention that the magazine pays them, even if the ostensible aim is to undermine it: 'Coitus eruptus. Why men's orgasms are never as good as yours (poor little squirts)' (*Cosmopolitan* cover, December 1992).

The 'poor little squirts' still concoct the rules of the games that *Cosmo* unravels every month for its upwardly mobile readers. SEX is fun in *Cosmo*, but the challenge of game-playing is daunting. In an article in the regular 'Sex and the Single Girl' slot, Cynthia Heimel outlines the dilemma: 'The manoeuvering and the basic strategies are so difficult that I've needed three advisers, plus a shrink. . . . To conduct successful courtship procedures, you require the iron will of a four-star general and the flexibility of Baryshnikov' (May 1992, p. 99). Feminism isn't much help. Best friend Jane advises the smitten author to play hard to get: 'I don't care about feminism; men need a chase' (ibid.). Tongue-in-cheek this may be, but the trick of ensuring that feminism is compatible with pleasure and with men is also financially shrewd. Recognizing that almost a quarter of its readers are men, *Cosmo* has little incentive, either, to query the nature of male sexuality.

Similar trends are visible in the magazines of the 1980s that target even younger women. EMAP Metro's fortnightly *More!*, introduced in 1988 for an 18- to 30-year-old market quickly acquired a following among a younger age group than *Cosmo* (82% of its readers are aged under 25, as against 36% of *Cosmo*'s – figures from July 1993 to June 1994 JICNARS Readership Surveys). Its focus on sex as a source of pleasure for women never lets its readers forget that satisfying men is a central aim. From features on 'What MEN think we do wrong in bed' (cover announcement, 24 June–7 July 1992) to 'SEXUAL DEPRESSION Handling his post-passion blues' (cover announcement, 19 August–1 September 1992), the magazine constantly reiterates the need to take stock of the nature of male sexuality, without in any way challenging its predatory characteristics. *Company* even invites its readers, in a 'chilling account', to consider 'why men rape' through the words of the men themselves (November 1993). More routinely, self-evaluation quizzes play on the young woman's insecurity about the adequacy of her own sexual experience and skills. A set of questions on sexual communication in *More!* (10–23 June 1992) suggests that even for the under 25-year-olds, sex may be 'flagging' and should be pepped up with more exciting sex talk.

The formulaic nature of advice in young women's magazines is often accompanied by disclaimers. Having established how young women might behave or consume, the magazine reassures the reader that she should follow her own inclinations. The postfeminist woman is, after all, 'positive, powerful, sexy and strong'. The monthly *19* (IPC, 1968–), aimed at a similar market to *More!*, warns its readers that undressing in front of your man is 'one of the . . . scariest things . . . Unless you're Cindy C' (July 1992, p. 6). It then disowns any anxiety this generates by reminding us that boys also worry about their bodies and 'still dream of having a penis that peeps out the bottom of their Levi's'. A similar pattern recurs in its advice on how to perfect a 'blow-job'. Maintaining an emphasis on the centrality of penetrative sex, *19* situates the ideal 'blow-job' as 'generally' occurring 'before or after intercourse' and admits that many women find oral sex distasteful (the Kinsey report is cited as evidence). The article nevertheless encourages its female readers to give it a try, because 'boys cannot physically do it to themselves . . . but they do like it' (July 1992, pp. 7–8). Having established the primacy of pleasing your man, using the variety of tricks the sexologists have outlined, the magazine adds a belated feminist coda: 'Sexual acts should be mutually enjoyable, not endurance tests or acrobatic feats, so never feel under pressure to do anything that you don't want to do' (ibid., p. 8). The contradiction between this advice and the cross-heading, 'Get on down', remains unresolved.

Despite their pretence to be open to their readers' voices, women's magazines often confine these to the problem pages. Readers have few opportunities to articulate their own desires and explore their own fantasies in the manner of the *Hite Report* contributors. This has two effects: it makes it easy for consumerist discourses to prevail in the discussion of female sexuality, and it heightens the sense that if sexuality is a problem in the late twentieth century, it is women, not men, who need to sort this out. The content of the advice has changed since women were encouraged in the 1950s to put the sanctity of the family before their own interests (Winship, 1983, pp. 46–7), but women continue to carry the burden of setting the interpersonal world to rights. By identifying the body and sexual issues as separable from the emotions or matters of the heart, several problem pages, especially in younger women's magazines, sharpen the distinction between the approaches of sexologists and feminists. Health experts offer sexologically inspired advice on sexual technique while feminist thinking filters into the recommendations of the 'agony aunts' on the solutions to emotional or interpersonal difficulties. As early as 1978, Irma Kurtz was exhorting a woman who couldn't make up her mind whether she should follow her partner when he moved to take up a new job: 'If you want him, and your career will suffer, then you must choose. That's what women's rights are all about, you know: the right to make your own choices and to take responsibility for the results' (*Cosmopolitan*, November 1978, p. 40).

Yet, the feminist nature of this advice is skin-deep. Advice to act decisively and assertively fits in with the aspirational drive of the monthly magazines, but it is logically flawed for women whose incapacity to solve their own problems suggests they are likely to be temperamentally reticent or possess at best a shaky self-confidence. Repeatedly, contemporary magazines suggest that women should initiate talk to solve their interpersonal problems ('Communication is an essential ingredient in making and sustaining relationships. You can't force him to live with you. But you can persuade him to talk about whatever is giving him cold feet . . . ', *19*, July 1993, p. 91); or that they should assert themselves ('stop being a doormat', *More!*, 19 August–1 September, 1992, p. 58; 'if you want someone with maturity and a sense of values, give this man the swift kick he deserves', *19*, July 1993, p. 90). This emphasis on self-reliance has been informed by feminism, but it repeats Irma Kurtz's version of 'what women's rights are all about': a matter of freedom, individual choice and self-determination. The conditions which make this difficult for women, and the responsibilities of men in relationships, are not tackled. Instead, the problem pages in women's monthly magazines reinforce the mythology that relationships are women's work, and that women have to take the initiative if improvements are to be achieved. The individualistic nature of the letter and answer format prohibits any consideration of the wider implications of feminist campaigns for personal equality.

Women are also able to speak out about their own sexuality in the first-person confessional feature. Largely reserved for those whose sexuality or sexual practices transgress the norms of heterosexual relationships perpetuated by the magazines, whether lesbians (*19*, November 1993), transvestites (*Marie Claire*, November 1993) or 'girls in porn' (*19*, July 1993), this sharpens the division between 'normal' and 'abnormal' sexuality. The erotic tradition of confessional accounts of sexual experiences translated into women's own words by men dates back to eighteenth-century novels, such as Samuel Richardson's *Pamela* (where Pamela's sexual victimization by her master is recorded in letter form), and John Cleland's pornographic parody of this in *Fanny Hill*. It continues even now to be incorporated in verbal accounts of sexual experiences in men's pornographic magazines. Women's magazines may not replicate the titillating and arousing discourse of these publications,

but the specialist use of first-person accounts to explore aspects of supposedly aberrant sexuality encourages a form of voyeuristic fascination
with the exotic.

The women's magazine treatment of lesbianism is symptomatic of this
trend. As Foucault points out, merely enabling a topic to get onto the
agenda does not of itself free up our attitudes to it. Although it is an
advance for women's magazines to recognize, in however fringe a manner, that lesbianism exists, they are happier to deal with it as a trendy
side issue rather than as an integral part of discussions of women's
sexuality. On the problem pages, at least in the glossies, lesbianism is
allowed more frequent mention. A recurring theme is the woman's fear
that she may be gay, or even bisexual. Advice varies from reassurance
that lesbian *fantasies* are a normal part of many women's heterosexual
love-making (*New Woman*, March 1993, p. 144) to suggestions that the
enquirer should contact relevant counselling groups to seek guidance
and clarify the nature of her sexuality (*More!*, 19 August–1 September,
1992, p. 58; *Company*, November 1993, p. 147). Even where lesbianism
does not feature explicitly on problem pages, young women's magazines
often recognize its existence by including lesbian and gay advice centres
or helplines in information boxes. While this is undoubtedly helpful, it
also enables the magazine to acknowledge lesbianism without committing itself to any meaningful discussion of the issue in its own terms.

Women's magazines have eagerly taken advantage of the dismantling
of moral taboos against the discussion and representation of female sexuality, but they have kept more than half an eye on the advertisers. In
the United States, the history of the women's magazine is similar in
many respects to the British, with those that have flourished, such as
Mademoiselle and *Seventeen* (and, of course, the American *Cosmo*,
Vogue and *Elle*) operating to the same formula as their British equivalents. Where the American publications differ most visibly is in their
greater segmentation by ethnicity as well as age. The size of the
non-white population makes it commercially viable to produce
magazines such as *Essence* for African-American women, or to run
Spanish-language editions of *Cosmo* for the Chicano population (see
McCracken, 1993, pp. 223–56 for further discussion).

The American magazine which most explicitly attempted to give
voice to feminist ideas was *Ms.*, founded in 1972. Dependent, like other
publications, on advertising revenue, it often produced contradictory
versions of female sexuality. By the late 1980s, advertisers were calling
the editorial tune (Faludi, 1992, pp. 134–5). Under the new ownership

since 1989 of Lang Communications, *Ms.* was relaunched in 1990 without advertising to enable it to pursue its feminist ideals. Relying on subscription, it will struggle for survival. Instead of glossy perfume advertisements on its back cover, it currently sports a 'No comment' feature displaying sexist advertisements collected by readers. *Ms.*, like its now deceased British equivalent, *Spare Rib*, retains an allegiance to feminism that provides a space for women to speak freely of their own desires. Its seriousness and its lack of visual appeal make it unlikely to entice readers away from its fun-loving competitors.

Advertising, as we saw in Chapter 3, responded to feminism with a cheeky sense of humour. The ability, in the wake of 'sexual liberation', to depict women as actively sensual was a bonus for agencies searching for new methods of appeal. As women in advertising were allowed sexual fantasies, the voice that spoke to these remained masculine. When the London Press Exchange introduced the Cadbury's Flake advertisement in 1961, it was a husky male voice-over that intoned the instruction to pleasure: 'By yourself. Enjoy yourself. Sixpence worth of heaven', over a black-and-white image of a woman lying back and erotically placing the Flake bar in her mouth. By the 1970s, the advertisement, now the responsibility of Leo Burnett, had developed its waterfall imagery and its more explicit (if mock-Freudian) sexual connotations, but the erotic voice was still male.

In the 1990s, the female voice is less coy. Some advertisers have awoken to the possibility of letting their women 'talk dirty' and express their own sexuality directly. The most controversial example at the time of writing in Britain is TBWA's 1994 campaign for Playtex Wonderbra. Featuring model Eva Herzigova, the advertisements use provocative captions to attract attention. The 'Or are you just pleased to see me?' caption (*see* Fig. 11) is a direct take-off of a famous Mae West line. The evocation of Mae West, most remembered for her single-line ability to taunt her men while inviting them into her boudoir, extends the distance between 'talking dirty' and having sexual freedom. While both Mae West and the Wonderbra model exude spirit and the enticement of pleasures to come, the game still revolves around pulling a man. If this reverses the conventional roles in predatory sexual play, it does little for rewriting the rules. The Wonderbra woman is nevertheless distinctive from Mae West in her ease with her own femininity. Mae West's self-conscious sashay and parodic acting draw attention to her performance as performance, in a way often reminiscent of the drag queen.

Fig. 11 1994 Wonderbra advertisement

Basic instincts or sleeping with the enemy?

In Chapter 4, I argued that film's recent explicitness in presenting sexually dynamic women perpetuated, rather than solved, the enigma of women's sexuality. In this section, I want to raise a number of more specific problems around the recent generation of sexually active women in film. How far can they be said to be exploring a specifically female sexuality? In particular, the use of lesbian and masturbation scenes in these films requires investigation. If, as I have suggested in relation to women's magazines, they are trying to rewrite the rules of sexuality for a liberated postfeminist age, we need to enquire whether male sexuality is correspondingly being toppled from its privileged position of the 'norm'.

The sexually predatory woman is not an invention of late twentieth century film. The 'vamp' and Mae West were early embodiments. A novel by Elinor Glyn, published in 1927 and translated into film, established Clara Bow as the 'It' girl, with 'It' defined in the late 1920s as a euphemism for sex appeal (Melman, 1988, p. 50). The erotically charged desert romance, *The Sheik* (1919), written by Edith Maud Winstanley under the pseudonym of E. M. Hull, also became a film starring the heart-throb of 1920s' female audiences, Rudolph Valentino (Melman, 1988, pp. 89–104; Gledhill, 1991, pp. 259–82). These novels and the films based on them recognized, well ahead of Nancy Friday, that women had sexual feelings and fantasies, but they kept alive the dominance of heterosexuality and the mythology of a submissive and even masochistic femininity by ensuring that a man initiated the sexual encounter, and that this was often violent and even brutal. The strict application of the Hays Code from the early 1930s until the 1960s cast a veil over the sexually precocious woman. As we saw in the case of film noir, alternative ruses had to be deployed to connote female sexuality.

Once the Hays Code lapsed, the film industry seized the opportunity to exploit the exciting and visually titillating potential of the 'liberated woman'. Male sexuality continued to be presented unproblematically as goal-driven and self-explanatory. As Molly Haskell pessimistically pointed out in the first edition of her *From Reverence to Rape* (1974), the 1960s and early 1970s were a bleak period for women's roles in American film. With the growing popularity of television in the 1950s and 1960s, the cinema's mass audience had been replaced by a more segmented and youthful clientele. Since this was assumed to be composed largely of single people, the 'women's film' and melodrama of the 1940s and 1950s became quickly extinct on the large screen, and reappeared as television soap opera. The decade that first allowed more explicit representation of sexuality turned instead to rape and brutality to establish its daring credentials. *Straw Dogs* (Peckinpah, 1972), with its infamous scene of Susan George yielding to the desires of her character's rapists, powerfully demonstrated that breaking the visual taboo on women's sexuality in popular culture could still be misogynistic and involved no necessary concessions to feminism.

In the same decade, *Looking for Mr Goodbar* (1977) focused on the sexually active woman, but was deeply ambivalent about her rights. A devoted teacher of deaf children by day, and a cruiser of singles' bars by night, Terry Dunn (Diane Keaton) uneasily straddles the divide between the 'good', nurturing mother-figure and the 'bad', hedonistic and pleasure-seeking 'whore'. Far from reconciling these oppositional paradigms of femininity, the film merely allows them to co-exist, offering the viewer points of identification with both positions. As Ann Kaplan points out, the camera films Terry's various sexual encounters from her point of view, but, in its narrative development, follows in the tradition of films which punish the single sexual woman for her moral transgression (1983, pp. 73–82). Terry, out on New Year's Eve for a final fling before altering her lifestyle, meets George, a homosexual whose inability to make love to her provokes her mockery and his revenge. Killed in a frenzied, violent rape, Terry receives the narrative punishment meted out in the 1940s to the *femme fatale*. The difference by the 1970s is that we are allowed to watch her perform sexually, as she openly takes the sexual initiative and is filmed enjoying her sexual pleasure.

In the 1980s and 1990s the sexual performance of the female characters has become more explicit and dominant. But while the well-publicized antics of a dominatrix-style Sharon Stone (*Basic Instinct*) or Madonna (*Body of Evidence*) have attracted most attention, other films, such as *9½ Weeks* (1985) and *Sliver* (1993) present a different, and more demeaning, version of female sexuality. Both these films retain the association between the sexually active woman, designer lifestyles and the creative professions (Elizabeth in *9½ Weeks* and Carly in *Sliver* work respectively in an art gallery and a publishing house). The central characters in these films are, however, portrayed as vulnerable and as prone to domination by men.

In *9½ Weeks*, Elizabeth (Kim Basinger) submits both to John's (Mickey Rourke) consumer whims and to his sadistic sexual tastes. She has no voice throughout the film to articulate her own feelings. John repeatedly ignores her point of view and expresses no interest in her thoughts on the expensive clothes he buys for her. The pattern repeats itself in their love-making, with Elizabeth submitting, sometimes willingly, to humiliating games to satisfy John's wishes. Visually, she is occasionally presented as sexually desiring, if ambiguously so. In one sequence she masturbates at home while watching slides. Shot in a style reminiscent of a lingerie advertisement (the film, like *Fatal Attraction*, was directed by Adrian Lyne, who has also worked in advertising), this scene connotes the wistfulness of the self-absorbed women familiar from the fashion features in women's magazines.

In another scene she strips and dances for her own and John's pleasure. Her silky underwear, and her playful brandishing of a whip, add emphasis to the fetishistic filming of her body in erotically angled and fragmented shots. Yet Elizabeth nevertheless reclaims the point-of-view often enough in this sequence to allow her to be the subject of her own sexual pleasure as well as the object of John's. These sequences are, however, contextually overshadowed by the more frequent scenes of Elizabeth being reluctantly blindfolded, or being intimidated into crawling across the floor on her hands and knees to satisfy John's obsessive and possessive sexual cravings. Although the coda at the end of the film tries to make a feminist statement, by having Elizabeth finally walk away from John's last charm offensive, this is tacked on unconvincingly.

Similarly, *Sliver* casts Sharon Stone in a role that reverses Catherine Tramell's strength and command of her actions in *Basic Instinct*. Carly Norris, despite her overt independence and designer lifestyle, has just come out of a bad marriage. The early scenes establish her vulnerability in the 'sliver' apartment block where she takes up residence by revealing her remarkable resemblance to Naomi Singer, seen plunging to her death in the opening shots of the film from the balcony of the same flat. As with Elizabeth in *9½ Weeks*, Carly is frequently lit and framed to accentuate her insecurity, and both women find themselves repeatedly in menacing locations. In addition, Carly is the object of a voyeur's attention as she moves around the 'private' space of her apartment. Even an early outdoor scene of Carly jogging in the park takes a sinister turn as she is pounced upon 'for fun' by Jack Landsford (Tom Berenger), who is one of the two men in the block pursuing her. The other, Zeke Hawkins (William Baldwin), she is drawn to like a magnet, despite her intellectual worries about his involvement in the mysteriously accumulating number of deaths occurring in the block. A weak plot is punctuated by their passionate love-making scenes, but the enigma of the killer's identity renders these threatening, too. Carly, unlike Catherine, is distinctly not in control. Like Elizabeth, her attempt to take command is withheld until the end of the film. Firing in disgust at the bank of screens on which her lover has been voyeuristically watching the antics of the entire block, including the death of Naomi Singer, she dismisses with contempt his soap-opera fantasies and exhorts him finally to 'Get a life!'.

What unites these films with *Basic Instinct* and *Body of Evidence* is the suppression of the woman's own voice and their unproblematic treatment of male sexuality. Catherine Tramell and Rebecca Carlson, as we saw in Chapter 4, remain ultimately as enigmatic as Elizabeth and Carly Norris. The absence of female friends excludes the possibility of confidences being shared about their sexual feelings. In *Sliver*, indeed, the rampant curiosity of Carly's colleague about every detail of her love life remains unassuaged, as Carly refuses to talk.

Male sexuality in all of these films remains predatory, opportunistic and fetishistic, turned on by silky underwear, or the toys of sadomasochism. This is one of the reasons why these films seem so misogynistic, despite the fantasies that some of them offer of female power. For the scenes of active female sexuality to be recuperable for women, they need to be accompanied by some questioning of the norms of male sexuality.

The forms that female sexuality takes in these films also leave women on the outside, watching from the position of the voyeur. Sex as performance, as 'taking' or 'being taken' maintains sexuality within a predominantly masculine paradigm, whatever the gender of the performer. Even the scenes of masturbation or lesbianism are employed in contexts that accentuate either the woman's vulnerability (*9½ Weeks* and *Sliver*) or her game-playing obsession with control (*Body of Evidence* and *Basic Instinct*). Although Sharon Stone comments fairly that the bath-tub masturbation scene in *Sliver* is not shot in the manner of 'an exhibitionistic sort of male fantasy', but as a private moment (*Empire*, September 1993), the privacy is questionable when the audience spectates on two levels: in colour as the actual film viewers, and in grainy blue film from the perspective of the 'sliver' voyeur. By accentuating our watching, these films replicate the voyeurism of pornographic films. Similarly, the lesbian relations of *Basic Instinct*, and Catherine's supposed bisexuality, remain matters of visible performance only. Indexed by embraces, touching up and exchanged kisses, they are tauntingly presented for our gaze through the eyes of the masculine onlooker. While the attacks on this film from the gay and lesbian community centred on the narrative associations between bisexuals and violence, this aspect of the film's textual construction remains problematic, also.

Despite its very different origins as an independent film, Spike Lee's *She's Gotta Have It* (1986) reproduces a number of these problems. The central character, Nola Darling (Tracy Camilla Johns), is black, independently minded, self-assured and, in her own words at the end of the film, definitely 'not a one-man woman'. As the film progresses, however, the audience is invited to consider whether Nola is, as one of her boyfriends, Greer, thinks, a nymphomaniac with a problem, who is using sex as a mask for a deeper search for truth or love, or a confident young woman at ease with her own sexuality who wants, as she claims at the end of the film, to retain control of her own body and her own mind. Both perspectives are on offer in the course of the film. We may be invited to laugh at Greer's self-important diagnosis of Nola's sexual desires, but they are also echoed in Jamie's repeated suggestion that Nola is merely using sex to search for some other source of fulfilment. At the same time, Nola sits astride her bed with the composure of a Buddha before a shrine.

Early in the film, the authority of the masculine voice is undercut by a humorous portrayal of male sexuality. In this respect, *She's Gotta Have It* contrasts with the other films discussed earlier. One of Spike Lee's aims in the film was to counter the one-dimensional caricature of black men in Alice Walker's *The Color Purple* (Simmonds, 1992, p. 210). We are invited to laugh at a succession of chat-up lines from a string of posturing aspirants for Nola's affections, and at the caricature of two of Nola's boyfriends. Mars (played by Spike Lee himself) is the joker, small in stature but wiry and intense with his baseball gear and his biking enthusiasm. Greer is the ego-tripping smooth-talker who thinks he can mould Nola as if she were 'a mere lump of clay'. But the third boyfriend, Jamie (Redmond Hicks), the most serious of the contenders, gradually assumes the dominant voice in the film, becoming increasingly impatient with what he perceives as Nola's uncertainty and fickleness. Narratively, the film begins to lend weight to his point of view.

In the early stages of the film, Nola talks directly to camera with a matter-of-fact nonchalance that leaves the men looking the more hysterical gender. Her self-possession and the authority of her voice are, however, seriously called into question both by the rape scene towards the end of the film and by the film's failure to allow Nola to comment directly on her sexual feelings. The events that lead up to the rape suggest that Nola's sexual self-assurance is cosmetic only. Frustrated by her reluctance to commit herself to him, Jamie has walked out of Nola's flat in a fury, to be replaced by Opal, her lesbian friend. When Opal makes sexual advances in an attempt to comfort Nola, Nola asks her to leave. What follows is a slow-motion sequence of shots of Nola's body as she begins to masturbate. From this the film cuts to Nola phoning Jamie and declaring that she needs him urgently. He reluctantly leaves his other girlfriend, imagining he is responding to an emergency. Feeling tricked by Nola, he brutally rapes her, taunting her verbally at the same time.

Through this sequencing, the audience is invited both to sympathize with Jamie's frustration and to see that Nola's sexuality is less self-confident and assured than her declarations would suggest. Both the scenes in the film which show Opal making advances suggest that Nola's rejection of her potential bisexuality is diffident rather than assured. As in the other films, lesbianism and masturbation are presented as performance, and as means of hinting at Nola's insecurity. Despite greater access to her voice than to that of most of the female characters considered earlier, we get no meaningful insight into her sexual feelings.

Nola's self-flagellating reaction to the rape leads Felly Nkweto Simmonds to conclude that the film does little to unsettle a predominantly masculine perspective. She argues that it endorses, rather than challenges, a disappointingly racist as well as patriarchal version of black female sexuality (1992, pp. 210–20). Yet, the last word in this film is Nola's, leaving an ambiguity over the status of her voice. Of her decision to go back to Jamie after the rape, she says that was 'a momentary weakness', and she asserts that her decision not to marry him is 'about control. My body. My mind. Who's going to own it, them or me?'. Although, as Simmonds suggests, we are by now sceptical of these claims, it does not seem to me that they are wholly undermined either. What the film does not pursue, however, is the interesting perspective of Nola's short-lived psychiatrist, Dr Jamison: 'If what you want is total female sexuality, be honest. The beautiful sex organ is between your ears, not between your legs'.

Lesbian sexuality

In the 1990s, lesbian sexuality moved occasionally out of the margins of representation to reappear in the guise of 'lesbian chic'. From the lesbian encounters in mainstream films, to Roseanne's contentious kiss with Mariel Hemingway to Cindy Crawford's dalliance with k. d. lang on the cover of *Vanity Fair*, lesbianism became a novel way of arousing interest and excitement. Lesbian chic's postmodernist and consumerist ring, and its defiance of meaning, comes from the association of lesbianism with celebrities such as Madonna, Sandra Bernhard and Martina Navratilova. While this enhances its gloss, it does little to explore what lesbian sexuality feels like, and mainly ignores its political significance to women for whom it is a deliberate choice.

Lesbian chic was preceded by a number of films in the 1980s which did attempt to explore lesbian relations in narrative terms. Out of three that had wide circulation, *Lianna* (1982), *Personal Best* (1982) and *Desert Hearts* (1985), only the last was directed by a woman. Made on a low budget, Donna Deitch's *Desert Hearts* goes furthest in exploring the lesbian theme, but even here the film is less an exploration of female sexuality than a love story with a novel slant. Jane Root suggests that the new popularity of gay films may stem from our continuing desire for romantic films in an age that can find no new drama in heterosexual relationships: 'maybe heterosexual sex no longer provides the thrilling images of illicit sexuality old-style Hollywood was founded upon? These days, the classic romance between two people held apart by society often looks happiest in a gay or lesbian context' (*The Guardian*, 31 July 1986). Where both *Lianna* and *Desert Hearts* differ from heterosexual romances is in showing one of the two women in each relationship being prised away from her heterosexual identity. In *Lianna* the central character is happily married and the mother of two children; in *Desert Hearts* the 'reluctant lesbian' is an uptight university lecturer who has travelled to Nevada in pursuit of a divorce.

Both films focus on initiation and education. Lesbianism, it appears, has to be learned, in a way that heterosexuality has not. In *Lianna* the student–teacher relationship underlines the learning experience, while in *Desert Hearts* Vivian's position as Columbian professor, and the more educated of the two women, is undermined by her inability to cope with the alien environment and lifestyle of the Nevada ranch. Vivian (Helen Shaver), literally, has to learn to let her hair down, and to acknowledge her doubts and fears about following her senses. For Lianna (Linda Griffiths), falling in love with her night-school tutor, Ruth, reactivates the latent lesbian desires she first experienced in experimental touching with a room-mate at a childhood camp.

Desert Hearts gives more access to the protagonists' thoughts and desires. In *Lianna*, as in the traditional romance, emotion is all. We spectate the central character's misery as she restlessly paces around her own spartan kitchen, throws a crisp packet at a television film in which a man asserts the claims of his wife over his lover, and sits disconsolately reading Radclyffe Hall's *The Well of Loneliness*! Similarly, we look on as she attempts to take a more positive attitude to her new independence, by taking more interest in her well-being, and grasping the challenge of going out to a lesbian club on her own. When Ruth has made her decision to return to her former lover, Jan, Lianna's tear-stained face is intercut with scenes of heterosexual love performed in mime by the group Lianna does lighting for, and with golden scenes of Ruth and herself enjoying their final embraces. The film skates around the contradictions posed by Lianna's affair with another woman while Ruth is away, or by her attempt to combine her lesbian lifestyle with motherhood. At the end of the film, her neglected relationship with her best friend, Sandy, is re-established, suggesting doubts about the permanence of her commitment to lesbianism.

In *Desert Hearts*, desire and longing are more overtly spoken. What makes this film particularly poignant is its focus on the older women's longing to break out of the constraints that shackle their sexual desires. Frances, Cay's spirited stepmother, has to abandon her possessiveness and disapproval of Cay's sexuality, and learn to live with her yearning for her dead male lover who 'reached in and put a string of lights about my heart'. It is the boomerang effect of these words, when Cay (Patricia Charbonneau) uses them to explain her own feelings for Vivian, that eventually softens Frances's opposition to their relationship. Vivian, in turn, has to learn how to 'be free of who I've been' and risk the vulnerability of falling in love with Cay. The passion in this film resides in Cay, the risk-taker, who publicly appeals to Vivian at the family table to join her at her friend's wedding. It is Cay who also initiates the sexual contact between the two women, and who resists Vivian's pleas to her to leave when she follows Vivian back to the motel.

Despite the gender of the protagonists, both of these films follow the basic structure of heterosexual romances, with lesbianism providing the thrill of a new form of sexual expression. *Lianna* traces the despair of an affair that does not deliver on its early promises while *Desert Hearts* ends on a more positive note with Cay joining Vivian's departing train at least until the next station. The ambiguity as to whether this relationship will prove durable is maintained. As in the best romances, the ritualistic motion of the action between attraction, obstacle and resolution is played as sufficient bait to win and hold the audience's attention.

In *Personal Best*, lesbian sexuality has a more peripheral role than in the other two films, playing second fiddle to the sporting rivalry between the protagonists. Male perspectives play a prominent role in this film, both in terms of narrative direction and shot composition. *Personal Best* both redefines the female body for the male gaze, stressing its power and vigour, and reminds us of its more typical construction as sexual object, both in the lingering slow-motion crotch shots as the team practise the high-jump, and in the distracting view of Chris's body in the swimming pool and (in another crotch shot) as she assists her boyfriend at training. While, as Linda Williams (1986) points out, not all women commentators have seen these shots as voyeuristic, there are other indices of the attention that we are invited to pay to masculine discourses in the course of the film. The male coach has a significant role in shaping both women's development, and Chris redefines her sexuality in the second half of the film, abandoning her lesbian 'phase' in favour of 'mature' heterosexuality.

SEX 'N SPICE

The advance of film recognizing that lesbian sexuality exists is muted by the delicacy with which it is treated. The love-making scenes, however audacious for mainstream cinema, are both less passionate, and more romanticized in the way they are shot, and in their accompanying soundtracks, than their heterosexual counterparts of the 1980s. Tenderness and gentleness dominate, ensuring that lesbianism fits easily into standard paradigms of femininity. Within limits, they do, however, give the audience more insight into the ramifications of sexuality as a social as well as a private issue than do any of the heterosexual films. Society's disapproval of lesbianism, or at the very least, its reluctance to accept it as normal, features as a narrative element in all of these films. Heterosexual relations, on the other hand, like masculine sexuality, being regarded as 'natural', appear to require no such investigation.

Sexual violence against women

The ideological framework that regards male sexuality as unproblematic and female sexuality as dangerous and titillating has powerfully informed popular media coverage of sexual crimes against women. Despite growing information about the nature of rape and sexual assault crimes, and slowly changing attitudes on the part of the police and legislature, the popular media still replay the madonna/whore dichotomy, and focus in a way untypical of any other crime on the victim or, as many support groups would now prefer to characterize her, the survivor.

In her book, *Virgin or Vamp* (1992), Helen Benedict argues that a number of rape myths still affect news coverage. Journalists often believe mistakenly that rape is a crime of sexual release, rather than a violent assault with intent to injure, humiliate and degrade the victim. The view that women incite rape by the way they are dressed or behave, or by the location they are in, survives despite the derision likely to accompany a comparable suggestion that a householder leaving a window open was *culpable of provoking* a burglary. Sympathy for rape victims in the media is also often tempered by the suspicion that many women bring false accusations against men for purposes of revenge, despite the trauma of testifying in court, and the obstacles lying in the way of a successful conviction. These suspicions feature strongly in the so-called 'date rape' cases, although these cases are least likely to succeed in the courts. Against this background, and the fact that the majority of rapes are carried out by men known to the victim, the chances of women in large numbers willingly distorting evidence seem very remote.

Popular newspapers continue to classify rapes into two varieties: those against women who are regarded as 'disreputable', such as prostitutes or women with highly active sex lives, and those carried out against 'respectable' women such as wives, mothers or young, sexually inactive girls. As Kate Clark (1992) demonstrates, the British tabloid, *The Sun*, regularly employs terms such as 'sex fiend' or 'sex beast' to refer to men charged with rape against 'good' women, but prefers in the case of women they define as 'bad' to place the implicit blame on the victim, not the perpetrator. Similar strategies in the popular American media were also evident in the four cases Helen Benedict examined. Benedict also found that a woman was more likely to be regarded negatively by juries if she previously knew the rapist, if she was young and attractive and if no weapon was used (despite the fact that use of a weapon is not part of the legal definition of rape).

British soap operas have made an attempt in recent years to deal with rape from the woman's point of view, showing the agonies of the event itself, and the trauma that ensues as the woman wrestles with the decision of whether to prosecute. Channel 4's *Brookside* in 1992 built a plot line around an alleged 'date rape', and allowed a number of different perspectives to emerge, inviting the audience to reflect on the issues for themselves. The American film, *The Accused* (1988), based on a real-life case (described by Benedict, 1992) also raised public awareness of conventional attitudes to rape. By focusing on the attempt of Sarah Tobias (Jodie Foster) to extract justice out of a hostile judicial system, and by showing the rape in an extended flashback towards the end, this film makes its audiences explore their own attitudes to the rape of a woman whose behaviour could stereotypically be labelled as 'provocative'. Shown drinking, dancing invitingly and flirtatiously before the rape, and dressed in a mini-skirt and low-cut top, Sarah is presented as the archetypal 'looking-for-trouble' young woman. Yet this characterization is complicated by our previous exposure to her pain, her articulateness about her own dilemma, and her awareness of the bedrock of human rights that has been infringed by what has happened to her. In addition, the controversial rape scene is shot in an approximation to real time, with frequent shots from Sarah's point of view reminding us of the brutal and relentless squashing of her will. The length of this scene, and the nature of its editing, prevent the titillation that ironically intruded in the cut versions.

Yet this rape scene encourages us to identify with masculine dilemmas, too. In particular, through the characterization of Ken Joyce, the college student who witnesses the gang rape but fails to intervene, we are invited to feel the contradiction between the young man's private respect for women and his public need to prove his virility and machismo. His position, caught between condemnation and fascination, is a surrogate for the audience's. We, too, are invited to indulge both a compulsive voyeurism and our moral disgust. By counterpoising the stampeding brutishness of the rapists with the concerned gaze of a more sensitive male onlooker, *The Accused* allows its audience an escape route from the contradictions between male and female sexual desire otherwise suggested by the film. When Joyce finally agrees to testify in court, and enables Sarah and her lawyer to win their case, his emergence as a hero legitimates our identification with his point of view. This may not undermine our ability to identify with Sarah Tobias's pain and anger, but it offers an alternative and less contradictory viewpoint.

A study into women's reactions to violence on the screen that included a screening of *The Accused* found a difference in the responses of women with experience of violence and those without. Although there was a strong consensus that the men who taunted their mates to participate in the rape were implicated in what happened, women with previous experience of violence were more eager to attribute guilt to those bystanders; women without experience of violence were more willing to identify with the pressures produced by male bonding (Schlesinger *et al.*, 1992, pp. 158–61). This research also reminds us of the multiple viewing positions that a film such as *The Accused* allows. The women in this 1990 study recorded their unease that many men might find the rape scene titillating, despite the aims of the director to prevent this. *The Accused* of itself is incapable of changing the viewing patterns of male audiences used to seeing rape exploited for dramatic and voyeuristic ends.

In conclusion

By representing women actively enjoying sexual pleasure, the popular media have helped to publicize the findings of the sexologists. They have also fetishized and commodified female sexuality by associating it closely with beautiful young bodies and the trappings of a glitzy lifestyle. From the white silk scarf Catherine Tramell uses to tie her victims to the bedposts, to the desirable lingerie and the array of body lotions guaranteed to make the skin silky smooth, recommended in women's magazines, foreplay is in danger of being removed from the bedroom to the shopping mall. By attending to media representations, we might easily forget that fat, ugly, disabled or wrinkled women have sexual desires, too, and that stretch marks are not incompatible with sexual pleasure.

Although women are now shown in controlling sexual positions, they are rarely enabled in mainstream representations to speak of their own sexual desires and feelings. This lessens the media's ability to explore the possibilities of moving away from the traditional masculine paradigm of a predatory and goal-directed sexuality towards more open forms of sexual pleasure. Simply reversing the positions of the sexual performers does not achieve this. Nor does pretending that female sexuality can change without putting at least a question mark opposite male sexuality. Unproblematic attitudes to male sexuality have especially damaging repercussions in the supposedly factual area of news reporting in the popular media, which derive many of their palimpsests from surviving mythologies.

A more intractable problem confronts the visual media even if they aim to expand our perceptions of female sexuality. Because of the history of representing the female body for the male gaze, when new images are produced, they are often looked at through old spectacles. Kathy Myers explores this dilemma in an article written as long ago as 1982. Arguing that objectification of women's bodies for commercial purposes does not mean that objectification itself is always harmful, she urges feminists seeking a new erotica not to be afraid of using visual codes already employed from male perspectives. By taking them over and redeploying them, she feels that power to encourage new ways of looking will follow. Feminist artists have grappled with the complexities of achieving this. One solution is to particularize the woman in the image, so that she cannot be seen as a symbol (see discussion of Susan Valadon's nudes in Betterton, 1987), while other artists, such as Judith Chicago, have preferred to take a more metaphorical approach. Her famous *Dinner Party* exhibition constructed place settings for famous women in the shape of vaginal imagery. Despite the difficulties in encouraging novel ways of seeing even in art, it is at least freer of the commercial pressures that haunt the popular media.

In literature, too, it is more possible to experiment with the diversity of what female sexuality might potentially mean. The history of women's literature and writing about sexuality in the twentieth century suggests that verbal texts are particularly capable of struggling with definitions of women's sexuality in women's own terms. Writers such as Angela Carter, Margaret Atwood, Alice Walker and Toni Morrison in their various ways attempt to 'say things for which no language previously existed', in a 'slow process of decolonising our language and our basic habits of thought' (Angela Carter's words in Wandor, 1983, p. 75). Often controversial and discomfiting, they can both more easily allow their female characters to speak for themselves, and use metaphoric freedoms to leap the colonial barriers. In the women's magazines, and in many mainstream films, when the colonizer shows signs of departing, it is the entrepreneur who moves in.

7

Refashioning the body

There is nowhere to go but the shops. . . . The only meaningful struggle
left is between the individual body and the impersonal, life-denying forces
of the state.
(Dick Hebdige, *Hiding in the Light*, 1988)

Adornment of the body is an issue that blurs the borderline between
representation and practice. In deciding whether to diet or not, whether
to wear make-up or not, how to dress, how to style their hair, women
are actively participating in a system of meaning-creation that also
invites their response in magazines, advertisements and other media
forms. It is this investment in appearance as a key identity marker that
makes representation of the body a particularly crucial area for defining
or redefining femininity. Distinguishing virgins from whores, mothers
from sexual beings, 'feminine' women from 'feminists', or, more banally,
the beautiful and valued from the ugly and devalued (Ussher, 1989,
pp. 13–16), the body requires us to work at fashioning our own identity,
and to practise as well as respond to signification. It is this duality of
the body and appearance that makes them an appropriate place to end
this book.

In recent years, the most optimistic writing on women and culture
has come from a wing of feminist cultural studies that concentrates on
what women do with media images and discourses, especially in the
areas of fashion and bodily adornment and movement. This chapter
will consider the polarity that is emerging between writers such as
Naomi Wolf who, focusing on media representations, see 'the beauty
myth' as a conspiracy to suppress the gains of feminism, and writers
such as Angela McRobbie and Elizabeth Wilson who, concentrating on
cultural practices, interpret positively the opportunities that women
take in their own lives to play with the codes of fashion and appearance,
and to create new and liberating meanings for themselves.

The body, gender and identity

In the 1992 film *Just Another Girl on the I.R.T.*, the central character, Chantel, an African-American teenager living in Brooklyn, boldly asserts her rights to independence, educational success and a bright career as a doctor. When an unexpected pregnancy threatens to thwart her plans, she rejects offers of help from her penitent if panic-stricken boyfriend, claiming that, since her body belongs to her, she alone is entitled to make decisions about its future. Her clarion declaration is made with all the passion of the women's liberation movement of the 1970s, even if her decision – to refuse the abortion option – might not endear her to that generation of feminists. In the 1990s, with renewed and often virulent attacks on women's rights to make choices about their own bodies, especially from the anti-abortionist lobby in the United States, Chantel's claim still has the power to provoke dramatic tension. *Just Another Girl* indeed reminds us that sovereignty over the body is easier to assert rhetorically than to establish in practice. Emerging from a labour whose unruliness hovers on the brink of farce, Chantel decides finally to keep the baby and allow motherhood to restrict her other aspirations.

The body has historically been much more integral to the formation of identity for women than for men. If women had defined for themselves the ideals of their bodily shape or decoration, this would not be problematic. It is the denial of this right in the history of western cultural representation, in medical practice, and in the multi-billion dollar pornography, fashion and cosmetic industries, that has granted women only squatters' rights to their own bodies. At the same time, and increasingly since the 1970s, the body as a sign has allowed groups threatened by cultural invisibility to assert their presence in innovative and striking ways. Gay men and lesbians, Afro-Caribbeans, young unemployed men who spend their time 'working out', or adolescents following their favoured rock group, have all transferred their claim to power from the public arena to the dressing up or cultivation of the body. Decisions to sport dreadlocks, shaved heads, bulging muscles or plaster-white make-up, privately and personally taken, translate into signs, readable on the street and demanding of attention. Whether representations of these changes have the same dynamic charge as their practice is a question to which this chapter will return.

The body's traditional centrality to feminine identity can be sub-divided into a variety of codes of appearance: ideal bodily shape and size; appropriate forms of make-up and cosmetic care of skin and hair; and the adornment of the body through clothes and accessories. It is not the body, but the codifying of the body into structures of appearance, that culturally shapes and moulds what it means to be 'feminine'. For women, the relation between identity and the body may take many other forms, which are much less visible in the mainstream media: the impact of regular menstruation or the effects of the menopause; gynaecological disorders that produce pain or discomfort; distortions of shape and bodily functioning produced by childbirth or osteoporosis; the sense of loss ensuing from removal of breasts or womb. What this partial list reminds us is that it is not the body as a functioning or dysfunctioning system that has been culturally related to female identity, but those aspects of the female body that are attractive to men. In contrast, male bodies connote masculinity through associations of bodily functioning and performance (sporting or sexual) and of powerful and energetic activity.

As the last chapter indicated, women have long been encouraged to view their bodies as intrinsically related to their sexual desirability. Female sexuality, in media and advertising discourses, is normally perceived to end by the time a woman enters her forties. By associating sexual feelings with bodily perfection, the point of view remains firmly masculine. One of the reasons why women regard soap opera as offering a positive representation of their lives is its willingness to include older women who still take pride in their appearance and who refuse to deny their sexuality. Women's magazines, on the other hand, replace sexuality with romance for the older woman. As the joke goes, *Vogue* will tell you how to have an orgasm with style, but *Woman's Weekly* (aimed at older women) will tell you how to knit one. Male sexuality has floated free of the constraints of age, with concepts such as 'virility' and 'potency' relating for the duration of a man's life to the energetic and active functioning of the body rather than its aesthetic quality.

For women, ageing is constructed as a process to be feared and avoided as long as possible, while for men it often enhances status and prestige. The different cultural perception of the process of growing older by men and women in the western world has attracted considerable attention (see, for example, Itzin, 1986; Arber and Ginn, 1991). Because of the close relationship for women between appearance and identity, the signs of ageing trigger worries about loss of social value and esteem that have no equivalent for men (even hair loss – despite its more dramatic visual impact than wrinkles or greying hair – raises more muted anxieties). Historically, in western industrialized societies, old women have been characterized as witches, hags, old maids and crones, while in other cultures, as Arber and Ginn point out, the older woman can be regarded as a source of wisdom and leadership (1991, p. 48).

The fear of ageing is stimulated by the glossy women's magazines and driven by advertisers of the multitude of products claiming age-delaying or even age-reversing properties. By the mid-1980s, skin-care products and eye gels were using scientific or quasi-scientific discourse to sell themselves to the affluent reader (most of these products were and are expensive). Women, the traditional carers of others, were now invited to devote as much nurturing attention to their own skins. Preventive action was encouraged, as advertisers targeted younger rather than older women's magazines. Lancôme was in the 1980s one of the first manufacturers to claim a breakthrough in the battle against 'the pressure of time'. The discovery of Niosomes™ as 'unique microscopic spheres which match the skin's natural supporting structure' formed the 'principle [sic] constituent of Niosome Système Anti-Age' (Cosmopolitan, December 1986, pp. 42–3).

This was easy to follow compared with the language of 1990s' advertisements, addressing a readership now well versed in the ageing properties of sunlight and polluted atmospheres. 'Liposomes' (Vichy) and 'Ceramides' (Elizabeth Arden) enlarged the reader's vocabulary at the same time as they promised to extend the anti-ageing resistance of her skin. For the sceptical, quantifying the advantages was meant to offer reassurance. Elizabeth Arden's claims for its moisturizing cream were typical: 'supercharged with HCA, a unique alpha-hydroxy complex, ceramides and other skincaring essentials; boosts skin's hydration level over 450% after one hour' (Marie Claire, November 1993, p. 134). Even more frightening are the statistics provided by the advertisement copy for Lancaster skin therapy: 'At 30, the skin's oxygen content is already down by 25%. Fine lines are the first tell-tale sign. Lancaster has developed a revolutionary technology: pure oxygen molecules encapsulated in a smooth, light cream are channelled deep into the epidermal layers' (Marie Claire, November 1993, pp. 36–7). By increasing oxygen in the skin, the advertisement claims, 'wrinkle depth is reduced by 40%'.

By employing quasi-scientific discourses, these advertisements replaced skin-care's association with narcissism and beauty with an address to the postfeminist woman: aware, self-reliant and taking responsibility for her own future and well-being. The products' long-researched chemical structure also, of course, justified the inflated prices charged for the products. Caring for the body, a developing obsession of the 1980s, was never going to come cheaply, as manufacturers took advantage of the new navel-contemplation, and the worlds of sport and casual fashion became increasingly intertwined. Cycling shorts and shell suits, trainers and baseball caps indicate how interwoven the connections between sport, fashion and identity became during this decade. A trend of the 1980s that extended across the gender and ethnic boundaries, this syndrome had an added urgency for women.

In the economic and cultural context of a society that devalues older women in other ways, by debarring them from many employment opportunities, removing them from prominent visual positions in the media, and discounting the management and negotiating skills that many older women have acquired within their child-rearing roles, advertising discourses that imply that grey hair and wrinkles are signposts towards the scrap-heap acquire additional power. Middle-aged and older women as voices of authority (in, for example, television news and current affairs programmes or documentaries) are not yet routinely established, although they are edging their way into visibility. Female film and television stars, likely to become recognized at an earlier age than their male counterparts, also have a much shorter shelf-life than their male equivalents (Levy, 1990, pp. 251–7). Older female stars, such as Joan Collins, become best known for their curiosity value and their dependency on the aids of the beauty industries.

Women philosophers and artists have increasingly over the last two decades questioned the traditional relationship between female identity and the body. Luce Irigaray has pointed out the importance of touch in women's experience of their bodies. For women, she claims, the experience of touching takes the sensual place occupied by looking for men (Moi, 1985, pp. 143–4). As we saw in the last chapter, visual representation in the popular media, with its problematic relation between text and audience, poses difficulties for exploring new approaches to female sexuality. In the arts, women have more scope to explore new relationships between artefact and spectator. The three-dimensional and tactile nature of sculpture offers particular freedom. Niki de Saint Phalle's vibrant and exuberant sculptures of the female form ('Les Nanas') suggest the possibilities of a different relationship between looker and constructed form. Encouraging participation and touch (one giant Nana invites the spectator to walk in through the vagina), and exalting size, energy and colour, her sculptures celebrate

female vitality and pleasure. Larger than life, unruly but never grotesque, her women's outsize bodies invite admiration, not disdain. Her
inspiration for this work came from her antipathy to the Twiggy craze
of the 1960s, and was no doubt intensified by her own experiences as
a model for American *Vogue* and *Harper's Bazaar* in the 1940s.

In the medium of photography, too, the process of reclaiming
women's bodies for the exploration of women's own experience is well
developed. Both Cindy Sherman and Jo Spence, in collaboration with
Rosy Martin, have used photography as an autobiographical medium
to challenge the simplicity of the correlation between bodily image and
identity that prevails elsewhere in culture. Their projects are sharply different, with Sherman exploring her own body in a number of poses
from imagined film narratives in *Untitled Film Stills,* or playing with
the conventions of the centrefold spread to unsettle the 'male gaze'.
Spence and Martin courageously express the psychic and physical
anguish of the woman struggling with identity against the ravages of
both a repressive culture and a destructive disease (Jo Spence used
photography as a therapeutic means of dealing with her breast cancer).
Breaking down our voyeuristic inclinations by declaring openly that
these are images of themselves, these photographs put subjectivity
within the frame, and force us to explore our own relationship to the
visual representation of bodies that we are more accustomed to viewing
in objectified form.

The ideal body

Notions of the ideal white female body have undergone a number of
transformations through time. Again, there is no parallel for the male
body. In the Renaissance period, as has often been pointed out, the ideal
female body, depicted in oil paintings of the time, was full and well-
rounded. By the Victorian era, maternal roundness was pinched into
the hour-glass figure, in triumphant tribute to the achievements of cor-
setry. During the twentieth century, change has increased in pace, with
the 1920s' Chanel- and Patou-inspired boyish flapper image giving way
in the 1930s to the slinkier, bias-cut look, and being reversed totally
in the post-war 'new look', led by Christian Dior. Curvaceousness
remained the norm throughout the 1950s, but rapidly gave way in the
1960s to the 'Twiggy' look, as hemlines rose dramatically and the age
of the mini-skirt arrived. The ideal of the slender body has remained
supreme since then, although fashion continues to dress it up in novel

and distinctive ways. The 1990s' catwalk, as we saw in Chapter 4, has seen the advent of the girlish, vulnerable look, with waifish bodies combining with sexually knowing faces to produce a disturbingly ambiguous image.

What is obvious from even this potted history is that versions of the ideal female body shape are interconnected with the evolving fashion industry. To pose this as a male conspiracy is to oversimplify a complex set of interactions. Susan Bordo (1990) argues that the slender female body was, for men, a response to the anxiety produced by female sexual desire as women moved increasingly into the public sphere and, for women, a welcome refuge from the maternal and reproductive definitions of femininity triggered by the ample female form. Naomi Wolf, in a similar but cruder argument, contends that Twiggy's arrival was welcomed by women because of her opposition to maternal iconography and by men because, coming at the same time as the contraceptive pill, she 'cancel[led] out its most radical implications' (1991, p. 184).

These theses ignore two significant factors. First, the ideal of the slender body, openly disregarded in the typically curvaceous models posing in soft-porn photo-spreads for men, forms an unconvincing male invention, even if we were to accept Susan Bordo's suggestion that women's presence in the public sphere of work made men uncomfortable with a more fetishized female form. Anecdotal evidence indicates also that many men prefer their female partners not to be too thin, and masculinist references to breast size and ideally proportioned figures persist in the popular media. Second, although the fashion industry remains male-dominated, two of the main designers responsible for introducing the leaner look were women (Coco Chanel in the 1920s and Mary Quant in the 1960s). A simple thesis of masculine conspiracy leaves a number of unanswered questions.

From the interwar period up until the 1960s, interactions between the fashion, advertising and film industries did nevertheless set unmistakable norms for the ideal white female form. For non-white women, the comparative lack of model images has produced a curious freedom. As film director Gurinder Chadha explains: 'Asian women are not turned mad in the way white women are about their looks. We adorn ourselves in bright, wonderful colours and jewellery, which celebrate what we are and life itself' (*The Guardian*, 27 August 1992). While Afro-Caribbean and African-American women have historically come under pressure to conform to white ideals of black beauty (helped by Naomi Campbell's image), resistance to this has also been serious enough to become a political issue for black women.

By the 1980s and 1990s, even for white women, the relatively straightforward relationship between dominant media images and the construction of a template to aspire to has given way to a more complex and fragmented set of signposts. From being leaders, the industries with an investment in image and appearance now promote themselves as responding to women's own varying self-concepts and desires; enablers through fantasy, rather than prophets on the mountain with tablets of stone. As the supermodel replaces the model, the fashion industry learns from the rag trade, and the diet industry thrives against awareness of anorexia and bulimia, something more complex is taking place than a simple conspiracy of money-makers.

Modernism began the process of detaching image from reality, but it is in the shift to postmodernism that detachment becomes dislocation. While modernism encouraged women to emulate the ideal images they encountered in magazines and on film, postmodernism produced a more sceptical and 'knowing' relationship with image. Achieving the ideal now becomes a hybrid and contradictory mix of rigorous bodily control and playful experimentation with dress, make-up and accessories. While this is liberating in freeing image for self-expression, it masks less happily the gap between the image and women's continuing socio-economic struggles.

The flapper image of the 1920s and early 1930s was, as Martin Pumphrey (1987) points out, cleverly in line with modernity. What was now on offer to women was, for the first time, a set of images of how they might be that was classless, internationalist and that confidently breached the norms of femininity of their mothers' generation. The opportunity of modernism was, for women, embodied in a 'look' that held the promise of freedom. Images of the female body, widely circulated for the first time to women as well as men, became as uprooted from their reality as the modernist cityscape was from its industrial and commercial functions. The fashion and film industries encouraged young women in particular to dream of a liberation from the tedium of their office and shop lives that was to be realized in leisure activities (removed from both work and home environments) and associated with the romantic worlds of Hollywood or Paris. Style and appearance were emerging as international languages through which femininity could become sophisticated and chic. The two-dimensional spatial relations of fashion line drawings began to resemble the technocratic outlines of the modernist era, in a move that distinguished fashion as the only area of culture to integrate women into modernity.

If cultivating a specific 'look' was the only key to freedom for the majority of women, it is not surprising that it should have acquired such significance. The growth of mass-produced fashion, and the transition from tailor-made to ready-made clothes, strengthened women's sense that democracy could be achieved more quickly through the new look than through the contested medium of the ballot box. Although fashion models were not yet established as household names (the model, as Jennifer Craik points out (1994, p. 77), took some time to establish her respectability) the lead in setting trends fell to prominent members of the aristocracy and to film stars. The distance from ordinary women this suggested was overcome by the availability of cheaper versions of their clothing, and the appearance in women's magazines and women's pages of patterns or ideas through which women could adapt high fashion to their own requirements. As Jackie Stacey demonstrates, in women's reactions to female film stars of the 1940s and 1950s, emulation was a dominant aim (1991, pp. 141–63).

With the move to postmodernism, spectacle works to enlarge our fantasies, not bring us closer to identification with the particular. As we saw in Chapter 4, the supermodel is, in any case, an elusive role model. In an era where the fashion industry plunders its ideas from 'high' and 'low' culture, from film and popular music, from street wear and aristocratic chic, where advertising emulates the fantasy evocations of the catwalk, and film upsets the glamour bandwagon of the modern period by dressing its female heroines in jeans and denim shirts (as in *Thelma and Louise*), it is not surprising that reverential attitudes and aspiration have been unsettled by a new awareness of the processes of image construction. Emulation has not, of course, completely disappeared, but it now hits its peak in the adolescent, or even pre-adolescent, years. It is no accident that the prime age for Madonna worship has always been the teenage years of identity crisis and revolt against parental authority, with the 'wannabes' of one age quickly slipping into cynical disowners in the next.

Dislocation between image and identity in the postmodern period makes it more difficult for women to attain the ideal merely by 'putting on a face' or by 'dressing up'. Instead of external cultivation of ideal image, rigorous bodily discipline becomes the substitute route to regaining the homology of image and identity that would otherwise be lost. 'Feeling good' involves, for the postfeminist woman, success in career, sexual life and appearance: in all three cases, nothing is to be achieved without hard work and commitment. At the same time, fashion and cosmetics allow new freedoms in experimentation and play; a route to developing multiple subjectivities for women from work to leisure that ensures women feel freed from the obligations of less liberated periods. While the move from modernism to postmodernism and the social changes in women's roles and self-perceptions have clearly influenced these developments, they were aided and abetted by the promotional and marketing strategies of the industries who were set to gain most from the new complexity of women's relations with image and identity.

Body discipline

The diet industry, emerging in a culture of post-war affluence that ended the association between thinness and poverty, has become relentlessly persuasive in its encouragement of women to slim. Aided by a fashion industry consistently endorsing slenderness since the 1960s (despite occasional emphases on larger breasts), the expanding service sector has had ample opportunity to sell slimming aids, exercise machines, or establish health farms and support agencies such as Weight Watchers (set up in the USA in 1963 and in Britain four years later, and by the 1990s a profitable wing of the giant food company, Heinz). While women's willing participation in dieting would not have been possible without this multifaceted commercial stimulus, neither would it have occurred had bodily appearance not been so closely associated with identity for women. The contradictory impulses to pamper and indulge oneself, and yet submit to régimes that at times emulate torture, find an echo in Foucault's theory of the body as a central location in the contest for power. Commenting that mastery over the (implicitly male) body is achieved through strenuous exercise and other forms of control, he adds that this also triggers a reaction against regulation, in favour of pleasure and indulgence (1980, p. 56). It is this continual battle between opposing forces that encourages Foucault to see the body as *within* discourse, not poised innocently outside it.

In selling diet to women, discourses of looking after oneself predominate. Positive terminologies of 'fitness and health' and 'psychological well-being' mask the rigorous discipline required. Whether through physical working out or mind control, the rewards on offer are surprisingly similar: enhanced self-esteem, a better appearance and the ability to wear more fashionable clothes. By constructing the body as a work zone, women's magazines encourage women themselves to perpetuate the objectification of their bodies. With the aspiring secretary Tess in Mike Nichols' film *Working Girl* (1988), *Cosmo* girl and her friends can declare that they have cultivated 'a head for business, and a bod for sin'. The materiality of the body, which women feel to be such an intrinsic part of their own subjectivity and identity, becomes a detachable asset, malleable to whatever aspirational purpose postfeminist woman chooses.

Throughout the nineteenth and early twentieth centuries, disciplining the body was perceived as a social duty. The need to build a healthy and resilient army, or to ensure that absenteeism did not hinder western industrial competitiveness, and the desire for a strong child-bearing stock in an era when infant mortality was still high, led to the care of the body being talked about in terms of civic duty. As we saw in the last chapter, even the more enlightened campaigners on behalf of women's sexual rights in the early decades of the twentieth century employed eugenic discourses to support their argument.

Since the interwar period, the immense advances in public health and in sport and leisure facilities coupled with the advances in birth control methods have shifted discourses of bodily care from public to private duty. For men, lacking the historic link between body and perceptions of self-identity, this has led to an often obsessive concern on the part of some with training and physical development. The unseen enemy for them is not primarily loss of sexual attractiveness (although this may be a significant influence for gay men), but physical decrepitude through illness or decay. For women, the new discourses of fitness and health have a different echo. The forms of exercise most widely publicized in women's magazines and on videos targeted at the female market are those related to appearance. Where beauty, in the Victorian ideal, was seen as attainable through spiritual purity, and more recently through sufficient sleep and healthy eating, it is now more actively to be worked for in the aerobics class or on the step apparatus.

These 'feminine' forms of exercise reinforce the link between beauty and health, making both a matter of self-discipline and will-power, and blithely obliterating the contribution of the individual's genetic make-up. The collective nature of classes encourages women to survey their own bodies competitively. In addition, as Susan Willis points out, the association of working out with women famous for their appearance (Jane Fonda in the 1980s, Cindy Crawford in the 1990s) makes it difficult to separate the exercise routines from the rituals of dress and self-presentation associated with them: 'for women, poised body line and flexed muscles are only half the picture. Achieving the proper workout look requires several exercise costumes, special no-smudge makeup, and an artfully understated hairdo' (1990, p. 7). The glamour of aerobics, and its supposed role in fending off the ageing process (Fonda was already in her forties when her book and video were published) does little to suggest that diverse shapes are compatible with health and high self-esteem. The emphasis on aerobics has also meant that different forms of exercise, such as swimming, which might be better routes to fitness and physical well-being for women, are culturally undervalued. Ironically, when swimsuits appear in fashion spreads in women's magazines, they are more likely to be discussed as garments for being seen in on the beach than in the unglamorous and chlorine-scented swimming baths.

Young women in the 1980s began to work-out, diet and subject themselves to systems of self-discipline that would have made the etiquette rituals of the Victorian era seem mild by comparison. The discourses through which this attention to bodily reformation was encouraged emphasized pleasure and choice. Magazines addressed to teenage girls applauded fitness and health while overtly discouraging fasting or forcing the female body into the straitjacket of an ideal shape. More! in the summer of 1992 was running a series of features called 'Suit your shape', designed to advise young women on how to make the most of themselves, whatever their shape or size. Yet at the same time, a fitness feature was counselling 'the great swimsuit shape-up' through a variety of exercises guaranteed to 'blitz your wobbly bits'. The three routines outlined, labelled 'leg lengtheners', 'tummy toners' and 'bum busters', were exemplified by a camera-aware young woman with an ideal shape and a healthy tan (More!, 24 June–7 July 1992, pp. 29–31).

In the next age range, represented by magazines such as Company and Cosmopolitan, care of the body is frequently linked to positive states of mind, and feeling generally good about oneself. The aspirational young woman is encouraged to cultivate positive thinking as well as rigorous work-outs. For superwoman, living is not enough: 'superliving' is the target. An up-beat ten-page guide in Company (September 1992) links the exercising of 'mind', 'body' and 'sex' as the route to making 'superliving' a possibility for all its readers. The mode of address is exhortatory and encouraging, focusing on agility in all three areas as the passport to perfect happiness. New Woman, similarly, promises the achievement of 'SUPERHEALTH' through mind control. 'The single most powerful weapon in the fight against ill health is your mind. With it you can control your body's natural defences, safeguard your health and think yourself into a state of wellbeing' (March 1993, p. 63). Willpower, discipline and self-control have passed out of the language of constraint and self-denial to become key words in the postfeminist's vocabulary. The carrot is visually enticing: lithe and athletic tanned bodies, nude or in swimsuit in *Company*; golden-hued and mystically contemplative in *New Woman*.

Advertisers have also recognized the potential of postfeminist discourse for persuading women to buy expensive trainers. Nike has been particularly creative in its campaigns to win its share of the market from competitors Adidas and Reebok. Taking women's lack of contentment with their own appearance as its theme, it urges readers to 'make your body the best it can be for one person. Yourself. Just do it'. One 1993 advertisement in women's magazines presented six almost-nude women (one holding a baby) with the caption 'it's not the shape you are, it's the shape you're in that matters'. Another (*see* Fig. 12) uses an appealing toddler to gently mock the reader's own dissatisfaction with her body, brought on, in the advertisement's small print, by influences such as 'puberty', 'boys' and (ironically) 'magazine images'. From the blissful innocent state of ease with the body, the advertisement suggests, women have learned anxiety and self-criticism:

Suddenly the mirror is no
longer your friend.
So who defined your
template of beauty?
Who said you weren't OK?
Get real.

Exercise and fitness are the implied routes to self-satisfaction; making the most of oneself the advice. Yet this advertisement, too, while cleverly avoiding producing its own adult 'template of beauty', reminds the reader that worrying about appearance, and trying to disguise the flaws, is the normal, if pathological, condition of femininity.

Slimmer versions

In the slimming magazines, it is the crossing of psychological barriers that is emphasized. Implicitly addressing a female readership, these

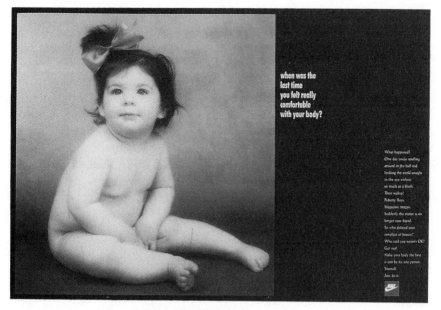

Fig. 12 1993 Nike advertisement

publications offer confessional 'before' and 'after' accounts of the transformation achieved in people's lives by losing weight. These histories follow a routine narrative structure. Starting with the obstacle of the protagonists failing to recognize their weight as a problem, the stories relate how this was triumphantly overcome, to reach the euphoria of the post-conversion state. Mixing first-person narrative and the interviewer's evangelizing commentary, the tone is up-beat and proselytizing. It is a message reiterated in the magazines' advice columns where, for example, the medical expert advises a $13\frac{1}{2}$-stone, 41-year-old woman not to go on a crash diet but to tackle the emotional problems at the root of her condition by changing her outlook and attitude: 'you need to work on your mind' (*Slimmer*, February/March 1994, p. 98).

The benefits to be gained by coming to terms with weight are remarkably material and commodified for such a spiritual journey: along with renewed self-confidence comes, we are repeatedly told, an increased interest in clothes and fashion and a greater participation in social and leisure activities. Fashion is particularly emphasized in photo displays which often indicate where the clothes modelled on the younger, slimmer woman can be bought (*Weight Watchers Magazine* and *Slimmer* both contain such features). Although increased sexual desirability rarely appears as an overt incentive (indeed, several narratives relate how happy partners were with the women's appearance before dieting), a glow of satisfaction is occasionally derived from acquaintances' mistaken belief that their partners have started a relationship with a younger, more attractive woman. Reinforcing women's fear that age (or the appearance of age) reduces their sexual attractiveness, these asides provide added incentive for readers.

While most 'before' and 'after' accounts focus on women, occasionally heterosexual couples are featured. The different motives reported for the men and women to lose weight reveal a great deal about cultural constructions of masculinity and femininity. Men worry about health and fitness; their female partners yearn principally for improved self-esteem and appearance. In a feature entitled 'Love is . . . losing weight together!', the husband comments: 'I think Jayne was more concerned with the way we looked than I was. It was the health aspect of being overweight that worried me'. The objectives the couple set themselves also varied. For Richard, the challenge was to be fit enough to undertake a demanding walking trek; for Jayne, it was to 'wear size-10 clothes and shop in Paris' (*Slimming*, February 1994, p. 124).

The slimming magazines constantly return the reader to the consumer benefits of self-control and psychological tenacity. Far from being cast within a paradigm of self-denial or rigorous and painful discipline, losing weight is part of a positive discourse about responding to a challenge, making the most of yourself and feeling good. Lest we be in any doubt, these slimming magazines are, ironically, dominated by fetishized and lavishly shot displays of food. Fasting is out: 'scrumptious', 'delicious', 'tasty', 'nourishing', 'filling', 'mouth-watering', 'healthy', 'wholesome' food is in. Sensuous images of low-calorie chocolate cakes, fish and chips, larger-than-life bread rolls give the lie to the notion that slimming requires sensory deprivation, as features merge into advertisements and promotions, all singing to the same tune.

In the United States, where evangelical religions and psychotherapy are both more common than in Britain, direct accounts of spiritual victories over the demon of weight need less consumer dressing. As Kathleen Rowe (1990) reminds us in her discussion of Roseanne as an 'unruly woman', fatness and looseness of tongue or behaviour are often linked in the history of the 'grotesque' woman. Excess weight implies a lack of moral and spiritual fibre. Oprah Winfrey, in proselytizing mode, publicized her own eventual victory in her battle against her weight as a confrontation with 'the truth' (*Oprah Winfrey Show*, Channel 4, 19 January 1994). 'The truth', she argued, means recognizing the source of hurt in one's life that manifests itself through excess eating, much as the alcoholics at the Victorian temperance meeting might be encouraged to see the demon drink as the projection of their spiritual problems.

What is not explained in either the discourse of 'fitness and health' or 'psychological control' is why losing weight should be such a clear symptom of success. Evidence suggests that most women (contrary to the confessors in the slimming magazines) are likely to believe they are overweight, even when they are not (Brumberg, 1988, p. 32). Where fitness and health are at stake, we might expect a greater variety of advice on exercise and medical issues than most magazines provide. By demonizing 'flab', the magazine press, together with the fashion and advertising industries, encourages the aspiring woman to tackle an obstacle course that consists not of glass ceilings, low pay, domestic inequalities or excessive caring obligations, but of cellulite-ridden thighs and the temptations of 'wicked' chocolate gateaux. There is nothing new in alleging that the mind interacts with the body, but suggesting that all failures of the flesh can be overcome by power thinking carries medical dangers, too.

Young women's magazines take care to distance themselves from the more direct prescriptions of the slimming publications. Far from telling young women what to do, they explicitly urge them to make the best of their shape and be wary of quick cosmetic fixes. This stated position is often at variance with the image, and, in a pattern already familiar from their approach to sexuality, rejection of a particular point of view has an uncanny way of boomeranging back to leave its mark. *Just Seventeen*, for example, discounts bodily perfection as an essential ingredient in attracting a boyfriend: 'As girls, we are bullied into being self-conscious. We believe that thighs you can bounce a brick off, skin like velvet and a model-girl pout are normal . . . Quite the reverse is true' (7 November 1990, p. 16). Yet the same magazine regularly features fashion and advertisement models who give the lie to the undesirability of a perfect shape. Negation curiously becomes a form of affirmation, as the reader is reminded, even by denial, of what 'normal' girls worry about.

In parallel with the teenage women's magazines' denial of dieting and slimming as recommended pathways to health and fitness, magazines such as *Cosmopolitan* and *Company* carry occasional articles warning women against the commercial exploitation of their bodily anxieties. A feature in *Company* (November 1993, pp. 60–7), despite advertising itself by the title 'Thin Thighs in An Instant!', consists of the recounted experiences of two reporters who have subjected themselves to different treatments for cellulite, described melodramatically here as '20th-century woman's biggest enemy', but by Naomi Wolf as 'an invented "condition" that was imported into the United States by *Vogue* only in 1973' (1991, p. 227).

The before, during and after photographs, in contrast to those that feature regularly in slimming magazines, include badly bruised buttocks and thighs, and legs bandaged after one of the volunteers 'woke up in a pool of blood'. Information boxes evaluate different forms of treatment and warn about unqualified practitioners. The tone of the first-person accounts is sombre and the descriptions of the agony the investigators endured vividly evoke milder forms of torture. While this might be the basis for an 'all-worth-it-in-the-end' conclusion, the reader is left with a more ambivalent verdict. Laura, subjected to cellulolipolysis ('the removal of cellulite using needles attached to an electric current'), declares that even if she could have sustained the full extent of the treatment she would have refused, while Clare, experiencing the delights of liposuction ('the removal of fat cells by suction'), enjoys the benefits of being able to wear, for the first time, a 'stretchy Lycra tube skirt', but still asserts 'I'd never do it again'.

These features remind us that the magazine is our trusted friend, independently exploring what is good for us. Turn to the back pages, though, and advertisements for clinics offering cosmetic surgery or liposuction predominate. Unlike a politically committed magazine such as the now defunct *Spare Rib* or the American *Ms.*, the reader is still addressed as someone obsessed with her body. Ambivalence, never far below the surface, sometimes obtrudes with staggering crudity. The issue of *Company* that ran the special feature on 'superliving' follows this with fashion features (manly pinstriped clothes, succeeded by erotically-enticing leathers and fishnet tights), advice on how to make the most of your eyes, and then a romantically illustrated article on 'Body Love' which offers this advice: '**STOP** being a slave to shape . . . Now we're into the Nineties, you can set yourself free from the misery of dieting and worrying about weight. It's called learning to love yourself, and as long as you're healthy, you've got the **LOOK**' (September 1992, p. 93). Ridiculing the notion that women can change their bodily shape at will, this feature nevertheless raises anxieties and offers advice for action. The fear of cellulite raises its bumpy head again, with five recommended courses of action, including the use of proprietary creams. Crash dieting is explicitly condemned, but the initial commentary is as unstable as the flesh it refers to: 'Wide hips and wobbly thighs are probably your biggest body worry. Sure no one wants to wobble, but your curves go towards the beauty of being a woman. Your pelvis has to be wider than a man's to allow for childbirth' (ibid.).

By explicitly rejecting extreme measures, young women's magazines stay on the right side of the fence in an era in which public concern about eating disorders, particularly among girls and young women, is increasing. Women's magazines (especially in the United States) helped to spread awareness of the extent of anorexia nervosa (initially intentional but then uncontrollable weight loss) and bulimia (a repeated cycle of bingeing followed by vomiting) in the late 1970s and 1980s, although the conditions themselves have a longer history. Their treatment of these issues now remains occasional and surprisingly remote, if we attend to the nature of these magazines' readerships; less so, if we remember the extent of these publications' dependence on advertising revenue.

Although it is well established within academic literature that eating disorders have complex psychological, biomedical as well as cultural causes (e.g. Brumberg, 1988, pp. 24–40), popular commentators have often blamed the slimming and fashion industries, and their distillation through the women's magazine press, for, as Naomi Wolf melodramatically puts it, locking women 'into one-woman hunger camps' (1991, p. 181). With waifs on their fashion pages, and svelte models featuring in the advertisements, the glossies' kid glove approach is highly motivated. It is their readers, research indicates, who are most at risk, with both anorexia nervosa and bulimia especially prevalent among young, white, middle-class women in the most developed countries (Brumberg, 1988, pp. 12–13). But there is no incentive, in these aspirational publications, to deal with the pathology and disorder in the relationship between body and psyche.

Ironically, the anorexic and bulimic body, painfully thin and even emaciated, is the true unruly body, the body that has escaped the control of the mind. For the sufferer, the body ceases to obey instructions. As a 29-year-old anorexic and bulimic featured on BBC2's *40 Minutes* documentary series put it, in the week before Oprah's confessional

(*Caraline's Story*, BBC2, 11 January 1994): 'If I just pared the layers of flesh off my thighs, I could wipe away the sins of the fathers and the mothers' (she had been abused by both her parents). Removing unwanted flesh in this instance has little to do with producing an attractive body (indeed, Caraline says that her behaviour means that she is never capable of 'wearing [her] body with pride'); but has everything to do with self-contempt and a self-destructive thirst for love.

Although occasional articles on anorexia and bulimia do appear in the monthly women's press, their preferred method of dealing with the subject of eating disorders is to print replies to their own surveys on the issue. As with their approach to lesbianism (see Chapter 6), this allows them to deal with the topic without committing themselves to their own opinion. In 1992, *Cosmopolitan* provided a questionnaire on its readers' relationship with food. The results, published in the March 1993 issue, were hailed by the magazine as 'astonishing' in what they revealed about the proportion of the 7,000 respondents who confessed to eating disorders. The finding that 30 per cent of those who claimed to diet regularly had at some point made themselves vomit either routinely or from time to time was described as 'heartbreaking' in its demonstration that 'so many of you feel so bad about yourself that you will go to such damaging lengths'. It did not appear to occur to *Cosmopolitan* that its own ethos and journalistic practice might fuel that sense of dissatisfaction, or, indeed, that the statistics it uncovered merely echo those widely suggested in earlier, much publicized writing on the subject. At the end of the article, writers Tania Unsworth and Rachel Shattock conclude that 'dieting should carry a health warning' and that we should think more about the reasons why we eat (including psychological problems) and less about what we consume. No advice, or telephone helpline, was offered to the 28 per cent of those completing the survey who had answered that they either currently were, or had been, anorexic or bulimic.

I am what I wear

In the 1980s, at the same time as régimes of bodily discipline were becoming more systematically marked out, new freedoms opened up for experimentation with dress and personal style. Dress and fashion, operating as both visible and readable cultural practices and as semiotic systems, raise particularly interesting issues in relation to redefinitions of femininity. These have been increasingly explored within feminist cultural studies by critics who see women participating actively in the creation of meaning through dress and adornment. This approach contrasts with the early feminist view of fashion, and also with Naomi Wolf's belief that the ideologies promoted by the beauty industries have conspired to suppress feminism as effectively as the ideologies of domestic slavery which, in her view, they replaced.

Early feminist reactions to fashion were often overtly hostile. Seen as a prime means of restricting women's identity within an extremely narrow definition of femininity, the criterion of elegance against which society judged women was influentially described by Simone de Beauvoir as a form of 'bondage' (1972, p. 548). De Beauvoir also observed that the sophisticated woman who translated her sexuality into a highly coded dress system was, by restraining its overt expression, the more erotically appealing to men (p. 191). A generation later, Rosalind Coward argued that being fashionable was essential for any woman concerned to avoid being cast as sexually conservative. While she saw the promotion of fashion as a complex system, extending beyond the marketing efforts of the fashion industry, she adamantly rejected the notion that women were using fashion to experiment with their own subjectivities: 'one thing that fashion is quite categorically *not* is an expression of individuality' (1984, p. 29).

Second-wave feminists' rejection of fashionable 'feminine' clothing, and their adoption of dungarees and boiler suits, triggered a wave of anti-feminist mockery and stereotyping in the popular press, and led to accusations from more thoughtful analysts of either bad faith or muddled thinking. Philosopher Janet Radcliffe Richards, describing herself as a 'sceptical feminist', claimed that if saving time and effort were the objectives, feminists would sport the first item of clothing they came across in a jumble sale 'even if it happened to be a shapeless turquoise Crimplene dress with a pink cardigan', but adds acerbically, 'no feminist would be seen dead in any such thing' (1982, p. 225). The photographer Rosy Martin similarly describes feminism as curtailing her pleasure in dressing up: 'I felt a peer-group pressure, a "thou shalt not" dogma, the safest solution to which would be a couple of pairs of jeans, lumberjack checked shirts and short, short hair. But what of my own delight in style, and playing with visual contradictions?' (Martin and Spence, 1987, p. 274).

The suspicion expressed by Janet Radcliffe Richards and Rosy Martin that feminist attitudes to fashion were both hypocritical (replacing one 'feminine' uniform with another 'anti-feminine' one) and puritanical, found support in the writing of cultural theorists in the 1980s. Elizabeth Wilson, responsible for pioneering the re-evaluation of fashion within feminism, characterizes the differing attitudes of feminists towards it as a battle between the 'authentic' and the 'modern' view of identity. The 'authentic' followers believe that women's task, as an oppressed group, is to discover their true nature, and to remove the dust of ages that obscures their genuine essence. Fashion, on this reading, is one of the masks that serves to hide what women are really like. The 'modernists', on the other hand, accept that modern social life depends on the cultivation of image as part of the forging of identity, and consequently accept fashion as an inevitable ingredient in this process. Put succinctly, she argues, the question is: 'Does [fashion] muffle the self, or create it?' (1985, p. 231). Her own answer to this question supports the latter perspective, believing as she does that the notion of a 'natural' self is romantic and essentialist.

At the same time, Wilson is not naïvely euphoric about fashion's potential as a means of liberating women and enabling them to explore different subjectivities. It is perfectly possible, she says, to 'acknowledge that dress is a powerful weapon of control and dominance, while widening our view to encompass an understanding of its *simultaneously* subversive qualities' (1992, p. 14). In many work contexts, dress still serves as a more serious constraint for women than it does for men. Often forbidden from wearing trousers, and always required to exhibit a more varied wardrobe than their besuited male colleagues, women are subjected to continuing explicit or implicit restrictions on what they wear.

It is these rules of dress that are sent up in the 1988 film *Working Girl*, as Chanel-inspired superexecutive Katherine Parker (Sigourney Weaver) comes to a bad end and awkwardly dressed secretary Tess McGill (Melanie Griffith) rises to the top. Pretending to be Katherine (now convalescent after a skiing accident), Tess gets the dress codes wrong, turning up at a business cocktail party in a sparkling little black number, while the other women sport dull masculine-style suits. It is this *faux pas* that brings her to the notice of Jack Trainer (Harrison Ford) and sets her on course to success. His comment that she is 'the first woman I've seen at one of these damned things that dresses like a woman, not like a woman thinks a man would dress if he was a woman' confirms the association between 'authentic femininity' and Tess that runs throughout the film and ensures that she, not Katherine, will reap the final rewards. It is, paradoxically, in line with the film's moral endorsement of the 'authentically' feminine that in her hour of triumph she should be wearing jeans and a sweater.

Angela McRobbie's writing on young women, fashion and style relates new possibilities for experimentation with subjectivities and identities to the influences of both popular culture (most specifically popular music and dance) and the altered economic environment within which fashion trends evolve. As the worlds of popular music and fashion collided to produce dress styles that could shock by transgressing codes of femininity or masculinity, of 'good taste' and vulgarity, the freeing up of appearance released a surge of energy that liberated younger women from some of the conventions that had emerged during the modernist period. Punk, especially, broke every rule of appearance, sweeping feminine hairstyles, make-up and clothing within its black dustbin-liner, and mocking jewellery and adornment conventions by transferring them from their usual place on the body to new and more obtrusive locations (for a further discussion of women and punk, see Evans and Thornton, 1989, pp. 17–34). Angela McRobbie describes 'punk do-it-yourself fashion' as transforming fashion 'into pop art' (1989, p. 40). Young women's magazines, and most especially *Just Seventeen* in Britain, helped to project the idea that adapting style and creating something new were more trendy than slavishly following fashion. Improvisation and excess began to take the place of imitation and conformity (1991, pp. 177–9).

McRobbie also traces the interrelation between street-market fashion and high fashion in an economy that pushes former art school students into the commercial slipstream of market trading, and young upwardly mobile women (such as students) into at least temporary poverty. Both forms of improvisation transform financial necessity into creative fun. McRobbie cites the example of leggings which, despite their humble origins as men's long underpants on Camden Market stalls, set more of a fashion trend in the 1980s than the creations of big-name designers. Charity and second-hand clothes shops in the same decade became such standard sources for stylish buying by students and other young people that the term 'retro-chic' was coined to describe the phenomenon. Both the overlapping of street and high fashion, and the mixing of styles from different periods to create a stunning effect might be argued to bring these developments within the territory of the postmodern. By grounding her analysis in material conditions, however, McRobbie refuses the version of postmodernism that concerns itself only with cultural signs. At the same time she acknowledges that the new play with style emerges out of a celebratory 'knowingness'; a self-conscious awareness of the dislocation between image and identity epitomized also in 1980s' female music performers such as Bananarama or – again – Madonna (1989, pp. 23-49).

Youthful playfulness with dress codes co-exists, of course, with the continuing power of the fashion industry to set trends and parameters within which experimentation is possible. Young women, emerging through punk or Gothic affiliations, or merely accustomed to mixing without matching clothing and accessories, are, though, less likely to perceive the fashion industry as oracle; more likely to perceive it as an enabler of a variety of subjectivities that can be used for self-expression at work or in leisure pursuits. In this sense, young women's readings of the fashion features in women's magazines (discussed in Chapter 4) may take the form of 'bricolage' rather than imitation. Hebdige defines bricolage as the dislocation of signs from their original location to forge new meanings. Subcultural groups take the codes of dominant fashion and use them in ways that subvert their original intention (1979, pp. 103-4). Young women arguably respond similarly to the fashion displays in magazines. The accessory and separates market has especially enabled creativity to extend well beyond those able to afford designer outfits. Within the cultural practice of fashion, the fabricating of a single uniform identity is now seen as a mark of profound conservatism: indeed, it can be argued that it was the well-off careerists of the 1980s (referred to as the 'yuppies', or young upwardly mobile people) who most slavishly adopted 'the look' on offer from designer stores.

While the liberating aspects of this creativity and bricolage are obvious, the extent to which they redefine femininity is less clear-cut. 'Dressing up', or as the concept of the masquerade would phrase it, playing with the masks of womanliness, has long been an integral part of learning to be feminine. What is new, however, about the recent trends is that the play takes place in the public arena of the urban streets or rave venue, not in the private space of the bedroom. The effect of this is to turn even the non-participant into a more knowing decoder of fashion and style than her earlier sisters. 'Retro', for example, by bringing together past and present codes both subverts the essential newness and nowness of high fashion and establishes a dialogue between past and present constructions of femininity (Silverman, 1986, pp. 150-1). Whether the 'ironic distance' between image and identity that is established in the practice of fashion carries over equally into our readings of its representations is another matter. This becomes a particular issue in relation to the practice and representation of cross-dressing.

Cross-dressing

Cross-dressing would appear on the surface to be one of the most direct ways of challenging gender expectations. Yet the power hierarchy ensures that it is more transgressive and unsettling for men to dress in female clothing than the other way round. As Barthes puts it: 'there is a social prohibition against the feminization of men, there is almost none against the masculinization of women: Fashion notably acknowledges the *boyish look*' (1985, p. 257). A woman attired as a man may be seen either as 'power dressing', or as adopting the mannerism of the lesbian. In film, the deliberately androgynous look has been cultivated in a number of films since Marlene Dietrich's appearance in top hat and tails in von Sternberg's *Morocco* (1930). In a development seen by Walter Benjamin as a by-product of modernism, lesbians, at least in Paris, were already by that period establishing male dress as both fashionable and shocking (Wilson, 1985, pp. 128, 164). Coco Chanel, in mainstream fashion, had as early as the 1920s been designing clothes for women that adopted a masculine look. In von Sternberg's film, the subversive power of his star in mannish attire may, for its contemporary audience, have been perceived more in sexual than in gender terms. But its challenge to convention is also questioned both by Dietrich's glamour and the narrative development of the film. In the role of Amy Jolly, a nightclub singer, her donning of male evening wear is presented as a masquerade aimed to win over a hostile audience. Enabling her to command her audience, reject unwelcome advances, and remain in control, she projects enough charisma to kiss a woman on the lips.

This sexual gesture, like the cold but passionate kiss that Catharine bestows on Alex towards the end of *Black Widow*, takes the audience by surprise and may momentarily shock heterosexual expectations, but it also reminds us that the glamour of male dress, even in its lesbian connotations, has erotic appeal to men as well as women. It is the men in the audience who cheer Amy Jolly's audacious act. In Adrian Lyne's *9½ Weeks*, Elizabeth's adoption of moustache and tuxedo to parade as John's business associate in an expensive restaurant increases her attraction to him and becomes another episode in his plans to reconstruct her. The narrative development of *Morocco* also makes it difficult to read

this scene as a direct challenge to conventional gender or sexual identities. In her next act, Dietrich reappears in the more familiar garb of
the feminine woman, dressed in frills and girly clothes, and posing as
a seller of apples. Her song makes the reference to Eve explicit as she
coyly exploits her sexual charms to persuade the audience to buy her
wares. Male dress becomes just one ploy in a series of 'dressing up' masquerades that Dietrich's films explore.

It is revealing that when we think of female cross-dressers in the
media the names that spring to mind are either glamorous women such
as Marlene Dietrich, Marilyn Monroe (in the delightfully effervescent
Some Like it Hot), and Madonna (who draws on both the earlier stars
for her acts), or models associated with glamour products, such as
Revlon's Charlie in the 1970s, striding about town in trouser suits,
exuding chutzpah as well as the manufacturer's fragrance. The exceptions in cinematic terms include Joan Crawford as Vienna in the variant
of the western of *Johnny Guitar* (1954) and Doris Day as Calamity Jane
in Warner Brothers' film of that title in 1953. Both these 1950s' films
depart from the celebration of domestic versions of femininity dominant
in American and British culture of the period. Even sexy women in this
decade's films were generally unthreatening and girlish, despite their
womanly shape. Doris Day's pertness and jauntiness in *Calamity Jane*,
her readiness to confront her opponents, match her androgynous
cowboy outfit. Ready to take on the world, she is nevertheless
transformed, partly through the conventions of the musical genre, and
partly through the film's narrative ending, into a woman masquerading
as a tomboy. When wild Bill Hickock says to her towards the end of
the film, 'You're a fake, Calam. You dress, talk, ride and shoot like a
man but you think like a female: a green-eyed, snarlin', spittin' female',
the audience is inclined to agree. In the best Hollywood musical tradition, the film ends with the romantic fanfare of a double wedding.

Johnny Guitar's darker atmosphere produces a more serious questioning of gender expectations. Although the film is named after the hero
who, as Vienna's ex-lover, finally rescues her from the clutches of the
posse seeking revenge for a stagecoach killing, it is Vienna who commands attention throughout the film. Joan Crawford, now operating as
a freelance star, changes persona in this film with a panache and
audacity that casts dress as a narrative player in the drama. Initially
garbed in sombre shirt, jeans and masculine necktie, when she resumes
her relationship with Johnny Guitar she is dressed seductively in low-cut
purple nightdress. The final melodramatic shoot-out between herself

and Emma Small (Mercedes McCambridge) sets the mourning-bedecked Emma (her brother was killed in the stagecoach attack) against Vienna's garish attire of yellow shirt, red necktie and blue jeans. In a clash between sombre black and bright primary colours, there can be scope for only one heroine.

The six dress changes that Vienna undergoes in the course of this film (three 'feminine', three 'masculine') mark out significant stages in narrative development, and establish the heroine as at her most seductive when most in control, and most androgynous in appearance and behaviour. Whereas in film noir, the *femme fatale* had a consistency of appearance that belies her duplicity, in *Johnny Guitar* the frequent and ostentatious reversals of Vienna's image paradoxically underline, as in the excess of the masquerade, the forthrightness and unwavering quality of her character.

Since the 1960s, the growth in unisex clothing that enabled women to dress more like men has made the dressing up of women in markedly male attire less common in the cinema. Instead, the trend has been glamorized in the world of high fashion. In the 1980s in particular Princess Diana's taste for tuxedo and tie, the cross-dressing of pop star Annie Lennox and, more ambiguously, of Madonna, have helped to reaffirm the place of pinstripes and masculine cuts on the designer agenda. Removing any hint of sexual or gender subversion from masculine dress, and re-presenting it as meaningless chic is a peculiarly postmodernist act. As a fashion feature in *Company* magazine displaying pinstripe suits and dresses puts it, 'from him, the confidence of many pinstripes. From you, the sex appeal of frankly feminine hair, elaborate shirts and high heels. It's a seductive combination that says Forties glamour, Nineties power' (September 1992, p. 75). Annie Lennox also claimed that her adoption of masculine clothing and an androgynous look aimed less to subvert the gender norms than to encourage people to take her seriously:

Before Eurythmics became established, I wanted to present myself as a woman that was not of the girlish, girly ilk, with little mini-skirts and legs, a sexy cutesy-pie dolly-bird type person. Which I'm not. I wanted to reinvent myself, so it was natural for me to wear more mannish clothes because it gave me more power.

(Interview with Adam Sweeting in *The Guardian*, 26 November 1986)

Even when what is being played with are the conventions of

masculinity, the effect may be more that of outrageous fun than subversion. A recent Jean Paul Gaultier advertisement poses the male model as a latter-day Marilyn Monroe, holding down 'her' dress with 'his' heavily tattooed arm, as the famous grille of *The Seven Year Itch* threatens to expose 'his' private parts. The joke is self-evident, but it works by appropriating the association between bodily exhibitionism and femininity rather than undermining our expectations of masculinity. Similar processes attend the drag artist or the female impersonator in media performance. Because the crossing of gender codes is necessarily exhibitionist in this context, the projection on the stage of the duality of masculinity/femininity (the drag artist never masks his male identity completely) appears anarchic rather than subversive. In performance, transvestism (men – usually, but not uniquely – dressing up in the other sex's clothing), differs markedly from its practice as a form of fetishistic sexual excitement (see Peter Ackroyd's distinction between 'anarchic' and 'fetishistic' transvestism in Evans and Thornton, 1989, p. 38). In contrast to drag as performance, practising transvestites are 'seriously committed to narrowly idealised conventional gender standards' (Evans, 1993, p. 176).

Drag performance questions gender stability, but it does not, as one might logically expect, challenge masculinity's power. From the pantomime dame, to Dame Edna Everage to Ru Paul, the adoption of women's clothing in performance is 'outrageous' (in a way that women's adoption of masculine attire is not) precisely because it so naughtily mimics the excesses of the feminine. As Judith Williamson puts it, 'There is nothing inherently radical about men dressing as women. After all, under all those skirts and stuffed bras there's still a perfectly safe penis' (1986a, p. 48). John Epperson, Lypsinka in his drag act, comments that playing this role is 'empowering', but adds with some bewilderment 'I didn't even know what I was doing when I started doing this. I didn't know it was subversive and now everyone's attaching a political tag to it. I just did it to be in show business' (*Without Walls* programme on Bodyism, Channel 4, 15 February 1994). Even within film narratives, men dressing up as women may temporarily destabilize our gender certainties, and, as Annette Kuhn points out, draw attention to our conventional way of looking at women on film, but in the end, 'many do so only . . . to reassert a "natural" order of fixed gender and unitary subjectivity' (1985, p. 57). Marjorie Garber's view that cross-dressing not only puts in crisis the categories of 'male' and 'female' but marks 'the necessary critique of binary thinking, whether particularized as male and female, black and white, yes and no, Republican and Democrat, self and other, or in any other way' seems exaggerated almost to the point of parody (1993, pp. 10–11). Even in its occasionally overt political manifestations, drag raised more anxieties than certainties about its subversive capacities (Evans, 1993, pp. 174–6).

In conclusion

Fashion, dance, and bodily adornment offer scope for play and experimentation with identity that is liberating, especially for the young. In these practices of the body, postmodernist optimism comes into its own. Angela McRobbie (1989, 1991, 1994) has written persuasively of the 'upbeat' case to be made for seeing those aspects of youth culture as breaking down old oppositions between femininity and feminism, and allowing new forms of self-expression to emerge for young women, challenging previous starched polarities of race, class or gender. While this is a convincing argument, even if, as McRobbie herself suggests in relation to rave culture (1994, pp. 167–74), the material control of the entertainment industries sometimes complicates the picture, it is harder to sustain in relation to representation. As with 'camp' or dance forms such as 'ragga', the escape from the limits of convention for those who participate is not necessarily replicated for those who watch.

The practice of 'camp', as Richard Dyer points out, enables many gay men to express their identity with wit, self-mockery and a celebratory sense of fun. But, he adds, 'something happens to camp when it is taken over by straights – it loses its cutting edge, its identification with the gay experience, its distance from the straight sexual world-view' (1992, p. 145). Watching 'camp' is even less inspirational, tending as it does to confirm stereotypes of gay sexuality rather than challenge them. Similarly, the testimony of black female ragga dancers suggests that, from their point of view, dressing up, putting on a persona that exposes their sexuality and commands erotic attention, enables them to contest the devaluation of black women's bodies in mainstream culture (*Arena*, BBC2, 12 February 1994). Watching ragga dancing, on the other hand, it may be difficult to resist the position of the voyeur, surveying images of female bodies reminiscent of pornography. The positive characteristics of ragga as dance also exist in tension with ragga as text on another dimension, as Angela McRobbie recognizes, given the homophobic nature of some of its lyrics (1994, p. 184).

When the focus is on texts, as it has been in this book, the grounds for optimism seem fewer. McRobbie sees the exploratory and celebratory practices of youth culture as 'changing the mode of femininity'. While in media representations, the myths of femininity have been modified in the course of this century in a variety of ways, what is disturbing is their tenaciousness, or the alacrity with which they have been defensively reinvented, against the cultural and social changes in women's lives. Emphases have changed, playfulness has taken over from seriousness, but the 'mode of femininity' has been tinkered with, not redrafted. Two lines of progress seem necessary to produce an 'upbeat' assessment here. Women need to have more opportunities to explore and articulate their own desires and their own diversities. But if this is going to amount to more than allowing women extra slots in the schedule, or an even wider range of women's magazines, myths of masculinity need to be more extensively destabilized and rethought, too.

At the same time, the gap between practice and representation is arguably less fixed than I am suggesting, as today's experimenters with identity in the dance-halls or street-markets spend a quiet night at the cinema, or collapse eventually into bed to consume magazines or MTV. The developments that are taking place in 'changing the mode of femininity' in youth culture cannot, in this sense, be detached from the experience of young people as consumers of the media. While I would not wish to endorse the simplicity and over-optimism of John Fiske's much celebrated view that we are all 'producerly' readers now, continually inventing our own scripts in tune with our own experiences from those the media offer us, it is clear that media readers who have already questioned conventional categories of gender, ethnicity or sexuality in their own practice have at least a chance of being more resistive readers than their conservative peers.

The danger is, that in passing from involvement in cultural practice to the less active role as audience of the text, parodic inventiveness will melt into Jameson's 'depthless' or 'blank' pastiche. We may all become more knowing spectators, more aware of playfulness, take-offs and reinventions, but intertextual sophistication will not of itself lead to change. Nor, necessarily, does a sense of irony, but the absurdity of the contrast between two levels of perception does at least introduce a grain of grit into the complacent eye. Playfulness has, as we have seen, become a recurrent mode in addressing women about their femininity. I have tended to present this as a ruse of consumerism anxious to revitalize worn myths without alienating an audience whose social and cultural position is changing. If, as Angela McRobbie's more positive interpretation suggests, this also, or nevertheless, succeeds in putting an ironic distance between text and reader, then hopes of progress are less fanciful.

While the female body remains an active battlefield, fashion and bodily adornment are now at least languages over which the media have lost full control. With the development of active subcultures, competing sites exist for youthful alliances. It is easy to argue that in a world of material inequality, in terms of jobs, money, security, opportunity and power, the realms of fashion and bodily appearance form only a peripheral distraction from the claiming of real citizenship rights. I have a lot of sympathy with this view. Yet in a world that devalues permanent work, that forces the young in particular to forge their identities in other ways, and that elevates the world of entertainment and leisure into a significant means of exploring who one is, at least part of the political ground is shifting. Questions of identity take on a new political urgency, and not just on the margins. For women, more used to adapting their personae, and playing different roles at the same time, this situation may paradoxically offer richer opportunities than for men. Those who have been held by generations of myths to be unknowable, multi-dimensional but yet faceless, may be less perplexed by an era of uncertainty than those who always thought they occupied a still place in a turning world. If this is so, it makes for interesting times, culturally and politically.

Glossary

Note: further guidance on many of the terms outlined here can be found in the following useful texts:

KUHN, A. and RADSTONE, S. (eds) 1990: *The women's companion to international film*. London: Virago.
O'SULLIVAN, T., HARTLEY, J., SAUNDERS, D., MONTGOMERY, M. and FISKE, J. 1994: *Key concepts in communication and cultural studies*. London: Routledge.

androgyny the state of exhibiting a combination of traditionally masculine and traditionally feminine traits.

avant-garde term often applied to art or films that challenge both the content and, even more importantly, the formal conventions dominant at the time. Avant-garde art or film tends as a result to be seen as difficult or demanding by audiences of the period.

bricolage adapting elements from a standard package of signs to an alternative purpose, thereby undermining their usual meaning.

code a system of signs that operates according to a set of rules that are widely understood within a culture or subculture.

commodification turning something into a commodity that does not belong intrinsically in the commercial sphere.

commutation test replacing one element in a communication (e.g. one word in a sequence) to highlight its particular contribution to the overall meaning (normally this is invisible because we are so familiar with the usual pattern).

connotation   the associations triggered by a particular sign.

co-option   the process whereby a dominant discourse apparently adopts elements of non-dominant discourses. By taking over surface elements only (e.g. key words, but not the ideas behind them), this drains the alternative discourses of their radical or oppositional implications.

deconstruction   a method of analysis (particularly associated with the French philosopher Jacques Derrida) that pays attention to gaps, silences and inconsistencies in a text in order to explore its unquestioned assumptions and internal contradictions.

determinism   laying all the responsibility for a phenomenon on specified causes (e.g. biological determinism places primary responsibility for social behaviour on the individual's genetic and physical make-up).

discourse   language understood as a social and institutional practice. Instead of viewing language as a neutral tool to produce meaning, discourse suggests that systematic ways of thinking about the world are already built into established patterns of language use. We, and the media, often reproduce these as if they were our own ideas. Discourse embodies ideology and therefore plays a major role in supporting or contesting power (e.g. feminist discourse contests sexist discourse).

essentialism   the belief that there is an intrinsic and inescapable difference between entities which does not need further explanation (in gender terms, this most often refers to intrinsic or natural differences between men and women). Essentialism holds that difference is prescribed and fixed, and therefore rejects the notion that gender differences, for example, are socially constructed.

ethnography   the adaptation by researchers into media audiences of a methodology developed in social anthropology. The ethnographic method includes observation of, and open-ended interviews with, real audiences in the surroundings in which they normally receive the medium being studied.

femininity   the attributes that are conventionally associated with the condition of being female within a specific culture.

folklinguistics   widespread cultural beliefs about the characteristics of language use by different groups. These function as myths and do not necessarily represent current realities of language practice.

hegemony   a consensual system of viewing and thinking about the world, arrived at not through coercion but by winning voluntary agreement that this is a sensible or even natural way of perceiving reality. In hegemony, ideologies are naturalized to appear as 'common sense'.

ideology   a system of beliefs operating widely, but often without us being conscious of it, in a particular society and sustaining specific power relations, e.g. of class, or gender, or ethnic dominance. Although some ideologies have higher status than others in our society, there is no single dominant ideology and a number of different ideologies compete continually for our attention and our support.

incorporation   see 'co-option'.

inscribed reader   the reader constructed by the media's modes of address (as opposed to the real reader, who may differ in many respects from this temporarily fabricated persona). (See also 'modes of address'.)

interpellation   'hailing' the reader or viewer, or strongly inviting him or her to adopt a particular stance in relation to the text.

224

intertextuality	the common practice in the late twentieth century of media texts referring to each other, often implicitly and with the assumption that the audience will pick up the references (this is particularly visible in British television advertising but is also, for example, a striking feature of Madonna's performances and of David Lynch's work). Our knowledge of these references contributes to the meaning that we derive from the intertextual text. (See also 'parody' and 'pastiche'.)
masculinity	the attributes that are conventionally associated with the condition of being male within a specific culture.
masquerade	literally this means putting on a mask or a disguise, but the term has been adopted in feminist film theory to suggest that when female stars exaggerate their feminine attributes, they denaturalize femininity and invite the audience to think critically and sceptically about the assumptions we normally make about it.
mise en scène	literally the staging of the scene for the camera, but now used to include the composition of the shot, choice of camera angle, framing and lighting.
modernism	a cultural movement extending from the end of the nineteenth century to the mid-twentieth century and characterized by a desire to break free from bourgeois conventionalism, and respond constructively to the new 'modern' social and technological environment. Modernism was caught between angst about the moral consequences of the speed of change and optimism about the potential for reshaping the world that this offered. In the arts, modernism was marked by a self-conscious attention to, and experimentation with, form.

modes of address   the ways in which the media address us. These are built on assumptions about our identities and interests, and often invite us to accept the personae that they invent for us. We may, of course, reject this position and find the modes of address jarring or off-putting (see also 'inscribed reader').

myth   a way of conceptualizing a subject that is widely accepted within a particular culture and a particular historical period.

parody   mimicking an original with ironic intent, in order to make a critical comment.

pastiche   mimicking an original for fun, with merely playful intent.

patriarchy   technically 'rule by the father or head of household' but now widely used to signify systematic male domination.

postfeminism   an ideological stance based on the belief that the aims of feminism have been largely achieved, and that women can now accomplish whatever they want to, provided they are prepared to make sufficient effort. Postfeminism substitutes individual endeavour for collective campaigning by feminists to change social institutions and the structural balance of power. Postfeminism is also associated with stylishness and the belief that it is possible to be both feminine and supportive of feminist objectives. Women who regard themselves as postfeminist will, however, usually reject the feminist label.

postmodernism   the cultural response, evident especially since the 1970s, to cataclysmic global changes in information provision, the economy, work patterns and technology. This response has been characterized by a loss of faith in meaningfulness and originality, and a celebration of fragmentation, surface texture and the breaking down of old boundaries (such as those between popular and élite culture or between masculinity and femininity).

poststructuralism   an analytical movement that challenges the notion of a unified subject, and the structuralist idea that meaning emerges from the clash of polar opposites. Influenced by psychoanalysis, it prefers to think of the individual as riven by fragmented subjectivities, and to approach the analysis of texts through the methodology of deconstruction (see also 'deconstruction' and 'subjectivity').

recuperation   see 'co-option'.

scopophilia   sexual pleasure derived from looking.

semiotics   an attempt to apply scientific principles to the study of signs in order to explain how meanings are produced.

sign   any physical manifestation (e.g. a sound or an image or a piece of writing) that refers to something beyond itself, in a way that is widely recognized. A red rose may, for example, signify a flower, or romance, or (in Britain) the Labour Party.

signification   the process of creating meaning through signs.

signifier   in the terms of the Swiss linguist, Ferdinand de Saussure, the physical manifestation that triggers the mental concept (or signified).

signified   in Saussure's terms, the mental concept triggered by the signifier.

structuralism   an approach to social and cultural phenomena that disregards surface appearances in favour of analysing the hidden polarities that govern the production of meaning.

subject   although this term is used in a variety of ways, including the sense of 'subjectivity' explained below, it is easier to separate these terms, and use 'subject' to refer to the concept of a coherent, rational and unified individual who has a significant measure of control over his/her actions, desires and thoughts. The origin of this view of the subject is often attributed to the eighteenth-century Enlightenment.

subjectivity

the persona that we are invited to adopt as a result of the way that we are addressed, either face-to-face or via cultural and media discourses. Each individual on this reckoning will experience a number of different, and even competing, subjectivities (for example, a woman may be torn between different subjectivities on the topic of abortion if she is both a feminist and a practising Roman Catholic).

voyeurism

deriving sexual pleasure from viewing titillating scenes from a clandestine position.

Filmography

Note: The film title is followed by the date of release, the production company and the name of the director.

The Accused (1988) Paramount (Jonathan Kaplan)
Alice Doesn't Live Here Anymore (1974) Warner Brothers (Martin Scorsese)
Aliens (1986) Twentieth Century-Fox (James Cameron)
Awakenings (1990) Columbia (Penny Marshall)
Baby Boom (1987) MGM/United Artists (Charles Shyer)
Basic Instinct (1992) Carolco/Le Studio Canal (Paul Verhoeven)
Beaches (1988) Touchstone Pictures (Gary Marshall)
Black Widow (1987) Twentieth Century-Fox (Bob Rafelson)
Blonde Venus (1932) Paramount (Joseph von Sternberg)
Body Heat (1981) Ladd Company (Lawrence Kasdan)
Body of Evidence (1992) Dino de Laurentiis Communications (Uli Edel)
Build My Gallows High (*Out of the Past*, in USA) (1947) RKO (Jacques Tourneur)
Calamity Jane (1953) Warner Brothers (David Butler)
The Color Purple (1985) Amblin Entertainment (Steven Spielberg)
Coming Home (1978) United Artists (Hal Ashby)
Desert Hearts (1985) Desert Heart Productions (Donna Deitch)
Double Indemnity (1944) Paramount (Billy Wilder)
Fatal Attraction (1987) Paramount (Adrian Lyne)
Fried Green Tomatoes at the Whistle Stop Café (1991) Fried Green Tomatoes Productions/Act III/Electric Shadow (Jon Avnet)
Gilda (1946) Columbia (Charles Vidor)
Girlfriends (1978) Cyclops (Claudia Weill)
The Good Mother (1988) Touchstone/Silver Screen Partners IV (Leonard Nimoy)

The Hand that Rocks the Cradle (1992) Buena Vista Pictures (Curtis Hanson)

Imitation of Life (1934) Universal (John Stahl)

Imitation of Life (1959) Universal (Douglas Sirk)

Jagged Edge (1985) Columbia-Delphi IV Productions (Richard Marquand)

Johnny Guitar (1954) Republic (Nicholas Ray)

Just Another Girl on the I.R.T. (1992) Truth 24 F.P.S. for Miramax (Leslie Harris)

Kramer vs Kramer (1979) Columbia (Robert Benton)

The Lady from Shanghai (1948) Columbia (Orson Welles)

A League of Their Own (1992) Columbia (Penny Marshall)

Lianna (1982) Winwood Company (John Sayles)

Longtime Companion (1990) Companion Productions/American Playhouse (Norman Rene)

Looking for Mr Goodbar (1977) Paramount (Richard Brooks)

Mildred Pierce (1945) Warner Brothers/First National (Michael Curtiz)

Morocco (1930) Paramount (Joseph von Sternberg)

9½ Weeks (1985) Jonesfilm/A Keith Barish Production in association with Galactic Films, Triple Ajaxxx (Adrian Lyne)

Norma Rae (1979) Twentieth Century-Fox (Martin Ritt)

Ordinary People (1980) Paramount (Robert Redford)

Out of the Past – see *Build My Gallows High*

Personal Best (1982) Geffen Company for Warners (Robert Towne)

A Question of Silence (1982) Sigma Films (Marlene Gorris)

She's Gotta Have It (1986) Forty Acres/Mule Filmworks (Spike Lee)

Single White Female (1992) Columbia Pictures (Barbet Schroeder)

Sliver (1993) Paramount (Phillip Noyce)

Steel Magnolias (1989) Tri-Star Pictures (Herbert Ross)

Stella Dallas (1937) United Artists (King Vidor)

Thelma and Louise (1991) Pathé Entertainment Inc. (Ridley Scott)

Three Men and a Baby (1987) Touchstone Pictures (Leonard Nimoy)

Three Men and a Little Lady (1990) Touchstone Pictures (Emile Ardolino)

Working Girl (1988) Twentieth Century-Fox (Mike Nichols)

Bibliography

D'ACCI, J. 1987: The case of 'Cagney and Lacey'. In Baehr, H. and Dyer, G. (eds), *Boxed in: women and television*. London: Pandora, 203–25.

ADVERTISING STANDARDS AUTHORITY 1982: *Herself appraised: the treatment of women in advertisements*. London: ASA.

ALCOCK, B. and ROBSON, J. 1990: 'Cagney and Lacey' revisited. *Feminist Review* 35, 42–53.

ALTHUSSER, L. 1971: Ideology and ideological state apparatuses: notes towards an investigation. In *Lenin and philosophy and other essays*. London: New Left Books, 121–73. (First published 1969.)

ARBER, S. and GINN, J. 1991: *Gender and later life*. London: Sage.

BAEHR, H. and DYER, G. (eds) 1987: *Boxed in: women and television*. London: Pandora.

BANKS, M. and SWIFT, A. 1987: *The joke's on us: women in comedy*. London: Pandora.

BARTHES, R. 1972: *Mythologies*. London: Jonathan Cape. Translated by A. Lavers. (First published 1957.)

BARTHES, R. 1985: *The fashion system*. London: Jonathan Cape. Translated by M. Ward and R. Howard. (First published in French, 1967.)

BEAUVOIR, S. de 1972: *The second sex*. Harmondsworth: Penguin. (First published in French, 1949, and translated in this form by H. Parshley, for Jonathan Cape, 1953.)

BEERE, S. 1991: Women's viewing patterns. In BBC Broadcasting Research Department: *BBC broadcasting research: annual review no. XVII*. London: John Libbey, 51–61.

BEM, S. 1974: The measurement of psychological androgyny. *Journal of consulting and clinical psychology* 42 (2), 155–62.

BENEDICT, H. 1992: *Virgin or vamp: how the press covers sex crimes*. Oxford: Oxford University Press.

BERGER, J. 1972: *Ways of seeing*. London: BBC/Penguin.

BETTERTON, R. (ed.) 1987: *Looking on: images of femininity in the visual arts and media*. London: Pandora.

BIRCH, H. (ed.) 1993: *Moving targets: women, murder and representation*. London: Virago.

BIRKE, L. 1986: *Women, feminism and biology: the feminist challenge*. Brighton: Harvester Wheatsheaf.

BLY, R. 1991: *Iron John: a book about men*. Shaftesbury, Dorset: Element Books.

BOBO, J. 1988: 'The Color Purple': black women as cultural readers. In Pribram, E. D. (ed.), *Female spectators: looking at film and television*. London: Verso, 90–109.

BORDO, S. 1990: Reading the slender body. In Jacobus, M., Keller, E., and Shuttleworth, S. (eds), *Body/politics: women and the discourses of science*. London: Routledge, 83–112.

BORDWELL, D. 1985: *Narration in the fiction film*. London: Methuen.

BOWLBY, R. 1985: *Just looking*. London: Methuen.

BROADCASTING STANDARDS COUNCIL 1994: *Research working paper IX: perspectives of women in television*. London: BSC.

BROWN, H. G. 1963: *Sex and the single girl*. London: Frederick Muller.

BROWN, M. E. 1990: Motley moments: soap operas, carnival, gossip and the power of the utterance. In Brown, M. E. (ed.), *Television and women's culture: the politics of the popular*. London: Sage, 183–98.

BROWNMILLER, S. 1976: *Against our will: men, women and rape*. Harmondsworth: Penguin.

BRUMBERG, J. 1988: *Fasting girls: the emergence of anorexia nervosa as a modern disease*. Cambridge, Mass.: Harvard University Press.

BRUNSDON, C. (ed.) 1986: *Films for women*. London: BFI.

BRUNT, R. 1982: 'An immense verbosity': permissive sexual advice in the 1970s. In Brunt, R. and Rowan, C. (eds), *Feminism, culture and politics*. London: Lawrence and Wishart, 143–70.

BRUNT, R. 1990: Points of view. In Goodwin, A. and Whannel, G. (eds), *Understanding television*. London: Routledge, 60–73.

BYARS, J. 1991: *All that Hollywood allows: re-reading gender in 1950s melodrama*. London: Routledge.

CAMERON, D. 1992: *Feminism and linguistic theory*. London: Macmillan.

CHAPMAN, R. 1988: The great pretender: variations on the new man theme. In Chapman, R. and Rutherford, J. (eds), *Male order: unwrapping masculinity*. London: Lawrence and Wishart, 225–48.

CHODOROW, N. 1978: *The reproduction of mothering: psycho-analysis and the sociology of gender.* Berkeley: University of California Press.

CIXOUS, H. 1992: The laugh of the Medusa. In Humm, M. (ed.), *Feminisms: a reader.* Hemel Hempstead: Harvester Wheatsheaf, 196–202. (First published in French, 1975.)

CLARK, K. 1992: The linguistics of blame: representations of women in 'The Sun's' reporting of crimes of sexual violence. In Toolan, M. (ed.), *Language, text and context.* London: Routledge, 208–24.

COATES, J. 1986: *Women, men and language: a sociolinguistic account of sex differences in language.* London: Longman.

CONRAN, S. 1975: *Superwoman.* London: Sidgwick and Jackson.

COOK, P. 1980: Duplicity in 'Mildred Pierce'. In Kaplan, E. A. (ed.), *Women in film noir.* London: BFI, 68–82.

COOTE, A. and CAMPBELL, B. 1982: *Sweet freedom: the struggle for women's liberation.* London: Picador.

COVENEY, L., JACKSON, M., JEFFREYS, S., KAYE, L. and MAHONY, P. 1984: *The sexuality papers: male sexuality and the social control of women.* London: Hutchinson.

COWAN, R. S. 1983: *More work for mother: the ironies of household technology from the open hearth to the microwave.* New York: Basic Books.

COWARD, R. 1984: *Female desire: women's sexuality today.* London: Paladin.

CRAIK, J. 1994: *The face of fashion: cultural studies in fashion.* London: Routledge.

CREED, B. 1993: *The monstrous-feminine: film, feminism, psycho-analysis.* London: Routledge.

DALY, M. 1978: *Gyn-Ecology: the metaethics of radical feminism.* Boston: Beacon Press.

DAVIDSON, C. 1982: *A woman's work is never done: a history of housework in the British Isles 1650–1950.* London: Chatto and Windus.

DELPHY, C. 1987: Protofeminism and antifeminism. In Moi, T. (ed.), *French feminist thought: a reader.* Oxford: Blackwell, 80–109. (First published in 1976.)

DOANE, M. A. 1987: *The desire to desire: the woman's film of the 1940s.* Bloomington and Indianapolis: Indiana University Press.

DOANE, M. A. 1991: *Femmes fatales: feminism, film theory, psycho-analysis.* London: Routledge.

DURKIN, K. 1985: *Television, sex roles and children*. Milton Keynes: Open University Press.

DYER, R. 1980: Resistance through charisma: Rita Hayworth and 'Gilda'. In Kaplan, E. A. (ed.), *Women in film noir*. London: BFI, 91–9.

DYER, R. 1992: It's being so camp as keeps us going. In Dyer, R., *Only entertainment*. London: Routledge, 135–47. (First published 1976.)

ECKERT, C. 1978: The Carole Lombard in Macy's window. *Quarterly Review of Film Studies* 3 (1), 1–21. (Also reprinted in Gaines and Herzog, 1990.)

EHRENREICH, B. and ENGLISH, D. 1979: *For her own good: 150 years of the experts' advice to women*. London: Pluto Press.

EVANS, C. and THORNTON, M. 1989: *Women and fashion: a new look*. London: Quartet.

EVANS, D. 1993: *Sexual citizenship: the material construction of sexualities*. London: Routledge.

EWEN, S. 1976: *Captains of consciousness: advertising and the social roots of the consumer culture*. New York: McGraw-Hill.

FALUDI, S. 1992: *Backlash: the undeclared war against women*. London: Vintage.

FISKE, J. 1989: *Understanding popular culture*. London: Unwin Hyman.

FOUCAULT, M. 1980: *Power/knowledge: selected interviews and other writing, 1972–1977*. Brighton: Harvester Wheatsheaf. Translated by C. Gordon *et al*.

FOUCAULT, M. 1981: *The history of sexuality, volume one: an introduction*. Harmondsworth: Penguin. (First published 1976.)

FRANK, L. and SMITH, P. (eds) 1993: *Madonnarama: essays on sex and popular culture*. Pittsburgh: Cleiss Press.

FRAZER, E. 1987: Teenage girls reading 'Jackie'. *Media, Culture and Society* 9 (4), 407–25.

FREUD, S. 1964: Lecture XXXIII Femininity. In *The standard edition of the complete psychological works of Sigmund Freud*. Translated by Strachey, J. *et al*., vol. 22, New introductory lectures on psychoanalysis (1933). London: Hogarth Press, 112–35.

FRIDAY, N. 1973: *My secret garden*. New York: Trident.

FRIDAY, N. 1991: *Women on top*. London: Hutchinson.

FRIEDAN, B. 1965: *The feminine mystique*. Harmondsworth: Penguin. (First published 1963.)

FRITH, S. 1993: The sound of 'Erotica': pain, power, and pop. In Frank,

L. and Smith, P. (eds), *Madonnarama: essays on sex and popular culture*. Pittsburgh: Cleiss Press, 87–92.

GAINES, J. and HERZOG, C. (eds) 1990: *Fabrications: costume and the female body*. London: Routledge/AFI.

GAMMAN, L. 1988: Watching the detectives: the enigma of the female gaze. In Gamman, L. and Marshment, M. (eds), *The female gaze: women as viewers of popular culture*. London: Women's Press, 8–26.

GAMMAN, L. and MARSHMENT, M. (eds) 1988: *The female gaze: women as viewers of popular culture*. London: Women's Press.

GARBER, M. 1993: *Vested interests: cross-dressing and cultural anxiety*. Harmondsworth: Penguin.

GERAGHTY, C. 1991: *Women and soap opera: a study of prime time soaps*. Cambridge: Polity Press.

GILL, R. 1993: Justifying injustice: broadcasters' accounts of inequality in radio. In Burman, E. and Parker, I. (eds), *Discourse analytic research: repertoires and readings of texts in action*. London: Routledge.

GILLIGAN, C. 1982: *In a different voice: psychological theory and women's development*. Cambridge, Mass.: Harvard University Press.

GLEDHILL, C. (ed.) 1987: *Home is where the heart is: studies in melodrama and the woman's film*. London: BFI.

GLEDHILL, C. 1988: Pleasurable negotiations. In Pribram, E. D. (ed.), *Female spectators: looking at film and television*. London: Verso, 64–89.

GLEDHILL, C. (ed.) 1991: *Stardom: industry of desire*. London: Routledge.

GOODMAN, L. 1992: Gender and humour. In Bonner, F., Goodman, L., Allen, R., Janes, L., and King, C. (eds), *Imagining women: cultural representations and gender*. Cambridge: Polity Press, 286–300.

GRADDOL, D. and SWANN, J. 1989: *Gender voices*. Oxford: Blackwell.

GRAY, A. 1992: *Video playtime: the gendering of a leisure technology*. London: Routledge.

HAMILTON, R., HAWORTH, B. and SARDAR, N. 1982: *Adman and Eve: a study of the portrayal of women in advertising carried out for the Equal Opportunities Commission*. Lancaster: University of Lancaster marketing consultancy and research services.

HARDYMENT, C. 1988: *From mangle to microwave: the mechanization of household work*. Cambridge: Polity Press.

HARRIS, T. 1991: The building of popular images: Grace Kelly and

Marilyn Monroe. In Gledhill, C. (ed.), *Stardom: industry of desire.* London: Routledge, 40-4.

HARVEY, D. 1989: *The condition of postmodernity.* Oxford: Blackwell.

HARVEY, S. 1980: Woman's place: the absent family of film noir. In Kaplan, E. A. (ed.), *Women in film noir.* London: BFI, 22-34.

HASKELL, M. 1987: *From reverence to rape: the treatment of women in the movies.* Chicago: University of Chicago Press. (First edition 1974.)

HEBDIGE, D. 1979: *Subculture: the meaning of style.* London: Methuen.

HEBDIGE, D. 1988: *Hiding in the light: on images and things.* London: Routledge.

HERZOG, C. and GAINES, J. 1991: 'Puffed sleeves before tea-time': Joan Crawford, Adrian and women audiences. In Gledhill, C. (ed.), *Stardom: industry of desire.* London: Routledge, 74-91.

HEUNG, M. 1987a: 'Black Widow'. *Film Quarterly* 41 (1), 54-8.

HEUNG, M. 1987b: 'What's the matter with Sarah Jane?': daughters and mothers in Douglas Sirk's 'Imitation of Life'. *Cinema Journal* 26 (3), 21-43.

HITE, S. 1977: *The Hite report: a nationwide study of female sexuality.* Sydney: Summit Books/Paul Hamlyn Pty Ltd.

HITE, S. 1987: *Women and love: a cultural revolution in progress.* London: Viking.

HOLLAND, P. 1987: When a woman reads the news. In Baehr, H. and Dyer, G. (eds), *Boxed in: women and television.* London: Pandora, 133-50.

HOLLINGSWORTH, M. 1986: Peace women at the wire: the Greenham factor. In Hollingsworth, M., *The press and political dissent.* London: Pluto Press, 170-207.

HOOKS, B. 1989: *Talking back: thinking feminist – thinking black.* Boston: South End Press.

HOOKS, B. 1993a: Power to the pussy: we don't wannabe dicks in drag. In Frank, L. and Smith, P. (eds), *Madonnarama: essays on sex and popular culture.* Pittsburgh: Cleiss Press, 65-80.

HOOKS, B. 1993b: Ending female sexual oppression. In Jackson, S. (ed.), *Women's studies: a reader.* Hemel Hempstead: Harvester Wheatsheaf, 245.

HUMM, M. (ed.) 1992: *Feminisms: a reader.* Hemel Hempstead: Harvester Wheatsheaf.

ITZIN, C. 1986: Media images of women: the social construction of ageism and sexism. In Wilkinson, S. (ed.), *Feminist social psychology: developing theory and practice*. Milton Keynes: Open University Press, 119-34.

JACKSON, S. (ed.) 1993: *Women's studies: a reader*. Hemel Hempstead: Harvester Wheatsheaf.

JAMESON, F. 1983: Postmodernism and consumer society. In Foster, H. (ed.), *Postmodern culture*. London: Pluto Press, 111-25.

JAMESON, F. 1984: Postmodernism, or the cultural logic of late capitalism. *New Left Review*, 146, 53-92.

JEWELL, K. S. 1993: *From Mammy to Miss America and beyond: cultural images and the shaping of US social policy*. London: Routledge.

JONES, D. 1990: Gossip: notes on women's oral culture. In Cameron, D. (ed.), *The feminist critique of language: a reader*. London: Routledge, 242-50. (First published 1980.)

KAPLAN, C. 1986: *Sea changes: essays on culture and feminism*. London: Verso.

KAPLAN, E. A. (ed.) 1980: *Women in film noir*. London: BFI.

KAPLAN, E. A. 1983: *Women and film: both sides of the camera*. London: Methuen.

KAPLAN, E. A. 1985: Dialogue on 'Stella Dallas'. *Cinema Journal* 24 (2), 40-3.

KAPLAN, E. A. 1992: *Motherhood and representation: the mother in popular culture and melodrama*. London: Routledge.

KARPF, A. 1987: 'Radio Times' - private women and public men. In Davies, K., Dickey, J. and Stratford, T. (eds), *Out of focus: writings on women and the media*. London: Women's Press, 169-76.

KENNEDY, H. 1992: *Eve was framed: women and British justice*. London: Chatto & Windus.

KINSEY, A. C., POMEROY, W. B., MARTIN, C. E. and GEBHARD, P. H. 1953: *Sexual behavior in the human female*. Philadelphia: W. B. Saunders.

KOHLBERG, L. and ULLIAN, D. 1974: Stages in the development of psychosexual concepts and attitudes. In Friedman, R., Richart, R., and Vande Wiele, R. (eds), *Sex differences in behavior*. New York: John Wiley, 209-22.

KRUTNIK, F. 1991: *In a lonely street: film noir, genre, masculinity*. London: Routledge.

KUHN, A. 1982: *Women's pictures: feminism and cinema*. London: Routledge and Kegan Paul.

KUHN, A. 1985: *The power of the image: essays on representation and sexuality*. London: Routledge and Kegan Paul.

KUHN, A. and RADSTONE, S. (eds) 1990: *The women's companion to international film*. London: Virago.

LAKOFF, R. 1975: *Language and woman's place*. New York: Harper and Row.

LAURETIS, T. de 1990: Guerrilla in the midst: women's cinema in the 80s. *Screen* 31 (1), 6–25.

LAWRENCE, A. 1991: *Echo and Narcissus: women's voices in classical Hollywood cinema*. Berkeley: University of California Press.

LECLERC, A. 1987: Parole de femme. In Moi, T. (ed.), *French feminist thought: a reader*. Oxford: Blackwell, 73–9. (First published in 1974.)

LeMAHIEU, D. 1988: *A culture for democracy: mass communication and the cultivated mind in Britain between the wars*. Oxford: Clarendon Press.

LEVY, E. 1990: Social attributes of American movie stars. *Media, Culture and Society*, 12 (2), 247–67.

LEWIS, J. 1984: *Women in England 1870–1950: sexual divisions and social change*. London: Wheatsheaf.

LIGHT, A. 1989: Putting on the style: feminist criticism in the 1990s. In Carr, H. (ed.), *From My Guy to sci-fi: genre and women's writing in the postmodern world*. London: Pandora, 24–35.

LIVINGSTONE, S. 1990: *Making sense of television: the psychology of audience interpretation*. Oxford: Pergamon.

LIVINGSTONE, S. and LUNT, P. 1992: Expert and lay participation in television debates: an analysis of audience discussion programmes. *European Journal of Communication* 7 (1), 9–35.

LLOYD, F. (ed.) 1993: *Deconstructing Madonna*. London: Batsford.

LOCHHEAD, L. 1986: *True confessions and new clichés*. Edinburgh: Polygon.

LOTT, B. 1981: A feminist critique of androgyny. Towards the elimination of gender attributes for learned behavior. In Mayo, C. and Henley, N. (eds), *Gender and non-verbal behavior*. New York: Springer-Verlag.

LOTT, B. 1990: Dual natures or learned behavior: the challenge to feminist psychology. In Hare-Mustin, R. and Marecek, J. (eds), *Making a difference: psychology and the construction of gender*. New Haven: Yale University Press, 65–101.

LOVELL, T. (ed.) 1990: *British feminist thought: a reader*. Oxford: Blackwell.

MACCOBY, E. and JACKLIN, C. 1974: *The psychology of sex differences*. Stanford: Stanford University Press.

MARCHAND, R. 1985: *Advertising the American dream: making way for modernity, 1920–1940*. California: University of California Press.

MARTIN, R. and SPENCE, J. 1987: New portraits for old: the use of the camera in therapy. In Betterton, R. (ed.), *Looking on: images of femininity in the visual arts and media*. London: Pandora, 267–79.

MASTERS, W. and JOHNSON, V. 1966: *Human sexual response*. Boston: Little, Brown & Co.

McCRACKEN, E. 1993: *Decoding women's magazines: from 'Mademoiselle' to 'Ms.'*. London: Macmillan.

McNAY, L. 1992: *Foucault and feminism: power, gender and the self*. Cambridge: Polity Press.

McROBBIE, A. (ed.) 1989: *Zoot suits and second-hand dresses: an anthology of fashion and music*. London: Macmillan.

McROBBIE, A. 1991: *Feminism and youth culture: from 'Jackie' to 'Just Seventeen'*. London: Macmillan.

McROBBIE, A. 1994: *Postmodernism and popular culture*. London: Routledge.

MELMAN, B. 1988: *Women and the popular imagination in the twenties: flappers and nymphs*. London: Macmillan.

MESSENGER DAVIES, M. 1989: *Television is good for your kids*. London: Hilary Shipman.

MILLETT, K. 1977: *Sexual politics*. London: Virago. (First published 1970.)

MILLS, J. 1991: *Womanwords: a vocabulary of culture and patriarchal society*. London: Virago.

MIRZA, H. 1990: *Young, female and black*. London: Routledge.

MITCHELL, J. 1975: *Psychoanalysis and feminism*. Harmondsworth: Penguin. (First published 1974.)

MODLESKI, T. 1982: The search for tomorrow in today's soap operas. In Modleski, T. (ed.), *Loving with a vengeance*. London: Methuen, 85–109.

MODLESKI, T. (ed.) 1986: *Studies in entertainment: critical approaches to mass culture*. Bloomington and Indianapolis: Indiana University Press.

MOI, T. 1985: *Sexual/textual politics: feminist literary theory*. London: Routledge.

MOORE, S. 1988: Here's looking at you, kid! In Gamman, L. and

Marshment, M. (eds), *The female gaze: women as viewers of popular culture*. London: Women's Press, 44–59.

MOORES, S. 1993: *Interpreting audiences: the ethnography of media consumption*. London: Sage.

MORLEY, D. 1980: Texts, readers, subjects. In Hall, S., Hobson, D., Lowe, A., and Willis, P. (eds), *Culture, media, language*. London: Hutchinson, 163–73.

MORLEY, D. 1986: *Family television: cultural power and domestic leisure*. London: Comedia.

MORLEY, D. 1992: *Television, audiences and cultural studies*. London: Routledge.

MULVEY, L. 1975: Visual pleasure and narrative cinema. Screen 16 (3), 6–18. (Reprinted in Mulvey, 1989.)

MULVEY, L. 1981: Afterthoughts on 'Visual pleasure and narrative cinema' inspired by 'Duel in the Sun' (King Vidor, 1946). *Framework* 15–17, 12–15. (Reprinted in Mulvey, 1989.)

MULVEY, L. 1989: *Visual and other pleasures*. London: Macmillan.

MYERS, K. 1986: *Understains: the sense and seduction of advertising*. London: Comedia.

MYERS, K. 1987: Towards a feminist erotica. In Betterton, R. (ed.), *Looking on: images of femininity in the visual arts and media*. London: Pandora, 189–202. (First published 1982.)

NICHOLSON, L. (ed.) 1990: *Feminism/postmodernism*. London: Routledge.

OAKLEY, A. 1974: *The sociology of housework*. Oxford: Martin Robertson.

O'CONNOR, P. 1992: *Friendships between women: a critical review*. Hemel Hempstead: Harvester Wheatsheaf.

O'CONNOR, B. and BOYLE, R. 1993: Dallas with balls: televized sport, soap opera and male and female pleasures. *Leisure Studies* 12, 107–19.

PALMER, P. 1986: *The lively audience*. Sydney: Allen Unwin.

PARKER, R. 1984: *The subversive stitch: embroidery and the making of the feminine*. London: Women's Press.

PARKER, R. and POLLOCK, G. 1981: *Old mistresses: women, art and ideology*. London: Routledge and Kegan Paul.

PERKINS, T. 1979: Rethinking stereotypes. In Barrett, M., Corrigan, P., Kuhn, A., and Wolff, J. (eds), *Ideology and cultural production*. London: Croom Helm, 135–59.

PHOENIX, A. 1987: Theories of gender and black families. In Weiner,

G. and Arnot, M. (eds), *Gender under scrutiny*. London: Hutchinson, 50–63.

PHOENIX, A., WOOLLETT, A. and LLOYD, E. (eds) 1991: *Motherhood: meanings, practices and ideologies*. London: Sage.

POLLOCK, G. 1988: *Vision and difference: femininity, feminism and the histories of art*. London: Routledge.

POSENER, J. 1986: *Louder than words*. London: Pandora.

POSTER, M. (ed.) 1988: *Jean Baudrillard: selected writings*. Cambridge: Polity Press.

PRIBRAM, E. D. (ed.) 1988: *Female spectators: looking at film and television*. London: Verso.

PRIBRAM, E. D. 1993: Seduction, control, and the search for authenticity: Madonna's 'Truth or Dare'. In Schwichtenberg, C. (ed.), *The Madonna connection: representational politics, subcultural identities and cultural theory*. Boulder: Westview Press, 189–212.

PUMPHREY, M. 1987: The flapper, the housewife and the making of modernity. *Cultural Studies* 1 (2), 179–94.

RICHARDS, J. R. 1982: *The sceptical feminist: a philosophical enquiry*. Harmondsworth: Penguin. (First published 1980.)

RIVIERE, J. 1929: Womanliness as a masquerade. *The International Journal of Psycho-analysis* X, 303–13.

RODOWICK, D. 1991: *The difficulty of difference: psychoanalysis, sexual difference and film theory*. London: Routledge.

ROHRBAUGH, J. 1981: *Women: psychology's puzzle*. London: Abacus.

ROIPHE, K. 1994: *The morning after: sex, fear, and feminism*. London: Hamish Hamilton.

ROOT, J. 1986: Distributing 'A Question of Silence' – a cautionary tale. In Brunsdon, C. (ed.), *Films for women*. London: BFI, 213–23.

ROSE, A. and FRIEDMAN, J. 1994: Television sport as mas(s)culine cult of distraction. *Screen* 35 (1), 22–35.

ROSE, J. 1990: Femininity and its discontents. In Lovell, T. (ed.), *British feminist thought: a reader*. Oxford: Blackwell, 227–43.

ROSEN, M. 1973: *Popcorn Venus*. New York: Avon Books.

ROWE, K. 1990: Roseanne: unruly woman as domestic goddess. *Screen* 31 (4), 408–19.

SCANNELL, P. (ed.) 1991: *Broadcast talk*. London: Sage.

SCHLESINGER, P., DOBASH, R. E., DOBASH, R. P. and WEAVER, C. K. 1992: *Women viewing violence*. London: BFI.

SCHWICHTENBERG, C. (ed.) 1993: *The Madonna connection:*

representational politics, subcultural identities and cultural theory. Boulder: Westview Press.

SEGAL, L. and McINTOSH, M. (eds) 1992: *Sex exposed: sexuality and the pornography debate.* London: Virago.

SIANN, G. 1994: *Gender, sex and sexuality: contemporary psychological perspectives.* London: Taylor and Francis.

SILVERMAN, K. 1986: Fragments of a fashionable discourse. In Modleski, T. (ed.), *Studies in entertainment: critical approaches to mass culture.* Bloomington and Indianapolis: Indiana University Press, 139–52.

SILVERMAN, K. 1988: *The acoustic mirror: the female voice in psychoanalysis and cinema.* Bloomington and Indianapolis: University of Indiana Press.

SIMMONDS, F. N. 1992: 'She's Gotta Have It': the representation of black female sexuality on film. In Bonner, F., Goodman, L., Allen, R., Janes, L. and King, C. (eds), *Imagining women: cultural representations and gender.* Cambridge: Polity Press, 210–20.

SPENDER, D. 1980: *Man made language.* London: Routledge and Kegan Paul.

STACEY, J. 1988: Desperately seeking difference. In Gamman, L. and Marshment, M. (eds), *The female gaze: women as viewers of popular culture.* London: Women's Press, 112–29.

STACEY, J. 1991: Feminine fascinations: forms of identification in star-audience relations. In Gledhill, C. (ed.), *Stardom: industry of desire.* London: Routledge, 141–63.

STACEY, M. and PRICE, M. 1981: *Women, power, and politics.* London: Tavistock.

STUART, A. 1990: Feminism: dead or alive? In Rutherford, J. (ed.), *Identity: community, culture, difference.* London: Lawrence and Wishart, 28–42.

TANNEN, D. 1991: *You just don't understand: women and men in conversation.* London: Virago.

TETZLAFF, D. 1993: Metatextual girl: patriarchy, postmodernism, power, money, Madonna. In Schwichtenberg, C. (ed.), *The Madonna connection: representational politics, subcultural identities and cultural theory.* Boulder: Westview Press, 239–63.

TICKNER, L. 1987: The body politic: female sexuality and women artists since 1970. In Betterton, R. (ed.), *Looking on: images of femininity in the visual arts and media.* London: Pandora, 235–53.

TOLSON, A. 1991: Televised chat and the synthetic personality. In Scannell, P. (ed.), *Broadcast talk*. London: Sage, 178–200.

TRENEMAN, A. 1988: Cashing in on the curse: advertising and the menstrual taboo. In Gamman, L. and Marshment, M. (eds), *The female gaze: women as viewers of popular culture*. London: Women's Press, 153–65.

USSHER, J. 1989: *The psychology of the female body*. London: Routledge.

VANCE, C. S. 1984: *Pleasure and danger: exploring female sexuality*. London: Routledge and Kegan Paul.

WANDOR, M. (ed.) 1983: *On gender and writing*. London: Pandora.

WARNER, M. 1985: *Alone of all her sex: the myth and the cult of the Virgin Mary*. London: Picador. (First published 1976.)

WARNER, M. 1987: *Monuments and maidens: the allegory of the female form*. London: Picador. (First published 1985.)

WHITE, C. 1977: *The women's periodical press in Britain 1946–1976*. London: HMSO.

WILLIAMS, F. 1969: *The right to know: the rise of the world press*. London: Longman.

WILLIAMS, L. 1986: 'Personal Best': women in love. In Brunsdon, C. (ed.), *Films for women*. London: BFI, 146–54.

WILLIAMS, L. 1988: Feminist film theory: 'Mildred Pierce' and the second world war. In Pribram, E. D. (ed.), *Female spectators: looking at film and television*. London: Verso, 12–30.

WILLIAMSON, J. 1986a: *Consuming passions: the dynamics of popular culture*. London: Marion Boyars.

WILLIAMSON, J. 1986b: Woman is an island: femininity and colonization. In Modleski, T. (ed.), *Studies in entertainment: critical approaches to mass culture*. Bloomington and Indianapolis: Indiana University Press, 99–118.

WILLIAMSON, J. 1988a: Having your baby and eating it. *New Statesman* 15 April, 44–5.

WILLIAMSON, J. 1988b: Nightmare on Madison Avenue. *New Statesman* 15 January, 28–9.

WILLIS, S. 1990: Work(ing) out. *Cultural Studies* 4 (1), 1–18.

WILSON, E. 1985: *Adorned in dreams: fashion and modernity*. London: Virago.

WILSON, E. 1992: Fashion and the postmodern body. In Ash, J. and Wilson, E. (eds), *Chic thrills: a fashion reader*. London: Pandora, 3–16.

WINSHIP, J. 1983: Femininity and women's magazines: a case study of 'Woman's Own'. U221 Unit 6, Open University second level course, *The changing experience of women*. Milton Keynes: Open University.

WINSHIP, J. 1987a: 'A girl needs to get street-wise': magazines for the 1980s. In Betterton, R. (ed.), *Looking on: images of femininity in the visual arts and media*. London: Pandora, 127–41.

WINSHIP, J. 1987b: *Inside women's magazines*. London: Pandora.

WOLF, N. 1991: *The beauty myth*. London: Vintage.

YOUNG, A. 1990: *Femininity in dissent*. London: Routledge.

Index

Faludi, S. 11, 96, 176-7
Fanny Hill 175
Fantasy 107, 116; revenge fantasies 99-100; *see also Thelma and Louise* sexual 98, 177
Fashion: features 107-11; feminism and 210-5
Fatal Attraction 11, 127-9, 147, 180
Fathering 148-51
Feminism 59, 109, 130, 172, 174-5; caring and 141-4; undermining of 127-9, 130-1, 144, 146-8; *see also* 'Backlash'; Recuperation; *see also* Advertising; Domesticitiy; Fashion; Psychoanalysis; Sexuality
Feminist magazines, *see Ms, Spare Rib*
Feminists 2-3, 22-3; radical feminists 165-6, 169
Femme fatale 51, 105, 113, 118-9, 130-1, 180, 217
Film: *see* individual film titles
Film directors: female 4, 43, 148, 154, 184, 193, 198
Film noir 105, 116-21, 139, 217; 1980s' versions 122-7, 130; *see also* Voice-overs
Film studies 2, 15, 23, 29
Fishman, P. 62
Fiske, J. 12, 220
Folklinguistics 54-66
Foucault, M. 38, 46-7, 92, 163, 164, 176, 201
Frazer, E. 5, 19
Frederick, C. 86
Freud, S. 22, 23-6, 29, 30, 105
Freudian ideas 27, 28, 40, 123, 135-6, 139, 165
Friday, N. 98-9, 167, 179
Friedan, B. 22, 86, 168
Fried Green Tomatoes 152, 156, 157-8
Friendships, female 132, 154-60, 160-1 *see also* Sisterhood
Frith, S. 116

Gaines, J. 29, 75
Gamman, L. 156
Garber, M. 218
Gender identity development, theories of; biological determinism 16-17, 26; cognitive-developmental 16, 17-19; social learning 16, 17, 19
Geraghty, C. 68
Gilda 116, 118, 119, 120-1
Gill, R. 51
Gilligan, C. 19-20
Girlfriends 154-5

Glamour 111
Gledhill, C. 29, 36, 137, 179
Golden Girls, The 56, 57, 154
Good Mother, The 143-4
Gossip 45, 54-5
GQ 110-1
Grace Under Fire 144
Gray, A. 37, 70
Guardian, The quoted 49, 52, 58, 87, 96, 198, 217

The Hand that Rocks the Cradle 152, 154
Hardyment, C. 80
Harpies and Quines 14
Harris, T. 111
Harvey, S. 116, 121
Haskell, M. 15-16, 155, 179
Hays Code 139, 179
Hebdige, D. 192, 214
Hegemony 86
Herzog, C. 29, 75
Heung, M. 127, 136
Hindley, Myra 123
Historical analysis 14, 30-3, 39-40, 121, 139-40
Hite, S. 63-4, 155, 167, 169-70
Hollingsworth, M. 161
Home Chat 74
Home to Roost 57
Honey 87, 171
hooks, b. 41, 72, 116, 169

Ideal body 197-201
Ideologies: Althusser on 35-6; competition between 5-6; in relation to 'public' and 'private' spheres 47-8; *see also* Discourse
Imitation of Life (1934) 136
Imitation of Life (1959) 136
In Bed with Madonna 115
Incorporation, *see* Recuperation
Independent, The quoted 128-9
Intertextuality 34, 110, 220
Irigaray, L. 66, 67-8, 72, 196
Irony 220-1
Itzin, C. 194

Jackie 5
Jagged Edge 122
Jameson, F. 33, 114, 220
Jeffreys, S. 169
Johnny Guitar 216-17
Johnston, C. 121
Joke-telling 57-59
Jones, D. 54-5
Journalists, women 49, 72